THE CAMBRIDGE COMPANION TO BOB DYLAN

A towering figure in American culture and a global twentieth-century icon, Bob Dylan has been at the center of American life for over forty years. *The Cambridge Companion to Bob Dylan* brings fresh insights into the imposing range of Dylan's creative output. The first Part approaches Dylan's output thematically, tracing the evolution of Dylan's writing and his engagement with American popular music, religion, politics, fame, and his work as a songwriter and performer. Chapters in Part II analyze his landmark albums to examine the consummate artistry of Dylan's most accomplished studio releases. As a writer Dylan has courageously chronicled and interpreted many of the cultural upheavals in America since World War II. This book will be invaluable both as a guide for students of Dylan and twentieth-century culture, and for his fans, providing a set of new perspectives on a much-loved writer and composer.

KEVIN J. H. DETTMAR is W. M. Keck Professor and Chair of the Department of English, Pomona College, California.

CAMBRIDGE COMPANIONS TO AMERICAN STUDIES

This series of Companions to key figures in American history and culture is aimed at students of American studies, history and literature. Each volume features newly commissioned essays by experts in the field, with a chronology and guide to further reading.

Volumes published:

The Cambridge Companion to Benjamin Franklin edited by Carla Mulford
The Cambridge Companion to Thomas Jefferson edited by Frank Shuffelton
The Cambridge Companion to W. E. B. Du Bois edited by Shamoon Zamir

Volumes in preparation:

The Cambridge Companion to Frederick Douglass edited by Maurice Lee
The Cambridge Companion to Malcolm X edited by Robert Terrill

THE CAMBRIDGE
COMPANION TO
BOB DYLAN

EDITED BY

KEVIN J. H. DETTMAR

CAMBRIDGE UNIVERSITY PRESS
Cambridge, New York, Melbourne, Madrid, Cape Town,
Singapore, São Paulo, Delhi, Mexico City

Cambridge University Press
The Edinburgh Building, Cambridge CB2 8RU, UK

Published in the United States of America by Cambridge University Press, New York

www.cambridge.org
Information on this title: www.cambridge.org/9780521714945

First published 2009
Fourth printing 2009

A catalogue record for this publication is available from the British Library

Library of Congress Cataloguing in Publication Data
Dettmar, Kevin J. H., 1958–
The Cambridge companion to Bob Dylan / Kevin J. H. Dettmar.
p.   cm. – (Cambridge companions to American studies)
Includes bibliographical references and index.
ISBN 978-0-521-88694-9 (hardback) – ISBN 978-0-521-71494-5 (pbk)
1. Dylan, Bob, 1941–Criticism and interpretation.
2. Singers–United States–Biography.   I. Title.   II. Series.
ML420.D98D48 2009
782.42164092–dc22   [B]   2008049667

ISBN 978-0-521-88694-9 Hardback
ISBN 978-0-521-71494-5 Paperback

CONTENTS

ACKNOWLEDGMENTS

Special thanks go to C. P. Lee, Dylan scholar *extraordinaire*, for his companionable help throughout the preparation of this *Companion*. And a shout out to a generation 2.5 Dylan fan, Adam Van Winkle, who provided invaluable help at a critical juncture in preparing the "Works Cited" and "Chronology of Dylan's Life." May you both stay forever young.

NOTES ON CONTRIBUTORS

ALEX ABRAMOVICH is a writer and editor in New York, and a frequent contributor to *Bookforum*, the *New York Times*, *Slate*, and other publications in and around the city. Currently, he's writing a history of rock & roll.

CARRIE BROWNSTEIN is a writer and musician. She was a member of the critically acclaimed rock band Sleater-Kinney. Her writing has appeared in *The Believer*, *Pitchfork*, *Slate*, and in various book anthologies. She writes a music blog for NPR and is an on-air contributor to NPR's "Day to Day." Brownstein is also one-half of ThunderAnt, a comedy duo with Fred Armisen. She lives in Portland, Oregon and is currently working on her first book of nonfiction.

ERIC BULSON received his PhD from Columbia University in 2004 and currently teaches in the Department of Comparative Literature at Yale University. He is the author of the *Cambridge Introduction to James Joyce* and *Novels, Maps, Modernity: The Spatial Imagination, 1850–2000*.

DEBRA RAE COHEN, Assistant Professor of English at the University of South Carolina, was, in her salad days, a rock critic for such publications as *Rolling Stone*, the *New York Times*, and the *Village Voice*, where she was one of the founding editors of the *Voice Literary Supplement*. In her academic incarnation she is the author of *Remapping the Home Front: Locating Citizenship in British Women's Great War Fiction*, and the co-editor, with Michael Coyle and Jane A. Lewty, of the collection *Broadcasting Modernism*. Currently, she's working on Rebecca West, modernist historiography, and the cultural poetics of the cover song, though not all at the same time.

MICHAEL COYLE, Professor of English at Colgate University, is founding president of the Modernist Studies Association and serves on the Boards of Directors for various author societies. He most often writes about modernist poetry and cultural history, or about jazz history and American musical vernaculars. His longtime involvement with college radio means that, by this point, he has been broadcasting longer than most of the student DJs at Colgate University's radio station, WRCU, have been alive. Helping keep the experience fresh, and his connection to music vital, is his work reviewing jazz records for *Cadence* magazine, where he regularly irritates his editor by being late with assignments.

ANTHONY DECURTIS is a contributing editor for *Rolling Stone*, and he teaches in the writing program at the University of Pennsylvania. He is the author of *In Other Words: Artists Talk About Life and Work* and *Rocking My Life Away: Writing About Music and Other Matters*, and he is the editor of *Present Tense: Rock & Roll and Culture*. He holds a PhD in American literature from Indiana University, and his essay accompanying the Eric Clapton retrospective *Crossroads* won a Grammy in the "Best Album Notes" category.

MICHAEL DENNING teaches American Studies at Yale University, and directs Yale's Initiative on Labor and Culture. He has written widely on popular culture and social movements, and his books include *Culture in the Age of Three Worlds* and *The Cultural Front: The Laboring of American Culture in the Twentieth Century*.

KEVIN J. H. DETTMAR is W. M. Keck Professor and Chair of the Department of English at Pomona College. He has published in the fields of modernist literature and popular music studies; he is the author of *Is Rock Dead?* (2006), and co-editor of *Reading Rock & Roll* (1999). His bi-monthly column on the intersections of popular music and everyday life, "Pop Life," runs in the *Chronicle Review*, the arts and ideas magazine of the *Chronicle of Higher Education*.

MARTIN JACOBI is Professor of English at Clemson University and co-author of *The Politics of Rhetoric* (1999). He has published on rhetorical theory, American fiction, and drama, with recent or forthcoming essays on Alan Bennett's *The History Boys* (*South Atlantic Review*), Sophocles's *Antigone* (*Journal of Drama Studies*), and the "fascist" novels of Jack London, Sinclair Lewis, and Philip Roth (*Philip Roth Studies*). He is currently working on the rhetoric of ancient and contemporary war drama.

JONATHAN LETHEM is the author of seven novels, including *The Fortress of Solitude* and *You Don't Love Me Yet*. His writing has appeared in the *New Yorker*, *Rolling Stone*, *Harper's* and many other journals and anthologies. His essays on popular culture are collected in *The Disappointment Artist*. He lives in Brooklyn and Maine.

ALAN LIGHT is the former editor-in-chief of *Spin* and *Vibe* magazines, and a former Senior Writer for *Rolling Stone*. He is the author of *The Skills to Pay the Bills: The Story of the Beastie Boys* and the director of programming for "Live from the Artist's Den" on the Ovation TV network. A frequent contributor to the *New York Times* and a columnist for msn.com, Alan is a two-time winner of the ASCAP-Deems Taylor award for excellence in music writing. He lives in Manhattan with his wife, Suzanne, and their son, Adam.

ERIC LOTT teaches American Studies at the University of Virginia. He has written and lectured widely on the politics of US cultural history, and his work has appeared in a range of periodicals including the *Village Voice*, the *Nation*, *New York Newsday*, *Transition*, *Social Text*, *African American Review*, *Representations*, *American Literary History*, and *American Quarterly*. He is the author of *Love and Theft: Blackface Minstrelsy and the American Working Class* (1993), from which Bob Dylan took the title for his album *"Love and Theft."* Lott is also the author of *The Disappearing Liberal Intellectual* (2006). He is currently finishing a study of race and culture in the twentieth century entitled *Tangled Up in Blue*.

LEE MARSHALL is a Senior Lecturer in Sociology at Bristol University. His research covers a range of areas within the sociology of culture that center around ideas about "authorship" that exist in modern life, most notably stardom, copyright, and popular music. His first book, *Bootlegging: Copyright and Romanticism in the Music Industry* (2005) won the Socio-Legal Studies Association's Hart Early Career Book Prize. His second book, *Bob Dylan: The Never Ending Star* (2007) offers a sociological account of Dylan's career in which he argues that to understand Dylan's work effectively, it is necessary to consider how wider structures of stardom and rock culture have constrained and enabled Dylan's creativity at various points in his career.

BARBARA O'DAIR is the editor of *Trouble Girls: The Rolling Stone Book of Women in Rock*. She has been a senior editor at *Rolling Stone*, *Entertainment Weekly* and the *Village Voice*, the executive editor of *Details*, *Harper's Bazaar*, *More*, and *Reader's Digest*, and the editor-in-chief of *Teen People* and *Us*. She has contributed essays, reviews and other articles to a wide variety of magazines, newspapers, and books. She holds an MFA in poetry and lives in New Jersey with her family.

ROBERT POLITO'S most recent books are the poetry collection *Hollywood and God* and *The Complete Film Writings of Manny Farber*. His other books include *Doubles* and *Savage Art: A Biography of Jim Thompson*. His previous writing on Bob Dylan appeared in *Bob Dylan's American Journey* and *Studio A*. He founded and continues to direct the Graduate Writing Program at The New School, where he is a Professor of Writing.

ANNE K. REAM is a Chicago-based writer whose essays and opinion pieces have appeared in the *Atlanta Journal-Constitution*, the *Chicago Tribune*, the *Los Angeles Times*, and *Washingtonpost.com*. She is the founder of The Voices and Faces Project (voicesandfaces.org), a national documentary initiative created to give voice and faces to survivors of sexual violence, and author of an in-progress book by the same name. A past finalist for the Dorothea Lange–Paul Taylor Documentary Prize and a longstanding advocate for women's issues, she is also the executive producer of *The Voices and Faces Project, Volume One* (canasongsavetheworld.com), a benefit album that features many of today's hottest indie rock acts. Finally, she is the co-author of Girl360.net, a forthcoming book and webzine program created to introduce history's groundbreaking women to a new generation of girls.

DAVID R. SHUMWAY is Professor of English, and Literary and Cultural Studies, and Director of the Humanities Center at Carnegie Mellon University. He has written *Michel Foucault* (1989), *Creating American Civilization: A Genealogy of American Literature as an Academic Discipline* (1994), and *Modern Love: Romance, Intimacy, and the Marriage Crisis* (2003), and edited *Knowledges: Critical and Historical Studies in Disciplinarity* (1993 with Ellen Messer-Davidow and David Sylvan) and *Disciplining English* (2002 with Craig Dionne). He is at work on a book about rock stars as cultural icons and a study of John Sayles.

R. CLIFTON SPARGO, a fiction writer and critic, is Associate Professor of English at Marquette University. His fiction has appeared in journals such as *Fiction*, *SOMA*, *Glimmer Train*, the *Connecticut Review*, and *Green Mountains Review*. His essays and reviews on American literature and culture have appeared in journals such as *Representations*, *PMLA*, *Mosaic*, *Raritan*, *Commonweal*, and the *Yale Review*. Formerly the Pearl Resnick Fellow at the Center for Advanced Holocaust Studies in Washington DC, he is the author of two scholarly monographs, *The Ethics of Mourning* (2004) and *Vigilant Memory: Emmanuel Levinas, the Holocaust, and the Unjust Death* (2006); and he is also co-editor with Robert Ehrenreich of *After Representation?: The Holocaust, Literature, and Culture* (forthcoming). For additional information, visit author's website: rcliftonspargo.com.

JEAN TAMARIN lives in Arlington, Virginia.

DAVID YAFFE is Gould Faculty Fellow in the Humanities at Claremont McKenna College and a music columnist for the *Nation*. He is the author of *Fascinating Rhythm: Reading Jazz in American Writing* (2006). His writings have appeared in many other publications, including the *New York Times*, *Slate*, the *Village Voice*, *New York*, and the *New Republic*. He is currently at work on the forthcoming *The Many Roads of Bob Dylan* and *Reckless Daughter: A Portrait of Joni Mitchell*.

1941   Robert Allen Zimmerman, son of Abram and Beatrice ("Beatty") Stone, born May 24 in Duluth, Minnesota.

1948   Abram relocates the Zimmerman family to Hibbing, Minnesota where Robert Allen spends the rest of his childhood.

1959   After playing in high school rock bands, he moves to Minneapolis and enrolls at the University of Minnesota. Hearing Odetta in a record store, he trades his electric guitar for an acoustic to begin performing folk music.

1960   Becomes involved in local folk scene, playing the Dinkytown area of Minneapolis. Adopts and performs under the name Bob Dylan (a nod to the Welsh poet, Dylan Thomas); legally changes name two years later.

1961   Moves to New York where he seeks out his ailing idol, Woody Guthrie. Begins performing regularly at folk clubs and coffee houses of Greenwich Village. Becomes romantically involved with the 17-year-old Suze Rotolo, whose political and artistic commitments make a profound impression on Dylan; the relationship survives many rough patches until the summer of 1964. His September show at Gerde's Folk City reviewed favorably by Robert Shelton in the *New York Times*; signed to a record deal with Columbia by John Hammond.

1962   First album, *Bob Dylan*, featuring two original songs, "Talking New York" and "Song to Woody," and covers of traditional folk material, released. Sells only 5,000 copies. Dylan referred to as "Hammond's Folly."

1963   Releases *The Freewheelin' Bob Dylan* in May; contains mostly originals ("Blowin' in the Wind," "Masters of War," and "A Hard

Rain's A-Gonna Fall") with two covers ("Corrina, Corrina" and "Honey, Just Allow Me One More Chance"). Refuses to play the *Ed Sullivan Show* after an attempt to censor his set list. Joan Baez invites Dylan to tour with her; they become romantically involved. Performs at the March on Washington for Jobs and Freedom in August.

1964   *The Times They Are A-Changin'* released. Meets the Beatles at Kennedy Airport in New York; reportedly introduces the group to marijuana. *Another Side of Bob Dylan* appears, marking the beginnings of his turn from the folk genre.

1965   Dylan gives "Mr. Tambourine Man" to Roger McGuinn; it becomes a major hit for the Byrds. Ends relationship with Baez; marries Sara Lowndes (sometimes spelt "Lownds"). Releases *Bringing It All Back Home* in March; the album has a decidedly different sound from the previous folk recordings, featuring heavy electric arrangements alongside some acoustic tracks. Dylan is booed when he performs an electric set at the Newport Folk Festival. Releases the all-electric *Highway 61 Revisited* with the definitive single "Like a Rolling Stone" in August. Hires backing band the Hawks (later the Band) featuring Robbie Robertson and Levon Helm for tour supporting the album.

1966   Records *Blonde on Blonde* in Nashville. Embarks on a world tour where he performs split sets at every stop, first performing solo on acoustic guitar and harmonica, then, backed by the Hawks, delivering a high-voltage electric set. In July, mysteriously crashes his Triumph 55 motorcycle outside Woodstock, NY. Dylan begins withdrawal from public performing and recording.

1967   While recovering, records several sessions with the Hawks in their nearby Woodstock basement (which become the first widely distributed bootlegs); sessions later released by Columbia as *The Basement Tapes* (1975). In October and November records *John Wesley Harding* in Nashville.

1968   In January, appears for the first time in public since his crash, performing three songs at the Woody Guthrie Memorial Concert.

1969   Releases an all-country album, *Nashville Skyline*. Appears on the first episode of Johnny Cash's television show in May, performing three songs with the host. Headlines the Isle of Wight festival in

England in August, having rejected offers to perform at the Woodstock Music Festival.

1970   *Self-Portrait*, an album comprised mostly of covers, is released and poorly received. *New Morning* released to more favorable reviews. On June 9, receives honorary doctorate in music from Princeton University.

1971   Performs at ex-Beatle George Harrison's benefit concert for Bangladesh. The single "George Jackson" is his only studio release of the year. Conducts recording sessions with Allen Ginsberg (still unreleased).

1972   Worked on Sam Peckinpah's film *Pat Garrett and Billy the Kid*, providing the songs (released on the 1973 soundtrack album) and acting as "Alias."

1973   Records *Planet Waves* (released in January 1974) with the Band, and begins rehearsing for a supporting tour after leaving Columbia for the Asylum label.

1974   The Bob Dylan and the Band tour recorded and released as *Before the Flood*. Begins recording *Blood on the Tracks* (1975) in September, once again on the Columbia label.

1975   Visits boxer Rubin "Hurricane" Carter in prison and pens "Hurricane," a single depicting the fighter's wrongful conviction in a triple-murder case in Paterson, NJ. Embarks on Rolling Thunder Revue tour, featuring T-Bone Burnett, "Ramblin'" Jack Elliott, Allen Ginsberg, Roger McGuinn, Joni Mitchell, and Joan Baez.

1976   As the Rolling Thunder Revue continues, Dylan releases *Desire* featuring collaborations with playwright Jacques Levy. It is his last number 1 album for thirty years. Appears at the Band's farewell concert, documented by Martin Scorsese (*The Last Waltz*).

1978   Releases *Street Legal*. Marriage to Sara ends in divorce. *Renaldo and Clara*, a four-hour film directed by Dylan, using concert footage of the Rolling Thunder Revue and starring himself alongside Joan Baez, is released to poor reviews.

1979   From January to April, participates in Bible study classes at the Vineyard School of Discipleship in Reseda, CA. Releases gospel-inspired *Slow Train Coming*, winning the Grammy for "Best Male Vocalist" for the song "Gotta Serve Somebody."

1980   Second "born again" album released: *Saved*. Tours, reviving songs from a number of his 1960s recordings.

1981   *Shot of Love* released, featuring both Christian-influenced and secular material.

1982   Travels to Israel; it is rumored that he rejects his born-again Christian status.

1983   Releases *Infidels* to critical acclaim.

1984   Appears in March on *Late Night with David Letterman*, backed by a punk band, performing three songs. *Real Live* samples the subsequent European tour.

1985   Releases *Empire Burlesque*. Performs to poor reception at Live Aid backed by Keith Richards and Ronnie Wood; performs to higher acclaim at Farm Aid, backed by Tom Petty and the Heartbreakers.

1986   Tours with Tom Petty and the Heartbreakers. *Knocked Out Loaded* released. Secretly marries backup singer, Carol Dennis (they divorce in 1992).

1987   Embarks on summer tour with the Grateful Dead (sampled on *Dylan and the Dead*, 1988), to mostly poor reviews. Has successful tour of the Middle East and Europe with Petty.

1988   *Down in the Groove* poorly received. Records with supergroup the Traveling Wilburys alongside George Harrison, Tom Petty, Roy Orbison, and ELO founder Jeff Lynne. Inducted into the Rock & Roll Hall of Fame, introduced by Bruce Springsteen. Begins "The Never Ending Tour" (and has continued touring to present).

1989   Records and releases the well-received *Oh Mercy* with producer Daniel Lanois. Accompanied by "Political World" music video on MTV.

1990   Reunites with the Wilburys (sans the deceased Orbison) for a second album: *The Traveling Wilburys Vol. 3*. Releases *Under the Red Sky* with contributions from George Harrison, Slash, Stevie Ray Vaughn, and Elton John. Named a *Commandeur dans l'Ordre des Arts et des Lettres*, France's highest cultural honor.

1991   Receives lifetime achievement award at the Grammy Awards ceremony; performs "Masters of War" in protest at the first US Iraq invasion on the show. *The Bootleg Series Vol. 1–3* releases a number of previously discarded but now praised Dylan recordings.

1992   *Good as I Been to You* released; features acoustic versions of old folk tunes.

1993   *World Gone Wrong*, an acoustic blues album, released.

1994   Appears at the twenty-fifth anniversary Woodstock '94 Festival. Performs on MTV's *Unplugged*, releasing a live album of acoustic versions of some of his electric classics.

1997   In January, reteams with Lanois to record *Time Out of Mind*. Before the album's scheduled spring release, suffers a near-fatal heart infection, pericarditis. Recovers to begin touring by mid-summer; performs for Pope John Paul II in the fall. *Time Out of Mind* released in September, peaking at number 10 on the Billboard charts, his highest position in twenty years. In December, President Clinton presents Dylan with a Kennedy Center Lifetime Achievement Award.

1998   Wins first "Album of the Year" Grammy for *Time Out of Mind*. Tours the U.S. in the fall with Van Morrison and Joni Mitchell. The legendary 1966 *"Royal Albert Hall" Concert* released by Columbia.

1999   Tours with Paul Simon.

2001   Single "Things Have Changed," written for the film *Wonder Boys* (2000) wins a Grammy, a Golden Globe, and an Academy Award for best song. The Oscar statue tours with Dylan atop an amplifier as he performs. Releases *"Love and Theft"* in September to high critical praise.

2003   Pens "Cross the Green Mountain" for the film *Gods and Generals*. Releases his own film (in collaboration with Larry Charles) *Masked & Anonymous* to poor reviews.

2004   Dylan publishes his autobiographical prose work, *Chronicles: Volume One*.

2005   The four-hour Martin Scorsese documentary *No Direction Home* is shown on television to a wide US audience, released to DVD, and accompanied by new bootlegs from the early 1960s. Records "Tell Ol' Bill" for the film *North Country*.

2006   Records and releases *Modern Times*. The album marks his first number 1 album in thirty years. At 65, Bob Dylan becomes the oldest living artist to hit the top spot. He also begins eclectic weekly "Theme Time Radio Hour" broadcasts.

2007   It is reported that Dylan is spearheading a collaborative project to record the lost Hank Williams catalogue (songs penned, but not recorded, by the country artist at the time of his death).

2008   In September Dylan publishes two poems, "17" and "21," in the *New Yorker*, from a forthcoming book, *Hollywood Foto-Rhetoric: The Lost Manuscript*. Bootleg Series *Vol. 8, Tell Tale Signs* – rare and unreleased recordings from 1989–2006 – is announced for October release by Columbia.

A NOTE ON DYLAN'S LYRICS

Lyrics quoted in the book are taken variously from writers' personal transcriptions of the recordings, Dylan's "official" website (bobdylan.com), and from the published collection, *Bob Dylan, Lyrics: 1962–2001* (New York: Simon & Schuster, 2004). In some cases the official published versions of song lyrics differ, sometimes significantly, from what one hears in the recordings; the contributors have used their discretion in determining which "version" of a song's lyrics to use.

KEVIN J. H. DETTMAR

Introduction

No other figure from the world of American popular music, of this or any other era, has attracted the volume of critical attention, much of it quite original and perceptive, that Bob Dylan has. Just as significantly, no popular-culture figure has ever been adopted into the curricula of college and university language and literature departments in the way Dylan has; critics have called James Joyce "God's gift to English departments," but Dylan is no less deserving of that designation. As early as 1972, articles started appearing in scholarly journals analyzing the songs of Bob Dylan, using the methodologies of literary studies; perhaps more surprisingly, *Scholastic Magazine*, with its audience of secondary-school students and teachers, featured an article on Dylan back in 1970. Dylan biographer Clinton Heylin calls his oeuvre "the most important canon in rock music"; this praise may actually understate the case, for arguably Dylan's is the most important canon in all of twentieth-century American popular music. And Heylin's unembarrassed use of that politically charged term "canon" serves to suggest, too, that Dylan has long since passed into the Academy, making a *Cambridge Companion to Bob Dylan* a logical addition to this distinguished series.

David Gates's description of Dylan as "the man who did to popular music what Einstein did to physics," while initially sounding like hyperbole, really isn't (62). (The error, if there is one, isn't in the parallel between these two innovators, but in equating these fields of innovation.) Dylan brought the long lyric line back to popular American song, much as Walt Whitman had restored it to populist American poetry a century earlier; and against the clear-sighted, sometimes childlike lyrics of the folk tradition, Dylan imported the French symbolists' strategy of suggesting rather than delineating his subjects, a style of lyrical impressionism fully consonant with the introspective (and sometimes hallucinogen-enhanced) listening styles of the time. Equally important as these two factors, Dylan from an early age boasted the voice of a seemingly old man – seemingly the very voice, to steal a phrase from Greil Marcus, of "old, weird America." In an era when pop (and even folk) stars were, as today, meant to sing like the nightingale, Dylan instead sang as the crow. But that croak, it seemed, contained a depth of feeling and passion and anger and joy and wisdom and disillusionment not hinted at by the songbirds; it came as a revelation. And it sounded like the voice of Truth.

As early as 1968, critic Nik Cohn could write, "Almost everyone has been pushed by [Dylan] . . . and almost everything new that happens now goes back to his source. Simply, he has grown pop up, he has given it brains . . ." (174). Dylan's influence has by no means weakened in the intervening years: One of the most talented and inventive American guitarists to achieve fame in the past decade, Jack White (the White Stripes, the Raconteurs), declared in a 2006 issue of *Rolling Stone*, "I have three dads: my biological father, God and Bob Dylan." And Gen-X director Todd Haynes's 2007 Dylan biopic *I'm Not There*, starring such Hollywood heavyweights as Cate Blanchett, Christian Bale, Julianne Moore, Richard Gere, and the late Heath Ledger, made self-conscious and explicit the mythological dimension that has always been an important part of Dylan's influence. Another new generation of musicians and artists is now falling in line to pay its devoirs to Dylan.

For Dylan's 1974 tour with the Band, 5.5 million people (nearly 4 percent of the US population) sent money by mail for advance-purchase tickets. While no longer enjoying that level of popularity (and given the fragmented state of American popular music today, no single artist does, or could), Dylan has recently been experiencing one of his periodic surges in appeal. New writing issues forth seemingly every month, some occasioned by Dylan's tell-some memoir, *Chronicles: Volume One*; Martin Scorsese's *No Direction Home*, produced first as a multi-evening television special and then as a DVD, attempted to take the measure of Dylan's achievement for a general audience, albeit considering only the earliest years of his career. Even Dylan's satellite radio program has provided a new kind of evidence of his influences, and provoked a new wave of writing.

The introduction to a *Cambridge Companion to Bob Dylan* must take up the vexed question of Dylan's status as a poet: the degree to which he is, and is not, a poet, perhaps in the context of other "rock poets" like Leonard Cohen, Joni Mitchell, Patti Smith, Paul Simon, and Lou Reed. Dylan himself has always insisted that he's not a poet – "Wordsworth's a poet, Shelley's a poet, Allen Ginsberg's a poet" is his response to being labeled a poet himself; and yet to some extent owing to the institutional needs of American colleges and universities, who first brought Dylan into the classroom under the only available rubric, as a "poet," some confusion exists about the status of his, and more largely rock, lyrics as poetry. As Robert Christgau has sensibly sought to remind us, "Dylan is a songwriter, not a poet . . . 'My Back Pages' is a bad poem. But it is a good song . . ." ("Rock Lyrics" 63).

Like Christgau, I would argue that Dylan is not a significant poet; but his contributions as a literary artist, understood more broadly, are of the first order. Hence this central paradox: Dylan is recognized as an important literary artist without ever having published a significant work of traditional "literary" merit (though some would now make that claim for the recently published memoir, *Chronicles: Volume One*). But Dylan's work is literary, I would want to argue, in the most fundamental of ways: his is a sensitivity, and a sensibility, that turns almost instinctively to the resources of literary language in order to manifest itself, "transmuting," as Joyce's Stephen Dedalus brashly proclaims, "the daily bread of experience into the radiant body of everliving life." At the close of the "Defense of Poetry," Shelley declares poets "the hierophants of an unapprehended inspiration," "the mirrors of the gigantic shadows which futurity casts upon the present," "the words which express what they understand not": and in this sense only, perhaps, Dylan is a poet. Without claiming him for a prophet, a designation he'd surely disdain, at the same time Dylan's writing has proven, time and again, to be prophetic, giving a shape and substance to those gigantic shadows of the future. And giving staying power and currency to the lessons of the past: "Masters of War," which suffered perhaps from straining just a bit too hard, sounding just a bit too paranoid, when it was released in 1963, gets more prescient every day. Every single day.

English departments first tried to put Dylan on the syllabus, and in the curriculum, as a poet because that was the nearest category available at the time (in the late 1960s and early 1970s); but as English departments have subsequently moved from literary to cultural studies, expanding the provenance of literary analysis into the sphere of popular culture and the everyday and broadening our understanding of "the literary," Dylan's status as a subject of literary inquiry has proven to be fully justified. What critic Andreas Huyssen has described as "the great divide" separating the texts of high and low culture in the early decades of the twentieth century has in large measure been bridged in the postmodern public sphere that Dylan inhabits; and so too in the academy, if somewhat belatedly, the arbitrary exclusion of the "low," the popular, from scholarly regard, is now a thing of the past.

In this revitalized, democratic and demotic environment, Dylan's work has become more valuable than ever in the literary classroom: his songs provide a wonderful set of texts in which to explore issues of intertextuality (borrowing as freely as they do from Dylan's forebears in the popular music traditions), irony, the rhetoric of political action, the limitations of formalist analysis, modernist textuality, the congruence of modern authorship and celebrity, and autoethnography, among others. If any reader of *The*

Cambridge Companion to Bob Dylan were to approach it with concerns about Dylan's credentials as a "literary" artist, those concerns would be laid to rest, I believe, in the chapters that follow. Let me turn now to those chapters.

The volume opens with a "Chronology of Dylan's Life." To a degree almost unprecedented even among celebrity-hungry and privacy-craving media figures, the biography of Bob Dylan is enveloped in clouds of myth, much of it self-generated; as Benjamin Hedin has written, "Dylan's creation myth is elaborate and well publicized" (3) – to which he probably should have added, "fantastic, self-contradictory, and often willfully, gleefully, demonstrably false." That said, there are of course a number of verifiable landmarks in his life and career to date, and those are conveniently sketched out in the "Chronology."

Part I of the *Companion*, "Perspectives," is comprised of nine chapters attempting to take the measure of Dylan's achievement and influence, as well as to place his work within an ongoing artistic and political tradition. Each identifies a "through-line" in Dylan's career, tracing a particular motif, concern, or influence in Dylan's work, or a response to his work, tracing it through the forty-plus years of Dylan's professional career. Dylan is famously a multi-faceted artist (Bernard Paturel: "There's so many sides to Bob Dylan, he's round"); he is also something like John Keats's "chameleon poet," all mask, no "essential" substance. Dylan has claimed, "I'm only Bob Dylan when I have to be"; and as Clinton Heylin writes, "The ability to reinvent who Bob Dylan was, and is, remains the primary characteristic of his art" (Behind the Shades 716). This combines, however paradoxically, with his fans' belief in his authenticity, transparency, and confessional sincerity.

Against a backdrop of familiar chord progressions and instrumentation, Dylan has relentlessly pursued his critique of the hypocrisy of American ideology, urging us, always, to do more to realize the great dreams upon which this nation was founded. Dylan stopped writing topical songs shortly after the release of *The Freewheelin' Bob Dylan* in 1963, just as the British were poised to invade American popular music, but he never stopped writing political songs; and just as not all topical songs are political, so too a song needn't be topical to have political importance. This distinction has too often been ignored. Dylan is the most political of our popular artists, and the most popular of our political artists. But he requires us to understand the term "politics" in its largest sense; and as a result, I have resisted the temptation to treat Dylan's politics as a separate category, choosing instead to underscore the political conscience that runs through his body of work, and to integrate discussion of Dylan's politics throughout these chapters.

David Yaffe opens the volume with a chapter on "Bob Dylan and the Anglo-American Tradition," with special consideration (echoed in Eric Lott's contribution on *"Love and Theft"* and Martin Jacobi's chapter on Dylan's collaborations) of the recent accusations of plagiarism leveled at Dylan's work. Both when acknowledged and when hidden, Dylan's debt to the traditions of Anglo-American popular music reach back to nineteenth-century musical practice and beyond, including folk, vaudeville, and minstrelsy. During the rediscovery of "roots" music that has characterized the past decade, Dylan's work has once again become newly suggestive and valuable; the consistent testimony of every new session man to play with Dylan, that rehearsals inevitably "[turn] into a whole series of informal workshops on American song," serves to suggest his value as a living repository of the popular music repertory, as well as an artist who can recombine and redeploy that repertory in fresh and surprising, sometimes revelatory, ways. During informal jam sessions in which he participated in the early 1980s, Charlie Sexton writes, "[Dylan] would just pick up his guitar and start singing and playing without any introduction or explanation... I'd keep asking him, 'Is this one yours?' and he'd just mumble in that gravelly voice, 'Nah, it's from the Civil War.'" In a somewhat surprising turn of events, given his reclusive reputation, Dylan's recent stint as a radio disk jockey of the old style, programming shows of thematically related music, suggests the newest outlet for his barely suppressed pedagogical impulses: Dylan is using the platform to teach his listeners about the shared musical heritage that lies just below the surface of our civic union, and tipping his hat, as well, to the music that has been most influential in his own artistic career.

In "Bob Dylan and Rolling Thunder," Michael Denning reads the Rolling Thunder Tour to tease out Dylan's performative politics during the Reagan era. Dylan had of course recorded his first album fully in the shadow of Woody Guthrie, whom he visited regularly at the Brooklyn State Hospital after his move to New York; but he became increasingly dissatisfied with the politics-on-its-sleeve modus operandi of the protest music movement, and weary too of the internal battles between folk purists, the folk-music equivalent of "original instrument" devotees in the classical-music world, and those who believed that the animating spirit of folk music endorsed its appropriation for contemporary political struggle. During the few years in which he operated squarely within the folk/protest idiom, Dylan wrote some of the best-known songs of the era: from the campfire fatalism of "Blowin' in the Wind" (made famous in the version by Peter, Paul, and Mary), to the newly electric anger of "Maggie's Farm," to explicit anti-war protest songs still (or newly) relevant today, such as Dylan's attack on the military–industrial complex, "Masters of War." Though uncomfortable always with the label "protest singer," Dylan has found ways over the years to make his voice heard, without restricting its range; his participation in the first Live Aid event, and his role in devising the subsequent Farm Aid concerts, are related manifestations of this desire. Indeed, as Denning persuasively argues here, it is the benefit concert itself that may ultimately prove Dylan's most durable political legacy.

In "Bob Dylan as Songwriter," Anthony DeCurtis focuses attention on both the continuities and innovations in Dylan's lyrical and musical production: for instance, his success in wedding the political urgency of Woody Guthrie et al. with the verbal energy, excitement, and suggestiveness of French surrealist poetry, and the second-person interrogative power of his most successful political ballads ("How does it feel?"; "You know there's something happening, but you don't know what it is, do you?"). While never reluctant to take credit for his lyrics (which he has consented to publish in stand-alone volumes), Dylan has never made large claims for his tunes, most of which he readily admits to having adapted rather freely from traditional sources; the title of his 2001 album *"Love and Theft"* is a wry nod to his lifelong love of, and theft from, the very tradition of which he is guardian, a topic given special attention in Eric Lott's chapter on that album, which closes the volume. But it is also generally conceded that Dylan has few if any peers as a pop lyricist; and attention to those lyrics, as well as Dylan's songwriting methods, commands DeCurtis's attention here.

In a relatively truncated time frame, Dylan was required to negotiate the transition from East Village coffee houses to international stadium concerts; and as iconic as his greatest albums remain for his fans, no rock performer's shows are more cherished by his fans than are Dylan's (only Bruce Springsteen really comes close). In "Bob Dylan as Performer," Alan Light vividly evokes what it's like to attend a Dylan performance. Not that the shows are always transcendent; Dylan's tours over the years, and the current Never Ending Tour (begun February 1988), have been famously uneven: revelatory one night, perfunctory (or even embarrassing) the next. But Dylan has committed himself to conducting his musical education in public; and "like a rolling stone," he refuses to stand still artistically, constantly challenging himself with new arrangements, new band mates, new phrasing and vocal colors, even new lyrics to the songs of his back pages. Dylan's most famous "instrument," of course, is that distinctive, unlovely voice; in his first national review, Robert Shelton called the voice "anything but pretty," and it remains the most-often (and colorfully) described voice in American popular music, of which Joyce Carol Oates's description may be the most evocative: "frankly nasal, as if sandpaper could sing." Though primarily regarded as the most significant songwriter of his generation, Dylan identifies himself as a performer first; as he explained in a 1991 interview, "What got me into the whole thing in the beginning wasn't songwriting... What interested me was being a musician... being a musician was always first and foremost in the back of my mind."

Though he has a well-deserved reputation as a loner, a study of Dylan's career also suggests the degree to which his creativity is dependent upon collaborative working relationships with other musicians – even, as Martin Jacobi provocatively suggests in "Bob Dylan and Collaboration," when one of those "other" musicians is an earlier version of himself. Dylan's formal songwriting collaborations are quite few (notably, with Jacques Levy on *Desire* [1976]); but his imagination seems to be sparked, in unpredictable ways, by informal interactions with other musicians, whether casual jamming, tour rehearsals, or the jamming-cum-rehearsals that often pass for Dylan recording sessions. This chapter also considers Dylan's more formal, sometimes more enduring working relationships with a varying roster of musicians, groups, and artists, such as the Hawks, the Band, Joan Baez, the Rolling Thunder Review, the Grateful Dead, the Heartbreakers, and the Traveling Wilburys.

Few of Dylan's celebrated collaborations have been with women; and the most famous of those, with Joan Baez, quickly became so one-sided that "collaboration" hardly seems a fit description. Barbara O'Dair, in "Bob Dylan and Gender Politics," mounts a suprisingly sympathetic reading of the status of women in Dylan's work. If Dylan was the fortunate inheritor in the 1960s of a newly liberated landscape of sexual and gender relations, he is also in some ways its spoiled child. Many critics and fans have tried, in many different ways, to deny or explain away Dylan's sexism, and yet nagging doubts persist; though often dismissed as anger toward specific women rather than a fear or mistrust of women more generally, the cumulative record of forty-plus years begins to suggest otherwise. Sometimes, Dylan's retrograde sexual politics are indistinguishable from simple egotism: including the plaintive (and beautiful) ballad "Sara" on the album *Desire*, for instance, and mustering the nerve to sing "Sara, Sara / Whatever made you want to change your mind?" – while at the same time engaged in one of his serial extramarital affairs – is an embarrassing example of blaming the victim, and one not reducible to simple misogyny.

The formalist critic Christopher Ricks is one of the few who continues to defend Dylan from all charges of sexism; but songs like "Rainy Day Women #12 and #35," with its nasty biblical allusion (Proverbs 27:15, "a continual dripping on a rainy day and a contentious woman are alike") and its rewriting of the New Testament story of the woman threatened with stoning at the well, with women now doing the stoning of poor Dylan ("Well, they'll stone you when you walk all alone / They'll stone you when you are walking home") – as well as its atmosphere of good ol' boy music-making – is hard to defend. Of course Dylan the songwriter and biographical subject is not identical to the persona in his songs; it would be wrongheaded to hamstring one of the most imaginative and innovative songwriters of our time by insisting on a direct equation between Dylan's own attitudes and values and those given voice in the narratives of his songs. Recounting her own experiences as a feminist-in-the-making encountering Dylan's work – especially, the (for feminists) notorious "Lay, Lady, Lay" – O'Dair manages to suggest how a feminist might still make room in her heart for Dylan.

A thoroughgoing religious thinker who is most comfortable with heterodoxy – his brief periods of orthodoxy, both Christian and Jewish, look like aberrations from this distance – Bob Dylan is the spiritual twin of the English Romantic poet William Blake. In "Bob Dylan and Religion," R. Clifton Spargo and Anne K. Ream treat not just Dylan's involvement with Christianity and his relationship to Judaism, nor do they simply consider his three explicitly Christian albums that followed in the wake of his 1979 conversion (*Slow Train Coming, Saved*, and *Shot of Love*). Rather, they tackle as well the larger religious logic of his most challenging work ("Highway 61 Revisited," "Gotta Serve Somebody") – what Christopher Ricks has called "Dylan's visions of sin," and his effective fusion of Judeo-Christian teaching onto something like an American political–civic religion. Like most of his positions on questions of great importance, Dylan's relationship to religion has shifted markedly, and often unpredictably, over the years; Clinton Heylin has described his career as "a very personal battle to construct a world view that retains his faith in both God and humanity" (*Behind the Shades* ix) – but he neglects to add, a world view that also reflects his profound skepticism of each. Dylan's most recently expressed understanding of the relationship of his faith to his art seems to balance brilliantly the different calls of each: "I find the religiosity and philosophy in the music. I don't find it anywhere else . . . I don't adhere to rabbis, preachers, evangelists . . . I've learned more from the songs than I've learned from any of this kind of entity. The songs are my lexicon. I believe the songs."

The songs – Dylan's songs – have by now become part of the lexicon of higher education, as well. As the New Critical method of "close reading" came to dominate American English departments, alongside the establishment of American Studies programs – and as the political unrest of the Civil Rights movement and Vietnam War protests forced their way into college classrooms – just at the right moment, the well-wrought lyrics of Dylan's sophisticated pop songs presented themselves as a legitimate means for making the teaching of American literature and cultural history "relevant." In "Bob Dylan and the Academy," Lee Marshall deals with the mutual construction of Bob Dylan's oeuvre and the critical apparatuses by which that work has been interpreted. Dylan's impressionistically suggestive, surrealistically charged songs proved wonderfully amenable to the close reading techniques championed by the New Critics, and his self-conscious adoption of literary, and especially biblical, allusion suggested his genealogy from the great poets of the English-language and Western European literary traditions. Dylan not only repaid close reading, but suggested in his own work the benefits of a careful literary apprenticeship. It was no mere caprice that in 1997 Dylan was first nominated for the Nobel Prize in Literature; in the words of the nominating letter, "His words and music have helped restore the vital, time-honored link between poetry and music, and have so permeated the world as to alter its history."

However, the narrowly formalist reading of Dylan's work favored by the New Critics requires the suppression of its obvious, anti-establishment political message; and advocates of "cultural literacy" within the Academy have too often approached Dylan's music blind to what Richard Goldstein calls their own "pop illiteracy," wresting the songs from the political, historical, and cultural contexts that are so integral to their functioning. Dylan has, of course, remained the privileged popular-culture subject of academic discourse to this day; as Benjamin Hedin shrewdly observes, "The excited teenagers and college students who stayed up all night hoping to decipher 'Maggie's Farm' became professors, journalists and other leaders of the educational hierarchy." The absorption of a popular-culture subject into university structures always involves both benefits and costs; owing to his early adoption by English professors, Dylan's is the most carefully studied body of work in all of American popular music (and Dylan has repaid the favor, naming his 2001 album after a work of literary and cultural criticism). But this scholarly work must stay cognizant of what Goldstein has called the "Rolling Tenure Revue," and the discipline of "Ph.Dylanology": a warning not that Dylan's work doesn't hold up to careful scrutiny, but instead that his songs are not the "well wrought urn" of New Critical ideology, but instead songs forged in the crucible of personal, national, generational, racial, sexual change, and can only be understood as such.

Thus while he seemed the perfect object for New Critical analysis, Dylan's music consistently, insistently gave the lie to one of New Criticism's central tenets: namely, the apolitical nature of all great literature. Though as careful in his artifice as any great writer, Dylan simultaneously wrote incisively about political hypocrisy, making him a popular-culture prophet for a culture that seemed to have lost its way, challenging equally those standing on either side of the "generation gap." Now that the generation that grew up with Dylan comprises the nation's ruling class – Dylan and his cohort recently turned 65 – he has been transformed into the perdurable icon of sixties idealism, artistic commitment, and rugged individualism. This has led to some confusingly contradictory gestures: Dylan has been inducted into the Rock & Roll Hall of Fame, nominated for the Nobel Prize in Literature, and at the same time has unabashedly transformed himself into a commercial brand, with his satellite radio program *Theme Time Radio Hour with Your Host Bob Dylan* and, more outlandishly, his TV commercial advertising lingerie for Victoria's Secret. Cultural critic David R. Shumway explores the contours of Dylan's ongoing self-creation and self-promotion in "Bob Dylan as Cultural Icon."

Richard Goldstein has written of the disservice to Dylan's artistic legacy wrought by the unthinking worship of Dylan the Icon: "He's the emblem of his generation's splendor. Beatified in his youth, he's cruising toward sainthood today." In fact, one might argue that this canonization began decades ago; as early as 1969, Dylan's mythic persona had begun to interfere with his receiving honest critical appraisal, as reflected in the fawning reviews of the second-rate *Nashville Skyline*. Goldstein's call for the rigorous criticism Dylan's rigorous oeuvre deserves is as urgent today as ever: "I don't believe in Dylan. His words are not the Word. And I come not to worship him but to complicate him."

For an artist with nearly thirty studio albums to his credit – not to mention six official live albums, a handful of film soundtracks, and an entire cottage industry in bootlegs, both black-market and the ongoing Columbia-authorized "Bootleg Series" – choosing a handful for closer discussion is an excruciating assignment. But that's precisely what we've done in Part II, "Landmark Albums." The eight albums spotlighted here begin to suggest the range and achievement of Dylan's recording career; each of these short pieces approaches one watershed Dylan album from a personal perspective and in a personal voice, helping to show, among other things, *what* and *how* Dylan's music means for those who love his work.

College and university courses in the US and Europe devoted to the study of Dylan's work are now so common as no longer to count as a curiosity. By far the majority of these courses are taught within departments of English or literature; the reasons for this are touched on in Lee Marshall's chapter on Dylan's relationship to the Academy, but the short answer is that Dylan came to public prominence at precisely the moment that departments of English were seeking to break down traditional barriers between "high" and "low" culture, and his highly literate and literary popular songs provided the perfect texts for classroom use and scholarly analysis. Hundreds of schools from Ruskin College, Oxford to Utah Valley State College, from Wofford to Harvard, from Brown to the Rhode Island School of Design to the Community College of Southern Nevada, now teach semester-long courses on Dylan; countless other courses examine Dylan's work within a larger literary, musical, or cultural context. Designed as a classroom text, *The Cambridge Companion to Bob Dylan* seeks to enrich the teaching of Bob Dylan's work by providing materials and perspectives to enliven and complicate discussions of his contribution to contemporary culture, exploring Dylan's ongoing appeal to teachers and students of literature as well as situating him within the field of American popular culture and popular music.

PART I

Perspectives

I

DAVID YAFFE

Bob Dylan and the
Anglo-American tradition

At the end of Todd Haynes's 2007 film *I'm Not There*, Cate Blanchett, one of the six actors playing a character inspired by Bob Dylan, sits in the back of a limo, smoking a cigarette, spouting fragments of dialogue directly transcribed from Dylan's 1966 *Playboy* interview with Nat Hentoff. Dylan was offering something new then – the rock concert – that would soon enough become as well worn as a Gerde's Folk City hootenanny soon enough. But the shock of the new was also entangled with archeological layers of vernacular tradition. Even in a rambling, opaque interview, Dylan – the character he played in *Playboy* who became the character played by Blanchett four decades later – manages to dodge and complicate his relationship to folk: a musical category he could never entirely ditch. When Dylan gives an interview, usually, nothing is revealed, yet Haynes's impressionistic riff on it – with nods to D. A. Pennebaker's 1965 Dylan tour documentary *Don't Look Back* and Fellini's *8½* – *does* reveal how the Dylan of our dreams remained tethered to something old, even when he was flying on amphetamines and snarling gnomic utterances over screeching feedback. Haynes cut and pasted through Dylan's interview patter, chock full of aphoristic non-sequiturs that already seemed fragmented: "jewels and binoculars hang from the head of the mule," he sang, mixing and matching. When Dylan was faced with a question about the "folk tradition," he neither accepted it as orthodoxy nor rejected it as defunct. He knew that he couldn't drown it out, no matter how high he turned up the amplifiers. The folk tradition was so thoroughly grafted into his DNA, he knew that it was a truth he could continue to tell, even if he told it aslant:

> As far as folk and folk-rock are concerned, it doesn't matter what kind of nasty names people invent for the music. It could be called arsenic music, or perhaps Phaedra music. I don't think that such a word as folk-rock has anything to do with it. And folk music is a word I can't use. Folk music is a bunch of fat people. I have to think of all this as traditional music ... Everybody knows that I'm not a folk singer.   (Hentoff, "Playboy Interview," 98)

Sentences from this interview are spouted while "Sad-Eyed Lady of the Lowlands" plays in the background, a song that gives a nod to Scots lowland balladry while riffing on the name of his first wife Sara Lowndes, with lyrics ("My warehouse eyes / My Arabian drums") that continue to divide listeners over whether Dylan was using "eyes" as a verb or a noun – not a question that would have troubled Scots balladeers. Dylan the partygoer may have eschewed the "old ballads," but Dylan the songwriter still soaked them up. Public Dylan was protesting the protest movement and all the ballads that went with it ("I'm always protesting," he droned in a 1965 press conference); private Dylan still looked back. "Traditional music is too unreal to die," he said. Not even the mod, usurping Bob Dylan of 1966 could kill it. Here is the Dylan who draws the distinction between what he would party to, what he would pray to, and what he would defer to. The partying would soon become too much as Dylan very nearly blazed to rock & roll suicide immortality. But he didn't snap his neck fatally (or perhaps not much at all). He retreated from the city to the country and eschewed his own advice: he looked back. "Tradition" became more of a big deal for him, a mountain to climb. Tradition was not just to be fucked with or conquered. It was a shrine. He did not join the Woodstock Generation. He was an upstate patriarch, a retiree at 26, learning to paint, perusing the Bible, and dusting off those Harry Smith 78s just like he did when he was couch surfing on Bleecker Street. For a while, it was a new, old morning.

OK: the backstory. If you are reading this for Rock & Roll 101, take notes, but do not plagiarize. Leave that to Dylan (but more on that later). This story has been blathered about in more than thirty books I see on my shelf right now (an Amazon.com count places the number of Dylan books at more than ten times that number), and if you have read them all and are among the faithful and your DVD of Martin Scorsese's *No Direction Home* has gotten pixilated from overusage, you may find your eyes glazing over in this paragraph, but here goes. Once upon a time, a lapsed bar-mitzvah boy named Bobby Zimmerman dusted the Midwestern snow off his boots and hitched a one-way ride to New York, which lead him, with his stolen records, to the Bleecker Street folk scene. There will always be an endless supply of pretentious 20-year-olds who think they can somehow make the world better than the one controlled by their lame parents and authority figures, but this group was special. They wanted to end racial segregation, stop Cold War foreign policy, and they did all this drinking coffee in joints with no liquor licenses. These kids were sweet. You had to at least find them adorable. Some of them – including Dylan and one Joan Baez with a vibrato that sunk a thousand megaphones – ended up marching with King and didn't just say they wanted to change the world but, in one sticky summer of 1963, actually did it.

But back to 1961: older folks who had paid their dues were among the heroes of Bobby Zimmerman and his pals. Zimmerman, as we know, became Bob Dylan (just as Elliott Charles Adnopoz became Ramblin' Jack Elliott). Ethnicity was left in the coat check and traded in for an amalgam of affected personae and ethnic posturing. So young, scruffy Dylan, with his carefully accessorized proletarian gear, genuflected at the bedside of Woody Guthrie as he was dying from Huntington's Chorea. Guthrie had a few blushing acolytes strumming "This Land Is Your Land" at the Bitter End, but none of them got his blessing like Bobby, who was working the old guy like a carnival barker. "Hey, hey Woody Guthrie, I wrote you a song," sang young Bobby on one of the two originals on his 1961 self-titled Columbia debut. The melody was shamelessly lifted from Guthrie's "1913 Massacre," but no one complained.

So one minute Dylan was kneeling at Guthrie's bedside and earnestly memorizing Carter Family finger-picking and kicking in a harmony with Pete Seeger. The next, Dylan was the voice of a generation. Then he plugged in at Newport and Pete Seeger, depending on whose story you believe, was either figuratively or literally threatening to cut the electrical wires with an axe (a threat literalized in Haynes's movie). *I'm Not There* gave us the Dylan of our imagination, the icon of our subconscious, and Haynes's Dylan – or one-sixth of it, the most intriguing one, the femme fatale – was providing acid-drenched copy for Nat Hentoff. Yet he was also emphatically distancing himself from "the folk tradition," well aware that he would be forever tethered to it. "Strap yourself to the tree with roots," sang Dylan in "You Ain't Goin' Nowhere." "Yet if the only form of tradition, of handing down, consisted in following the ways of the immediate generation before us in a blind or timid adherence to its successes, 'tradition' should positively be discouraged," wrote T. S. Eliot in "Tradition and the Individual Talent" (Eliot 38). Dylan had it both ways. All art is love and theft (see Eric Lott, p. 167). This is how the world ends, as usual.

Going to a Bob Dylan concert in the twenty-first century feels more like "A Prairie Home Companion" than anyone rebelling against anything. It is still thrilling to imagine Dylan as the transgressive who said that "folk music is a bunch of fat people," who drunkenly told the American Civil Liberties Union that he identified with Lee Harvey Oswald, but that was in another lifetime (filled with toil and blood). "Phaedra music," "arsenic music." Dylan was just asking for it when someone trying to start a folkie pogrom in Manchester called him "Judas!" The version of "Baby, Let Me Follow You Down" that he screeched through with the Hawks on the 1966 tour – and again a decade later, with the Band on *The Last Waltz* – bore little resemblance to the version he politely strummed on his 1961 debut. It was some kind of ugly – it smelled like apocalypse. Dylan said on that recording that he got it from Eric Von Schmidt, who said he first heard a similar song by Blind Boy Fuller, but no one knows for sure. The mutation has long outlasted its source. The Dylan of my dreams is forever mutable, transfiguring his words – sometimes with lyricism, more often than not with gravel – shortly after writing them. Dylan's true believers follow him down, even through the most clangorous and atonal changes. They say sing while you slave, but he just got bored, and those who truly love Dylan love his refusal to settle down. When he was on, no one could auto-desecrate better. "He who is not busy being born is busy dying," he famously intoned in "It's Alright, Ma (I'm Only Bleeding)," and way before the aphorism became worthy of inclusion in Bartlett's *Familiar Quotations*, he knew that inspiration was episodic, that it was all too easy to become sick of yourself and all of your creations. Through reissues, YouTube, and, now Todd Haynes, we can revel in the perpetual 1966, a never-ending tour of transgression, an everlasting *fuck you*, to feel, as Kurt Cobain later screeched to a flannel-clad Gen X, "stupid and contagious." Still, he could only play a few chords – never really that well, and often not even in tune – and so he never strayed from the structure of the old songs, even after he plugged in at Newport. How many roads could he walk down? He only learned a limited number of songs and just played them over and over, taking a composer's credit from that writer known as Traditional Arrangement. "That's the folk music tradition," he told the *Los Angeles Times* in 2004. "You use what's been handed down. 'The Times They Are A-Changin'' is probably from an old Scottish folk song."

From his earliest songs, Dylan was leaning on various traditions while, in his most inspired moments, his muse pointed the way to something new. In Martin Scorsese's documentary *No Direction Home*, Allen Ginsberg, looking like he's on his way to Desolation Row, recalls wistfully, and with not a little narcissism, that when he first heard the strains of Dylan's "A Hard Rain's A-Gonna Fall" back in 1963, he wept, not because of the song's apocalyptic sentiment, but because he felt that "the torch had been passed" (*No Direction Home*). The Beats had ceased to be the hipsters of the moment, the old road, for Ginsberg, was rapidly fadin', and this song, that seemed to evoke a Bleecker Street reaction to the Cuban Missile Crisis, pointed fingers which Ginsberg knew would gather more youthful spirits – and, not that this was the first thing on his mind, wallets and libidos (well, the latter *was* the first thing on his mind) – than the printed word.

But Ginsberg was surely aware that the torch was being passed with a tune that had survived centuries. "A Hard Rain's A-Gonna Fall" cribbed heavily from "Lord Randall," a ballad that some speculate was written about the sixth Earl of Chester, who died in 1232. Many centuries later, the story would still have legs. I saw Dylan sing "Hard Rain" in the spring of 2005 and, like Ginsberg, the song made me cry, but while 1963 listeners to the song heard Cold War anxiety, that night in 2005, a wave of applause flooded the Beacon in response to "the executioner's face is always well hidden," still topical a year after Abu Ghraib. Dylan was looking beyond the headlines as early as 1963 when, on a radio show, Studs Terkel proclaimed the hard rain to be a nuclear rain, only to be corrected by the young upstart: "no, no – it's a hard rain." It never got any easier. Keeping it general also kept it more like an anonymous and communal folk song – something that would last forever. The premise of Lord Randall is perennial: soldiers will always be sent off to war, the young will always face the prospect of death, and there will be balladeers to sing about it. Every generation sees the world end in its own way.

Incipient apocalypse provided an auspicious peg for Dylan when he wrote the song, right before Kennedy's and Castro's sabers started rattling. Dylan took the bare bones of "Lord Randall" and filled it with lyrics that alluded to *The Lord of the Rings* ("twelve misty mountains"), racial injustice ("I saw a white man who walked a black dog"), and an eerie wisdom well beyond his years ("I'll know my song well before I start singing"). The repetition is dazzling, overwhelming – like a Whitmanian list or a biblical incantation. The Anglo-American Folk Tradition was maybe just a bunch of fat people. Dylan had a cannibalistic feast before him – centuries to nosh and ruminate on.

So let's fast forward to 1965, when the boy who sat at the feet of Woody and Pete grew up too fast. The promotional film for "Subterranean Homesick Blues," used as the opening of D. A. Pennabaker's *Don't Look Back*, shows Bob Dylan at his most iconic, and it includes advice he was not inclined to follow. It was shot at the beginning of 1965; Dylan, not yet 24, stands in the alley of London's Savoy Hotel, holding signs scrawled with selected words from the song. With his baby face, James Dean sneer, and frizzy pompadour, he affects a calculated insouciance. While we hear the song playing, he is not lip-syncing, but tossing aside placards one at a time, stone-faced. He wants us to focus on the words – bad puns, clichés, and random maxims – but he also wants to give the impression that he couldn't care less about them. The recording spews out the associative lyrics faster than Dylan can toss aside "LOOK OUT" and "KID." By the time he gets to the end of each verse, he is throwing the placards faster and faster.

This is one of the most ubiquitous images in rock & roll, created a decade and a half before the launch of MTV, alluded to in videos by INXS, the Red Hot Chili Peppers, even a parody in the YouTube Democratic presidential debate in the summer of 2007. Some of these phrases were destined for

Bartlett's *Quotations*: "The pump don't work, 'cause the vandals took the handle," "Twenty years of schooling and they put you on the day shift." Others had more direct impact. "You don't need a weatherman to know which way the wind blows" was ominously co-opted by the radical group the Weathermen, that included three members who would accidentally die in an explosion in Greenwich Village, ignoring the advice he gives elsewhere in the song: "Don't follow leaders." In Pennebaker's iconic footage, Dylan, almost contemptuously, lets the placards reading "WIND BLOWS" fall aside like garbage.

Allen Ginsberg, who scrawled some of the words himself, hovers near a garbage can, dovening like an Orthodox rabbi, supporting the premise that Dylan took the aesthetic of *Howl* and set it to a rockabilly riff; he was an Elvis and a Kerouac in a Jewish punk with no shortage of attitude, who looks like he's too young to shave. This was the Dylan who inspired Bruce Springsteen to say at Dylan's 1988 induction to the Rock & Roll Hall of Fame, "The way Elvis freed your body, Dylan freed your mind." This was the young man who crowds still somehow want to see, even though he is as inaccessible as the era he had come to embody. "Subterranean Homesick Blues" combined derivative sources for an effect that was startlingly original. The song's lyrics had some striking similarities to Woody Guthrie and Pete Seeger's "Taking It Easy," its riff sounded appropriated from Chuck Berry's "Too Much Monkey Business," and its title was a nod to Jack Kerouac. He was not claiming purity in his findings – random utterances and recycled wisdom, and, in the promo, not even all scrawled in his own hand – even though he did claim a composer's credit. Did this vandal take the handle? And was that really the whole point? Dylan is heard singing "Don't steal, don't lift," while he is seen lifting a placard reading "DON'T LIFT." A year earlier, when Dylan was on the *Steve Allen Show*, he was asked, "Do you sing your own songs or other people's?" The cryptic response was pure Dylan: "They're all mine, now." He *was* being sincere – he had made the move from folk artist to original singer–songwriter; but he was also not far from the era where Dylan was emerging from the liquidity of the Gerde's Folk City days; back then, melodies were passed around like so many caps soliciting the cover charge, when a melody taught to Dylan by Paul Clayton could emerge as the breakup masterpiece "Don't Think Twice, It's All Right."

"Don't steal, don't lift." The line resonates over four decades later, but with a new irony. Dylan, who David Hajdu called the "Elvis of the mind," has been accused of stealing and lifting material for a growing chunk of his twenty-first-century output (Hajdu 277). Dylan essentially invented the genre of the singer–songwriter – the entire idea of a singer–songwriter – but recently he has been revealed to be leaning more and more on his source material, some well-known, some obscure. Sometimes he alludes, but other times he plunders and buries. "It's easy to see without looking too far / That not much / Is really sacred," he sang in 1965. Four decades later, what seemed like prophecy became fate: Dylan himself has become sacred to many, and it was disturbing to find that if you examined his recent work closely, you found a committee of muses.

"These fragments I have shored against my ruins," wrote T. S. Eliot in *The Waste Land*, and Dylan has been shoring up fragments against his own impending mortality, while perfecting the character of an older man in heartbreak. The blues he intones in a ragged croon or sometimes desperate croak sounds more authentic than it did in a younger man's snarl. Dylan has become the King Lear of rock & roll, raging against the heath, or at least the tie-dyed *hoi polloi* at his concerts. But the writing is more dependent on the words of others. Early Dylan always stole tunes, but later Dylan stole words. It was the latter category that had been the reason for worship, canonization, and inclusion on university curricula. What to do when the voice of a gene-ration was talkin' someone else's words? His two cover albums in the 1990s brought Dylan to the career renaissance he enjoyed with what was called – to his protest – his late career "trilogy": *Time Out of Mind*, "*Love and Theft*," and *Modern Times*. In 1992 and 1993, when the inconsistency of Dylan's later work seemed like a foregone conclusion, Dylan made two albums of traditional songs just as the craze in "roots" music was a fringe phenom-enon, a sliver of the cult of authenticity that dominated the folk scene that Dylan entered in 1961. Dylan had built up such loyalty among his fan base – which, it seemed, was dominating his critical base – that he could endure every plagiarism charge that came his way. "To live outside the law, you must be honest," sang Dylan in a famous line that resembled a similar one from Don Neil's 1958 film *The Lineup*. Living outside the law would be just fine for many in Dylan's audience, a law that was hardly ironclad to begin with. Going back to the source was just what the icon needed.

On October 16, 1992, Dylan gave a glitzy salute to his past at a Madison Square Garden concert celebrating his thirty years as a recording artist, and while there were notable, heartfelt versions of his songs from Neil Young, George Harrison, and others, it was most memorable for Sinéad O'Connor getting booed off stage, shortly after her career-destroying appearance on *Saturday Night Live* a week earlier when she ripped up a picture of the Pope. The mob who hooted O'Connor off stage were there to cheer on Dylan, who performed uncertain versions of his old standards, still trying to hit the notes he had belted out decades earlier, not sure about what his next incarnation would be. While he was certainly giving stronger performances on more inspired nights in lower-profile settings, clues to his next incarnation would appear in two traditional folk albums that would appear: *Good as I Been to You* (1992) and *World Gone Wrong* (1993). With his out-of-tune guitar and low-fi equipment – the albums were casually and quickly recorded in Dylan's garage – it was all too easy to dismiss them as mere obligations, fulfilling the end of a Columbia contract that would eventually be renewed. But Dylan sounds liberated singing the words of others, freed from the albatross of past expectations, from studio technology and from any sonic indication that he is living in the moment of, as he puts it in the *World Gone Wrong* liner notes, "celestial grunge." Celestial finger-picking, Carter Family-style, was preferable for Dylan, sitting out the zeitgeist in his Malibu garage.

Shortly after recording *Good as I Been to You*, Dylan said of the traditional material, "I treated them as if they were my songs, not like covers," and on both albums, his personality is stamped on every track: just as he told Steve Allen in 1964, they're all his, now. Some reviewers complained about the loss of range and dexterity in Dylan's voice, but they were missing the point. Dylan exploited every crack and crevice in an instrument weathered by decades of smoking. But what he lost in dexterity, he more than made up for in drama. Its wreckage, in fact, was crucial for the delivery. The title track of *World Gone Wrong*, slightly but crucially altered from the Mississippi Sheiks' "The World Is Going Wrong," is an example of how an aging rock star could summon a different kind of *Weltzschmerz* from the one of black depression-era troubadours who would go back to sharecropping a few years after recording the song. The chorus's refrain uses apocalypse as a convenient excuse for bad behavior: "I can't be good no more, just like I done before / I can't be good, baby, honey because the world's gone wrong." The Mississippi Sheiks play this for comedy, as if to show that, even in the face of depression, a scoundrel is still a scoundrel. Dylan, a few keys lower and a little slower, makes it sadder, more resigned, intractable. The world is not, in the words of the Sheiks' original title, *going* wrong. It has already gone wrong, with no turning back. For "Blood in My Eyes," the other Sheiks cover on the album (he recorded their biggest hit, "Tomorrow Night," on *Good as I Been to You*), Dylan made a video in which he wanders around London's Camden market in a jaded haze of fame, semiconsciously signing autographs, taking refuge in a café (the locale of the album's cover), where his intoning of the song's refrain, "Hey, hey baby, I've got blood in my eyes for you" is less about a young man's all-night binge than an older man's waning powers. The Sheiks' version is a young man's hyperbole; Dylan's anguished, strained delivery sounds almost literal. The Mississippi Sheiks broke up after 1935, and singer Bo Carter died destitute in 1964, while Dylan was on his unstoppable ascent.

For Dylan, though, the folk songs are like purgation, a musical *mea culpa*, a return to the land where it all began. "Lord, I'm broke and hungry, ragged and dirty, too," he sings on Willie Brown's "Ragged and Dirty," and he sounds convincing – at least for the latter claim. He looked to traditional songs as a ritual cleansing, with nothing but a murkily recorded acoustic guitar to back him up. Working without lyric sheets, it was as if he was summoning up Bleecker Street *circa* 1961, where he could have been performing the songs on a street corner, or in the West 4th Street subway station. When you ain't got nothing, you've got nothing to lose, he sang in 1965, and he sounded like he was just about there, singing American songs that stretched back to the nineteenth century, and English, Scottish, and Irish ballads that stretched back centuries further. The songs told tales of adultery, plundering, murder, and deceit – of a gypsy running off with a maiden, of Stagolee, willing to shoot a man for a Stetson hat, of women who quit men for no good reason, and of men who will kill for jealousy. It was a lawless past, certainly one without copyrights or credits – yet it had a code to which Dylan pledged allegiance, and he sang and played these songs as if his life depended on it. "You're gonna quit me, baby, good as I been to you?" sang Blind Blake, not as a guilt trip, just a settling of the romantic score. *Good as I Been to You,* announced Dylan's 1992 album title, reminding his listeners not to give up on him just yet, even if he wasn't using his own words to make the case. The world would continue to go wrong, but Dylan the songwriter would return. But, as he would write, you can always come back, but you can't come back all the way.

"I'm just going down the road feeling bad," Dylan sang on *Time Out of Mind,* and, from the sound of his voice, you were inclined to believe him, even though "Going Down the Road Feeling Bad" was a hillbilly standard warbled by Elizabeth Cotten and Woody Guthrie back when the Dust Bowl was aswirl; it was later covered by the Grateful Dead and, in an unreleased track, Dylan and the Band from the Basement Tapes sessions. The line occurs when Dylan is singing about a bottomless abyss on "Tryin' to Get to Heaven": "When you think that you lost everything / You find out you can always lose a little more." Dylan belts the lines out, exploiting his croak for all its wear and tear, emphasizing "lose" and "more" with an almost comical elongated percussive attack. How low can you go? Even lower down are the realms of Dust Bowl migration. The earliest known recording of "Going Down the Road Feeling Bad" is by Henry Whitter from 1923, and the song certainly provided the soundtrack to some harsh travels, far more arduous than that of rock & roll's most illustrious tour bus. Dylan sings the line like he is fighting for his life, and, indeed, the sessions were recorded shortly before he almost went to meet Elvis. Archaic language was wafted in elsewhere on *Time Out of Mind*'s atmospheric swamp. "I'll eat when I'm hungry, drink when I'm dry," Dylan grunted on "Standing in the Doorway," a maxim laid out on "Rye Whiskey," recorded by Woody Guthrie, and "Jack of Diamonds," recorded by Blind Lemon Jefferson back in 1926. "My heart's in the highlands, gentle and fair," he sang on the closing track "Highlands," doffing his cowboy hat to a 1789 Robert Burns lyric. Yet these lines were allusive, not plagiaristic, and they were yoked together to paint a portrait of a man out of time – hence the album's title, riffing on a line uttered by Shakespeare's Mercutio in *Romeo and Juliet*. Back in 1970, David Bowie sang about "a strange young man called Dylan / With a voice like sand and glue." Dylan was now a strange older man, and the sand and glue were mixed with deepening regret and despair, and maybe even something like maturity. Dylan, older than that now, did something Bowie, for all his fabulous, glimmering surfaces, could never achieve: he showed us how to age in public. Rock stars were supposed to burn out, not fade away. But Dylan was growing into the character he was playing with stoicism and grace, reaching back through centuries for what was becoming the grandest late-period self-elegy in rock & roll.

"Those old songs are my lexicon and my prayer book," Dylan said in 1997 when the album was released. "All my beliefs come out of those old songs, literally, anything from 'Let Me Rest on That Peaceful Mountain' to 'Keep on the Sunny Side.' You can find all my philosophy in those old songs. I believe in a God of time and space, but if people ask me about that, my impulse is to point them back toward those songs. I believe in Hank Williams singing 'I Saw the Light.' I've seen the light, too" (Pareles, "Wiser Voice"). In 1997, *Time Out of Mind* was a new record that somehow sounded like it had always existed. Dylan had created a compelling character out of the burned-out troubadour, and even if some words and phrases were cobbled together from outside sources, whose are not? "The party's over, and there's less and less to say," Dylan conceded on "Highlands," but on a seventeen-minute track that was cut down from a staggering thirty-five minutes, Dylan still had plenty to say indeed; his archaism was his way back into the game. It came out original, as a compelling work of aural theater. "I can't even remember what it was I came here to get away from," he croons on the heart-wrenching dirge "Not Dark Yet," but even if he conveys a sublimely disoriented ennui, he couldn't get away from those old songs. And to believe in a spiritual like "I Saw the Light" is to believe in a song of belief. The expression resonates beyond its subject matter; the words and sounds are intractable. If anonymous words that had resonated in the voices of Woody, Blind Lemon, or Elizabeth Cotten continue to be his lexicon, on *Time Out of Mind* he passed on the words, entangled with his own, his only lifeline to meaning.

Time Out of Mind sounded like a Sun Records session en route to deepest despair, but the belief in those old words burns out of every tortured syllable. It went triple platinum and ended up Dylan's first Album of the Year. In contrast to his muddled appearance in 1991, Dylan's 1998 Grammy walk was a triumph: he won a competitive award, did not flinch when an anarchist stormed the stage with "Soy Bomb" emblazoned on his chest (Dylan merely arched his eyebrows when he sang "I'm love sick," continuing a devastating performance until security eventually took the stage), and invoked Robert Johnson and Buddy Holly in a gracious acceptance speech. It took seven years for "Love Sick" to appear on a Victoria's Secret commercial, but before it became a lingerie soundtrack, it was a resurrection.

On June 10, 2007, while 12 million viewers were tuned in to "Made in America," the series finale of *The Sopranos*, 1965 Dylan surfaced on the episode's soundtrack, cutting and pasting his way into immortality. A. J. (Robert Iler) and Rhiannon (Emily Wickersham) are parked in the woods, sitting in his SUV pensively staring into space and listening intently to "It's Alright, Ma (I'm Only Bleeding)" from *Bringing It All Back Home*, the album that opened with "Subterranean Homesick Blues." Earlier in the episode, at an after-funeral reception where he is surrounded by mobsters uttering banalities, A. J., who had never been a particularly introspective character until a Yeats poem (he pronounced it "Yeets") and a breakup suddenly spurred him to attempt suicide, began a rather incoherent rant about American consumerism and foreign policy. "It's like, America . . . I mean, this is still where people come, to make it. It's a beautiful idea. And what do they get? Bling? And come-ons for shit they don't need and can't afford." Later, parked in the woods and watching Rhiannon pensively smoking a cigarette and taking in the song, he hears Dylan expressing a similar global frustration, a young man lashing out at everything around him, using a range of resources at his musical disposal. A. J. hears a man only a few years older than he is, who manages to allude to canonical literature without mispronouncing it. The hostility is focused, devastating, and, in contrast to the perception of much of Dylan's work, absolutely lucid. The Dylan of 1965 was no longer affecting the Woody Guthrie twang of a couple of years earlier, and was not yet the adenoidal troubadour he would become in middle age. A mix of influences abounds, but he's not channeling a particular dialect. The influence of the Beatles anglicized his inflections alongside the Dust Bowl and Delta-blues intonations.

This isn't exactly make-out music. They have been through a mental institution together and are listening for meaning. Rhiannon lights a cigarette. "Advertising signs they con / You into thinking you're the one . . ." goes the opening couplet, and you can see the flash of recognition in A. J.'s expression, remembering his inarticulate diatribe at the funeral, as if to say, "I wish I could have put it that way." "You kept telling me this guy was good," A. J. says. "It's amazing it was written so long ago. It's like about right now," Rhiannon replies. They soon move closer to each other and begin passionately kissing while Dylan continues coolly venting from the CD player. Rhiannon mounts A. J. and her bra is about to be unhooked when smoke begins pouring out of the air vent; A. J. made the mistake of parking the car on leaves. But before the car explodes, Dylan's voice can be heard slowing down: "While one who sings with his tongue on fire . . ."

"It's Alright, Ma" indeed had legs over forty-two years after its original recording. Twelve days after the *Sopranos* finale, Dylan included it in the set list of his summer tour, which saw his return to guitar after playing only keyboards in concert performance since 2003. In a show I saw at a casino outside Toronto, it was the highlight of the evening. The song had become a slower blues dirge, and Dylan's voice, reduced to a croak, just added drama to a lament that had become the lament of four decades. It surpassed many eras and occasions. Watergate and Clinton impeachment-era crowds had hollered at the line, "Even the president of the United States sometimes must have to stand naked"; Jimmy Carter and Al Gore had invoked the line, "He who is not busy being born is busy dying." And Dylan seemed to be living out the prophecy, doubtlessly continuing to let the song evolve still. Its particular power seemed as mystifying to its author as to anyone else. Dylan was already surveying an exhausted landscape when he wrote "It's Alright Ma." "The Great sayings have all been said," he wrote in the liner notes to *Bringing It All Back Home*. They are all his, now.

Dylan has, in effect, come to embody the cultural pastiche he wove together so inimitably from "Desolation Row" to "High Water," incongruous elements yoked together. Except that the yoking is less explicit in 2006, when he can assume that bloggers, English teachers, and librarians all across the globe will be scanning his words for attribution. The charges leveled against Dylan would prove ultimately inconsequential for his status as an icon. Dylan has been saying all along that he loves and he thieves, that he's one with Muddy, Cisco, Leadbelly, and all the other magpie hybrids of the American song he's been sponging off for nearly half a century. "Persons attempting to find a motive in this narrative will be prosecuted; persons attempting to find a moral in it will be banished; persons attempting to find a plot in it will be shot." The maxim from Mark Twain at the beginning of *Adventures of Huckleberry Finn*, a book cribbed for *Chronicles: Volume One*, should certainly apply to anything in rock & roll, an art form based on artifice, one that romanticizes the outlaw and banishes the scholar. Anyone with internet access knows that the blogosphere is filled with amateur and professional sleuths creating their own footnotes, tracking down Dylan and his increasingly avaricious muse. In many ways, Dylan's trajectory has been overdetermined. "I was young when I left home," he sang in 1961, a true statement, although he was trying to sound old when he sang it.

"Ain't talkin', just walkin'," he growled on "Ain't Talkin'," the track on *Modern Times* that stood out when the rest of it seemed so enervated, derivative, plagiarized. But it turned out that "Ain't Talkin'" could be the most mind polluting of all – lines and lines lifted from Ovid's *Tristia*. Dylan made other Ovid references on *Modern Times*, too (he says he's been studying "The Art of Love," which he rhymes, somewhat cloyingly, with "fit me like a glove"), but the *Black Sea Letters* and *Tristia*, poems written in exile after the poet was banished by Augustus, resonated most deeply of all. Ovid had been a rock star, perhaps even the voice of his generation in Roman antiquity. But he was also living in a moment of plagiarism – accused of plagiarizing Homer, in a culture that was generally plagiarizing ancient Greece – and, at 60, in the same age group as the Dylan of *Modern Times*, railed against the unfair forces that cast him away. "Ain't Talkin'," with a total of nine lines taken from *Tristia*, is a great Bob Dylan song anyway. He's at, in the words of Dylan and Peter Green's translation of Ovid, "the last outback at the world's end," intoning lines from Roman antiquity by way of the Mississippi Delta, Tin Pan Alley, the Confederacy, and God knows what else. "Walkin' with a toothache in my heel," croaks Dylan, a line from "Old Dan Tucker," a minstrel song first published in 1843. No one owns "toothache in my heel." Ovid, Henry Timrod, Bing Crosby are all public domain, the publishing Desolation Row, the dead-letter office of song. All textual sources are afloat in a voice that sounds older than his 65 years, nearly as ancient as his texts. "In the last outback, at the world's end," Dylan rasps before A Flat Minor becomes A Flat Major, word for word from Ovid's *Black Sea Letters*. It is a glorious finale, a sublime abyss of stolen fragments and appropriated personae. Dylan never claimed to be exactly who he seemed to be anyway. "It ain't me, babe," he told us, although he is not exactly Bing, Muddy, or Ovid either. In a 1962 interview, he was already making his confession: "Maybe I'm just all these things I soak up. I don't know." In 1965, Dylan sang *about* Desolation Row. In 2006, he made it there, number one with a bullet.

2

MICHAEL DENNING

Bob Dylan and Rolling Thunder

In the fall of 1975, just before embarking on the Rolling Thunder Revue tour, Bob Dylan recorded a raucous version of "Buckets of Rain" with Bette Midler for her album *Songs for the New Depression*. The album title was appropriate because Dylan, like Midler, had long drawn on the cultural memories of the Great Depression. The young Dylan emerged in the boom times of the early 1960s as a curiously anachronistic masquerade of a Depression singer – "in times behind, I too / wished I'd lived / in the hungry thirties," he wrote in an early liner note. If the ur-history behind the work of Great Depression-era artists like Orson Welles was the tale of the decline and fall of the Lincoln Republic, the ur-history behind Dylan's work was the epic tale of the Great Depression, of floods and dust bowls, race records and hillbilly records, Pretty Boy Floyd and Blind Willie McTell.

But the album title was also appropriate because the long boom of post-war capitalism was then collapsing into a new depression. The economic slump between the mid-1970s and the early 1990s stands as what we might now call the Great Recession, since the term "recession" had been adopted at the time as a euphemism for "depression," by then always associated with the "Great Depression" of the 1930s. Ironically, the term "depression" had itself been a euphemism of the 1930s, invented to avoid the even more terrifying memories of the "panic" of 1893. By the early 1990s, as one of the major economic studies of the period concluded, "the majority of Americans were worse off . . . than they were at the end of the 1970s," and "those in poverty in 1992 were significantly poorer than the poor in 1979" (Mischel and Bernstein 2, 7). And the Great Recession was not merely an economic watershed; it came to mark a distinctive period in US cultural history, the age of hip hop.

As the economic and political boom times of the 1960s receded into the Great Recession, Dylan embarked on his most ambitious political-aesthetic project since the *Broadside* era, the Rolling Thunder Revue of 1975. Dylan decided to assemble a troupe of performers – musicians, actors, and poets – to

barnstorm from town to town, playing small halls with little advance pub-
licity; along the way they would shoot a movie. It was at once a direct
political action – a campaign to free the imprisoned boxer Rubin
"Hurricane" Carter – and a utopian promise of a new artistic community,
a traveling Brechtian circus and a tale of America told on the road. If the
Rolling Thunder Revue was a failure – it never became the never-ending tour
it was imagined as, and the film was so thoroughly dismissed that it remains
the least-known work of Dylan's career – well, as he sang most every night,
"there's no success like failure, and failure's no success at all." Lashed by
the hurricanes of racial and sexual politics, the songs and performances
that made up the 1975 Rolling Thunder Revue and the subsequent 1978 film
Renaldo and Clara are not only Dylan's "songs for the new Depression," but
they illuminate Dylan's own relation to his times.

Placing Dylan in "his times" is difficult; he always claimed to be out of
time, even when he seemed to be of his time. Musically, his is the art of
prolonging or foreshortening time, adding or dropping beats and measures,
stretching or clipping syllables, resisting the tempo of his rhythm section.
While proclaiming that times are changing, he always tried to stop time, to
escape time, to get outside of time. As he told Allen Ginsberg in an interview
about *Renaldo and Clara*, "You wanna stop time, that's what you want
to do . . . In order to stop time you have to exist in the moment, so strong
as to stop time and prove your point" (Ginsberg 108). One might fairly say
that Dylan's work is made up of strategies of stopping time, techniques of
evading history.

His ballads are notoriously twisted and tangled, crafted with tantalizing
narrative non sequiturs, uncertain pronouns, and unresolved endings. The
pillaging of proper names from history, literature, vernacular song and
mythology – rearranging the faces and giving "them all another name" –
unmoors Dylan's tales from their historical context and severs his historical
allusions from their place. Moreover, he evades history by cloaking his songs
in the avowedly timeless music of blues, ballads, and gospel. Dylan's early
originality was his synthesis of two contrary wings of the folk revival, of
what Dave van Ronk calls, echoing its Latin American name, the "new song
movement" (Van Ronk, *Mayor* 196). On the one hand, Dylan was a "topical"
broadside singer, writing new songs, resurrecting the journalistic function of
the folk ballad; on the other, he, like those van Ronk calls the "neo-ethnics,"
sought to recapture not just the traditional songs but the performing styles
of traditional musics (Van Ronk, *Mayor* 200). Here time was never neatly
kept: one of his Rolling Thunder bandmembers (David Mansfield) later said
that "what I recall that was challenging to learn was his [Dylan's] phrase
lengths, [which] were totally unpredictable – they were [clearly] based on

American ethnic stuff, where it wasn't a neat eight bars, there might be a bar of 2/4, or it might just vamp on something for ten beats – a complete folk thing. I guess it all came from Appalachian music" (Quoted in Heylin 416). Thus, even Dylan's timely songs – from those of Hattie Carroll and Hollis Brown to those of Hurricane Carter and Joey Gallo – insist on occupying the time not of the present but of the past archaic.

Dylan also evaded time and history through his regular resort to the elements – wind, water, fire, and earth – and to an ahistorical geography of mountains, valleys, oceans, plains, and forests. If Christopher Ricks's categorization of Dylan's work by sin does capture the times of his confession – his sinning and repenting, his Saturday nights and Sunday mornings, the endless dialectic of blues harp and god box – it doesn't capture Dylan's elemental indifference, the reason that he is not finally a confessional or even a moral writer; as he sings with Baez on the Rolling Thunder tour, "maybe it's the weather or something like that." It was fitting that Dylan opened his Theme Time Radio Hour programs with a session on the weather. To capture this aspect of Dylan, one might need an analysis of "Dylan's Visions of the Elements."

However, if Dylan's songs of wind, water, and weather – "a change in the weather is known to be extreme" – are powerful naturalizations of history, they are at the same time historical allegories. Dylan's flood songs – from "A Hard Rain's A-Gonna Fall" to "The Levee's Gonna Break" – all have political and social resonances, like the great songs of the 1927 Mississippi Delta flood that Dylan has long been drawn to, from the Bessie Smith "Backwater Blues" that he sang at his first Carnegie appearance in 1961 to the Charlie Patton "High Water Everywhere" which receives an explicit homage on *Love and Theft.*

The very names that dominated the 1975 tour – Hurricane and Rolling Thunder – are examples of this rhetorical hesitation. Hurricane fused the natural force of the storm with the physical and political force of the imprisoned boxer. Rolling thunder was more enigmatic, and its meaning was debated throughout the tour. Dylan told Larry Sloman, a journalist traveling with the Revue, that it was simply the weather: "I was just sitting outside my house one day thinking about a name for this tour, when all of a sudden I looked in the sky and I heard a *boom*! Then *boom, boom, boom, boom*, rolling from west to east. So I figured that should be the name" (Sloman 55-56). "If it was Malibu it was probably the Vanderburg Air Force Base [that he heard]," Roger McGuinn later joked, "... it was probably sonic booms. The Sonic Boom Jet Revue" (Sloman 135). Others also heard jets; for them it was taken from the code name of the bombing campaign against North Vietnam, Operation Rolling Thunder. "Scarlet told me that," one tour member told Sloman, "she's very political. And get this. The planes that attacked Cambodia, the flights originated from the US base in the area, which is Guam," one of the nicknames for the Rolling Thunder band (Sloman 239–240).

Others heard an allusion to Native America; to the Indians it means speaking truth, Ramblin' Jack Elliott's road manager told Dylan, to which Dylan replied: "Well, well. I'm glad to hear that, man. I'm real glad to hear that" (Sloman 56). Rolling Thunder was indeed the name of a Cherokee medicine man, about whom a popular counterculture book had appeared the previous year; and Rolling Thunder himself joined the Revue briefly, coming from Nevada to lead a sunrise ceremony in Newport, Rhode Island.

Bombs over the Ho Chi Minh trail or the echo of the Trail of Tears? Rolling thunder became the master trope of the tour, triggering resonances emotional as well as political, historical as well as religious, sounds of gunfire and words of truth.

In thinking about the Rolling Thunder Revue, it is worth recalling that Dylan's fundamental long form, the frame for his songs, is not the album, but the concert and the concert tour. As Dylan said at the time: "Basically . . . I'm a live performer and want to play onstage for the people and not make records that may sound really good" (Allen 166). The long tradition of boot-legged Dylan "field recordings" is fundamentally a record of concerts and tours, whether public ones like the "Halloween" concert and the "Royal Albert Hall" or private ones like the "Minneapolis Hotel Tape" and the "Basement Tapes." Each of Dylan's films takes the concert or concert tour as its narrative skeleton, and all of them, including *Renaldo and Clara*, might be seen as replies to Pennebaker's film of the 1964 England tour, *Don't Look Back*.

Formally, the tour has four elements: the project, the cast, the itinerary, and the performance. The project of the Rolling Thunder Revue was both political and artistic. As a political intervention, it was a benefit concert. Hattie Carroll, Hollis Brown, Davey Moore, George Jackson: they were, in the words of the *Bringing It All Back Home* liner notes, "all dead." Hurricane Carter "sat like Buddha in a ten-foot cell," and the project of the song – a single released that fall – and the tour – culminating in the Night of the Hurricane in Madison Square Garden – was to break him out of jail: "this is a song about a man who is in jail right now," one version of Dylan's introduction went, "we're gonna try and get him out of jail" (Kokay 51). The longest sequence of the film (the opening of the second half) is the Hurricane narrative, where Dylan's recording of the song punctuates a montage that intercuts an interview with Rubin Carter, street interviews about the case with Harlem residents in front of the Apollo Theater, and the Revue's performance in a New Jersey prison.

Indeed Dylan's "politics" – a long-contested trope – might best be understood as the politics of the benefit concert. This may be an American form, a product of US mass culture: the first classic benefit concert was an earlier union of Patterson, New Jersey and Greenwich Village – the famous Patterson Pageant of 1913, when John Reed and the artists and intellectuals of the *Masses* brought together the Greenwich Village arts community and the New Jersey textile mill strikers of the Industrial Workers of the World (IWW). Though Dylan was, as he put it, no activist, his career could be measured in terms of historic benefit concerts: from the July 1963 voter registration rally organized by the Student Nonviolent Coordinating Committee (SNCC) in Greenwood, Mississippi to his appearance at the 1963 March on Washington, from George Harrison's Concert for Bangladesh in 1971 to Phil Ochs's Friends of Chile Benefit Concert in 1974, from Live Aid to Farm Aid, culminating in *Masked and Anonymous*, a film meditation on the very form of the benefit concert.

Alongside the political project of this "benefit" tour, the Rolling Thunder Revue was also meant to embody a new form of artistic community and collectivity. Analogies abounded: Dylan said it was like "those Italian troupes . . . those Italian street theaters . . . *Commedia dell'arte*. Well this is just an extension of that, only musically"; Baez called it a "medicine show" (Sloman 180, 184); perhaps it is best thought in its own words as a revue, in the spirit of those country music or rhythm and blues revues of the 1950s and early 1960s. Its cast mapped the lineaments of American arts, theater and music. Dylan enlisted the singers and songwriters of North American "new song," figures who had emerged out of the intersection of the folk music revival and the civil rights movement: among them were Joan Baez, Roger McGuinn, Ramblin' Jack Elliott, Joni Mitchell, Gordon Lightfoot, Kinky Friedman, Richie Havens, and Arlo Guthrie. The Revue was staged by a Brechtian theater director with roots in New York's experimental theater (Jacques Levy), and filmed by a radical documentary filmmaker (Howard Alk) whose earlier films had spanned music (the Newport folk festivals and Janis Joplin) and politics (the murder of Black Panther Fred Hampton and the 1968 Chicago convention, *American Revolution II*). From Robert Altman's *Nashville* (a film surely in Dylan's mind), the Revue borrowed the actor and singer Ronee Blakley.

The Revue also brought together a host of writers who not only performed on stage and in the film, but who eventually offered interpretations of its meaning: the playwright Sam Shepard who began as the film's "screenwriter" and was left capturing epiphanic scenes and dialogues; the gonzo rock journalist Larry Sloman obsessively recording the fear and loathing of the campaign while writing dispatches for *Rolling Stone*; and the poet Allen

Ginsberg who not only interpreted the song lyrics and film images, but articulated the ideology of the Revue, telling one journalist that "the Rolling Thunder Revue will be one of the signal gestures characterizing the working cultural community that will make the Seventies . . . this tour may not end as all the other tours have. There is some desire among us to have a kind of permanent community and Dylan is stepping very, very slowly to find out if that can work" (Ginsberg in Benson 142–3).

Much of the meaning of Rolling Thunder lay in the tour's itinerary, and this is accented in the film's editing of the tour. At the time, it was seen as a search for America on the eve of the bicentennial celebrations – "we have," Ginsberg said, "once again, embarked on a voyage to reclaim America" (Ginsberg in Benson 149). It would be easy – too easy – to place the Rolling Thunder Revue alongside the Basement Tapes and the folk cover albums of the 1990s as part of Dylan's quest for what Greil Marcus called that "old, weird America": it is surely Highway 61 revisited once again. But that would miss the specific nature of Rolling Thunder's "America," its peculiar history-writing by concert touring.

After all, the tour begins in the streets of Rome. Dylan's sets all opened, as does *Renaldo and Clara*, with Dylan – in a transparent Dylan or Nixon mask (it's too transparent to be clear) – and Bob Neuwirth singing "When I Paint My Masterpiece." More or less a 32-bar song (albeit with a truncated bridge that rhymes the old world "gondola" with the new world "Coca-Cola" without lasting the full 8 bars), it is a fitting opening because it is an allegory not only of artistic creation (the endlessly deferred promise that everything will be different, everything will be beautiful, when he paints "that" masterpiece) but also of the road – caught between Rome and Brussels, "it sure has been one helluva ride" – and the stage itself – "oh the hours that I've spent inside the Coliseum / Dodgin' lions and wastin' time." But it is also a tale of the debris and detritus of history itself: the song opens with "the streets of Rome are filled with rubble / Ancient footprints are everywhere"; it ends – in the *Renaldo and Clara* version – after the mandolin break with the verse that has left Rome and Brussels for some mythical place in the land of Coca-Cola: "Train wrecks runnin' through the back of my memory."

Moreover, the "America" that is reclaimed by the Rolling Thunder Revue is not the entire United States, but a specific geography, the northeast from Plymouth Rock to New York City by way of the streets and prisons of New Jersey. The following year, Dylan tried to re-enact the Rolling Thunder Revue along the gulf coast from Florida to Texas by way of New Orleans, but that tour never achieved the imaginative resonance of the northeastern swing (none of the footage of that tour was used in *Renaldo and Clara*).

Furthermore, the northeastern Revue was not simply a US tour; it crossed the border into Canada, recruiting Canadian musicians and incorporating Canadian settings and a little French dialogue. The landscape of Rolling Thunder is that of the north country (just as the landscape of *Masked & Anonymous* was to be Los Angeles); in the film, the Montreal concert performance of "Isis" begins with the fourth verse: "We set out that night for the cold in the North." *Renaldo and Clara* could easily have been titled *North Country Blues* or *Girl from the North Country*.

It is this north-country setting that places Rolling Thunder in the Great Recession. In the mid-1970s, the declining New England mill towns they played – Lowell, Providence, New Haven – were, together with the bankrupt New York, powerful emblems of the economic and social crisis, figures for the end of the post-war boom, train wrecks running through the back of the collective memory. Ancient footprints were everywhere, Dylan's Revue riotously retraced them, and the symbolic itinerary of the film maps a way of history-telling. In addition to countless bars, diners, streets, stations, trains and buses that make up the "road," a half-dozen or so locations come to dominate the Revue and the film: the Greenwich Village coffeehouses of the beat poets and the folk revival; the resort cabaret where Ginsberg reads *Kaddish* to the elderly Jewish women of the Mah-Jongg convention, sandwiched between cabaret versions of "Wilkommen" and "Morning of My Life"; the Tuscarora reservation schoolhouse near Niagara Falls where Indian activist Wallace Mad Bear Anderson welcomes the Revue and gives a history of the Iroquois Confederacy; the costumed theme-park history of Plymouth Plantation where the Revue meet a self-described "humble archaeologist dressed in seventeenth century garb"; the Lowell cemetery where Ginsberg and Dylan read "Mexico City Blues" at Kerouac's grave, and Ginsberg translates the francophone Stations of the Cross for Dylan; the street evangelists below the statue of George Washington on New York's Wall Street; the Trenton, New Jersey prison where Carter was being held; and the Dreamaway Lounge where the old singer Mama Maria Frasca reprises her recordings of Italian-language laments.

Through these "spots in time," often cut up and folded back on themselves and each other, Rolling Thunder touches down on the North Country's ethnic and racial histories – settlers, Indians, Africans, Italian and Jewish immigrants, the Québécois border country and mill towns – not as epic journey but as picaresque adventure. In the geography of Dylan's "tales of Yankee power," the northern borderlands (including Hibbing, Minnesota itself) are metaphoric equivalents of the southern borderlands, Dixie and Durango, Mississippi and Mexico. Dylan is not giving a history lesson as much as receiving one, finding it in odd curio shops as well as national monuments, New York streets as well as reservation schoolhouses. This history lesson always comes as a voice – preacher, poet, teacher, singer, politician, activist – trying to seduce and persuade, and, on the side, to pass the hat. No one can sing the blues like Mama Maria Frasca. And she'll sell you the record for a dollar.

Criss-crossing the north country and its borderline, Rolling Thunder staged a Brechtian comedy with performers in masks and painted faces. The show's director, Jacques Levy, recalled: "The thing was to make it appear like it was a spontaneous evening – totally impractical, like a travelling vaudeville show or a travelling circus – the jugglers and the clowns . . . We weren't using spotlight. All the lights were on the stage . . . The house would be dark, and there, down there, would be this little jewel box all lit up" (Bauldie 160). The core of the band had been assembled at the *Desire* recording sessions: its rhythm section was made up of bassist Rob Stoner, rock drummer and jazz pianist Howard Wyeth, and jazz percussionist Luther Rix. Over the rhythm lay a cacaphony of guitars and harmonized voices that juxtaposed vernacular musics like second cousins meeting uneasily at a family reunion: the acoustic dreadnought Carter licks of Guthrie-sidekick Ramblin' Jack Elliott, the British electric glam-rock of David Bowie partner Mick Ronson, the jangling West Coast twelve-string of Roger McGuinn, the lilting *tejano* guitar of T-Bone Burnett, and the explosion of fiddles, mandolins, dobros and pedal steels of the young virtuoso David Mansfield. Cutting through it all was Scarlet Rivera's "gypsy" fiddle, which took the place the organ had had in Dylan's earlier ensembles, weaving in and out of Dylan's vocal and harp phrases, its timbre often dominating the arrangements.

The show's basic sequence varied little, and is followed in both *Renaldo and Clara* and the *Live 1975* recording. At one level, the "story of the Hurricane" howls across the evening like rolling thunder, from Elliott's rendition of the first song he heard Woody sing – the Depression outlaw ballad "Pretty Boy Floyd" – to Dylan's revival of his civil rights ballad of justice betrayed, "The Lonesome Death of Hattie Carroll" (Hurricane's name echoes that of Hattie Carroll); from Baez's version of the Depression ballad "Joe Hill," about the Wobbly minstrel framed for murder (which she dedicates to the ongoing farmworkers organizing campaign) to the Baez/Dylan duet on Dylan's remake of "Joe Hill," "I Dreamed I Saw St Augustine" ("I dreamed I was amongst the ones / Who put him out to death"); from the Dylan/Baez duet on "I Shall Be Released," here fully resonant as a prison song ("All day long I hear him [Hurricane] shout so loud / Crying out that he's been framed"), to Dylan's culminating second-half performance of "Hurricane" with its update of "Pretty Boy Floyd" – "Now all the criminals in their coats and their ties / Are free to drink martinis and watch the sun rise."

At the time, Dylan's return to the "topical" song surprised many; it was, apparently, the product of Dylan's reading of Rubin Carter's autobiography and a subsequent visit to him in prison. In retrospect, his *corrido* about Hurricane Carter does not seem anomalous. Dylan's emergence as a songwriter had been shaped by the politics and aesthetics of the black liberation movement, and he had long been drawn to ballads of the wrongfully imprisoned. In 1971, he had responded to the death of the imprisoned black radical George Jackson by recording a single memorializing him: "Sometimes I think this whole world/ Is one big prison yard. / Some of us are prisoners, / Some of us are guards." In addition, Dylan's return to the form of the "topical" broadside that he had practiced in the early 1960s and then abandoned seems to have been inspired by the example of the Mexican *corrido*, with its roots in the Mexican Revolution ("We'll drink tequila where our grandfathers stayed/When they rode with Villa into Torreon" he sings in "Romance in Durango") which he had first attempted in his ballad, "Billy."

"Ashamed to live in a land/Where justice is a game," Dylan sings that the "story of the Hurricane . . . won't be over till they clear his name / and give him back the time he's done": Dylan wants not only to stop time but to take it and give it back. So the show can't end – "though I believe it's time for us to quit" – and the show's double ending points to two possible resolutions of the benefit concert. On the one hand, the prisoner feels he's "Knockin on Heaven's Door," the song rewritten without the badge and the guns; on the other hand, the ensemble insists that "This Land is Your Land," that, as Dylan says, "someday it'll [Guthrie's song] be our national anthem" (Kokay 51). The effect of the evening was to place Hurricane Carter in a long line of political prisoners and social outlaws, and to give new life and meaning to older, half forgotten, songs.

But Hurricane Carter was not the only hurricane on stage. History's ancient footprints were everywhere: the show opened with a half dozen songs by band members without Dylan, which not only sampled the musics he inherited, but conjured up the ghosts of that music, ranging from Bob Neuwirth's song about Hank Williams to Ramblin' Jack Elliott's channeling of Woody Guthrie. When Dylan took the stage, more ghosts were invoked – in different towns, it might be Poe, Melville, or Kerouac – and the evening's road narrative began. His opening set – a half-dozen story songs performed with the full band – were road songs, allegories of the Rolling Thunder Revue. "I hear them semis rolling too / If there's a driver on the road, then let him have my load," he sings in the exuberantly rewritten "Tonight I'll

Be Staying Here with You" ("You came down on me like rolling thunder," he sings in one of the evening's invocations of the ruling metaphor). Dylan's juxtaposition of the magical 6/8 journey to "the cold in the north" in "Isis" to a driving "Hard Rain's A-Gonna Fall" accented the latter's road trip of the "blue-eyed son," stumbling and crawling across misty mountains and crooked highways. "Romance in Durango" is here less a work of musical cinema – Dylan's 3-minute remake of Peckinpah's *Pat Garrett and Billy the Kid* – than a road song of "me and Magdelena on the run," with thunder rolling – "was that the thunder that I heard?" The music of the first half has the feeling of a rock & roll circus, a carnival of unorchestrated guitars jamming with clashing timbres.

The second half begins with what Sam Shepard called Jacques Levy's "one theatrical bravado act" (Shepard 112): the voices and guitars of Dylan and Baez are heard before the curtain rises on their acoustic duet of "Blowin' in the Wind." That theatrical "folk revival" is followed by a handful of Dylan/ Baez duets with a very different musical feel; they are joined by a full country band, dobros and steel guitars whining over "Mama You Been On My Mind," "I Shall Be Released," the folk lyric "The Water is Wide" and the Johnny Ace tune from the early 1950s, "Never Let Me Go." The show then turns to the Revue's "new song" figures, regulars and guests, who did short sets of their best-known numbers – among them, Baez's "Diamonds and Rust," Roger McGuinn's "Chestnut Mare," Joni Mitchell's "Coyote," and Gordon Lightfoot's "Sundown."

Dylan returned for a solo set of songs wrestling with the immediate past. In interviews at the time, Dylan regularly likened the 1960s to the Civil War: "the sixties were a shattering decade. The same thing happened in the 1860s." Now "it's a period of reconstruction" (Kotkin 45). The 60s "will always be felt just the same as the Civil War was always felt into 1870 and 1880" (Allen 168). "Tangled Up in Blue" was added halfway through the tour, and it came to serve as a rendering of that break. The Rolling Thunder version of "Tangled" recasts most of its "I"s in the third person, and the song's original search for a lost lover is displaced by a search for the entire political–artistic community, that lost world of "music in the cafes at night / and revolution in the air." "So now I'm going back again / I've got to get to *them* somehow": it stands as the starkest statement of Dylan's own goal for the Revue. In *Renaldo and Clara*, the song is the film's climax, and it follows a conversation in a diner about the "truth and love" that had made the "movement," and what happened when the movement went astray.

In this segment – which included "It's All Over Now, Baby Blue" with its command to "Forget the dead you've left / They will not follow you," and "Simple Twist of Fate" (in this version people tell him it's a crime, not a sin, fitting for an evening on criminal justice) – Dylan's acoustic guitar is a hyp-notic jingle-jangle; there is no finger picking, no blues work, no bass ostin-atos, none of the open tunings of *Blood on the Tracks*: just a strum with upbeat accents and cross-rhythms that tug against the vocal phrases. His harmonica never interrupts the lyrics; the harp solos are wordless codas to each song.

After that solo engagement with the "civil war" of the 1960s, the spare *Desire* band – bass, percussion, and Rivera's fiddle – joins Dylan for the climax of the show. These songs – here "Hurricane" shares a sonic space with "Oh Sister," where the brother's complaint is echoed in the interplay of Dylan's mouth harp and Rivera's fiddle, "One More Cup of Coffee," and "Sara" – seem weirdly out of place, set in another landscape than that of the north country. Largely written in minor keys, they have a remarkable sense of openness; they are the calm eye to the rest of the Revue's sonic hurricane, its heterophony of guitars and voices.

"One More Cup of Coffee" was not only the climax of the road narrative but, as Allen Ginsberg noted, the musical "high point" of the show: "it's Moorish, gypsy, Arabic, semitic," Ginsberg said. " 'Isis' and 'Hurricane,' I'm in sympathy with them in historical terms but this is sort of an archetypal song" (Sloman, 110, 113). With its Andalusian chord progression, it is one of those classic Dylan songs that have virtually no lyric content, or – rather – whose lyric content has been so concentrated in the great chorus that the verses are almost an afterthought: one thinks of "I Shall Be Released" or "Knockin' On Heaven's Door."

The entire traveling circus – including the poets like Allen Ginsberg – returned to the stage for the finale, three songs sung as anthems: "Just Like a Woman," the hymn-like "Knockin' on Heaven's Door," with Roger McGuinn singing the evening's final direct invocation of rolling thunder ("Mama, I can hear that thunder roll / Echoin' down from God's distant shore"), and Guthrie's "This Land is Your Land."

Wilfrid Mellers once suggested that Dylan's music is as much about self-loss as self-discovery, about finding oneself in the group, in a community. One can see this in the constant tension – among critics as well as in Dylan himself – between seeing him as essentially an individual performer ("No one sings Dylan like Dylan," as the early ad put it) and seeing him as a songwriter creating "standards" that would be adopted by a larger com-munity. Though Dylan recognized that he was never Pete Seeger, leading audiences to sing along, the dialectic between solo and group performance – between, to use Mellers' phrases, "the monody of deprivation" and the "heterophonic religious community" of the "white euphoria" (Mellers 43,58) – has been a constant of his performances from the civil rights performances to the electric blues bands (Dylan went electric so he could have someone to play music with) to the drunken revelry of the basement tapes. Rolling Thunder was one of Dylan's most powerful attempts not only to recreate the political-artistic community by force of will, but to counterpoint the monody of deprivation of his solo ballads (an enunciating mime in whiteface) with the euphoria of the Revue's carnivalesque singalongs.

The euphoria of the Revue's finale was brief; the Revue failed to become the "permanent community," an endless traveling coffeehouse where performers could always sit in for a few tunes. As tour memoirs later recounted, the Rolling Thunder Revue was no calm eye in the midst of the sexual and racial hurricanes engulfing American culture at the outset of the Great Recession. The conflicts over sexual politics were starkly figured each night when the cast of the Revue came together to sing an unlikely anthem, Dylan's "Just Like a Woman." Perhaps no song better embodied the ambiguities of Dylan's sexual politics – and the sexual politics of the 1960s counterculture – and it has long been the object of interpretative dispute (going back to Ellen Willis's classic feminist appreciation/critique of Dylan). Sung collectively at the end of the Revue, with Baez and Blakley taking verses, it is a figure not only for the impact of the women's movement on the Revue, but for the place of Dylan's love songs in the desire called Rolling Thunder. A great musical work, Jacques Attali reminds us, "is always a model of amorous relations" (Attali 143), and Dylan's Revue was such a model. Indeed from the beginning, the prominence of the women musicians on the tour distinguished it from Dylan's earlier electric tours with the Butterfield blues band and the Band. Not only did Joan Baez and Ronee Blakley have solo segments within the Revue, but Dylan's vocal duets with Baez and his instrumental duets with Scarlet Rivera became musical allegories of the love lyrics performed.

Renaldo and Clara tried to elaborate the Revue's love songs into a narrative, punctuating the musical performances with improvised skits of time-worn folk tales of the road: the rock-and-roller sweet-talking the farmer's daughter; the truck driver offering a ride to two women in a diner; the virgin boy in the whorehouse; the guitarist choosing his music over his lover; the cowboy trading a woman for a horse. These classic tropes of the masculine road narrative were fused to the goddess feminism of the era, the recovery of the eternal feminine in feminist mythographies like Mary Daly's *Gyn-Ecology*. This aesthetics of gender is played out in Dylan's newly-composed love lyrics: his invocation of the goddess "Isis"; his fusion of sister and wife, brother and husband, in "Oh Sister"; his daughter of the outlaw who "never learned to read or write" in "One More Cup of Coffee."

Like Kerouac's road novels, Dylan's road film ended up half *roman à clef* –
luring its audience with the promise of *cinéma verité* (particularly in the
confessional song, "Sara") – and half archetypal fiction, where all the men
were Renaldo (the one with the hat), and all the women Clara (the one with
the rose). Despite its dose of goddess feminism, the film's sexual politics were
at best enigmatic and at worst simply embarrassing. As Sara Dylan later
recalled of her role in the film, "After all that talk about goddesses, we
wound up being whores" (Quoted in Heylin 424).

It is also telling that the Revue's finale – the anthemic performance of
Guthrie's "This Land is Your Land" – was cut from *Renaldo and Clara*,
Dylan's four-hour film deconstruction of the tour. In its place, the film ends
with a "found" performance that was not part of the Rolling Thunder
Revue: a lounge singer's cover version of the Bee Gees's hit, "Morning of My
Life," performed by the obscure soul singer Hal Frazier. One might take this
revised ending as a disenchanted, ironic comment on the failure of the
Rolling Thunder Revue ("There were no jewels, no nothing, I felt I'd been
had"). On the one hand, despite winning a new trial, Hurricane Carter was
convicted at a second trial and did not win his freedom for another decade.
Moreover, though the tour was meant to culminate in a fusion of the folk-
country harmonies of the Revue with the call-and-response of black soul
music at the Night of the Hurricane in Madison Square Garden, it never did
connect with contemporary black musical culture: though Muhammed Ali
and Coretta Scott King appeared on stage, neither Stevie Wonder nor Aretha
Franklin made it and only Roberta Flack sang. Though Stevie Wonder did
perform at a subsequent Night of the Hurricane in Houston, the utopian
climax – a Dylan/Wonder duet – did not occur (ironically, it took place a
decade later when they appeared at the 1986 Martin Luther King Jr.
birthday concert). The creation of a beloved community in the name of
Hurricane was not to be in 1975.

As Shepard wrote of the Madison Square Garden concert when Roberta
Flack joined them, "There's a definite taste of black-white tension going on
backstage … Nothing weird or violent, just these two totally different
streams of musical culture swimming by each other without mixing" (Shepard
164). One sees this also in the awkward group performance of "Knockin'
on Heaven's Door" in the New Jersey prison, where Dylan turns as if Flack
will join him at the microphone but doesn't find her. Compared to the
legendary performances by Johnny Cash at Folsom Prison and B.B. King at
Cook County Jail, Dylan's jailhouse rock is anticlimatic. The forlorn hope
of Hal Frazier's "Morning of My Life" stands in place not only of "This
Land is Your Land" but of the yet-to-be-sung Dylan/Wonder duet. With all
its utopian promise, the Rolling Thunder Revue remained largely a white

country-folk ensemble, rarely crossing the color line; what is perhaps most striking about the Revue's music in the context of Dylan's own career is the absence of the blues (the only exceptions are Dylan's 16-bar blues march, "It Takes a Lot to Laugh, It Takes a Train to Cry" and the blues vamp version of "Hard Rains A-Gonna Fall"). Dylan himself seemed to recognize the formal and political incongruity of Rolling Thunder: after the disastrous reception of the film in 1978, he reversed course musically, abandoning the "rag rock" (his description of the music in 1976 [Hickey 107]) of Rolling Thunder for the soul studio at Muscle Shoals, and replacing the folk and country harmonizing of Baez, Blakley, and Emmylou Harris, with the gospel harmonies of Carolyn Dennis, Helena Springs and Regina McCrary.

Dylan's songs for the new depression seem to stand more as the end of an era than as the new beginning he had imagined. The Great Recession was to be not the age of Rolling Thunder but the age of Reagan, not the era of Hurricane but the era of hip hop. In *Chronicles: Volume One*, Dylan, writing of his lowest moment in the Great Recession, says: "Ice-T, Public Enemy, N.W.A., Run-D.M.C. These guys definitely weren't standing around bullshitting. They were beating drums, tearing it up, hurling horses over cliffs. They were all poets and knew what was going on ... The music that Danny [Lanois] and I were making was archaic. With Ice-T and Public Enemy, who were laying the tracks, a new performer was bound to appear, and one unlike Presley" (Dylan 219). Though Dylan sat in on the age of hip hop, joining Kurtis Blow on "Street Rock," he knew that he was out of time, too much like Presley.

Nevertheless, in retrospect, Dylan bears uncanny resemblance not to Presley but to that other prodigious American artist who imagined himself as Shakespeare, Orson Welles. If Welles re-imagined Elizabethan theatre in Hollywood film, Dylan re-imagined Elizabethan ballads in the recording industry. Welles was of course the fat man, Dylan the thin man. If Welles was, as he said, condemned to play the king roles, Dylan wondered why he must always be the thief. Midwesterners who headed east to New York, they were prodigies in left-wing political-cultural formations that gave them subjects, forms and collaborators. Both went electric, taking their avant-garde performances to the mass audiences of broadcasting and recording. In a sense they never repeated their astounding youthful triumphs: the Harlem *Macbeth*, *Citizen Kane*, "Blowin' in the Wind," *Highway 61 Revisited, Blonde on Blonde*. The political moment passed, their collaborators disappeared, and they barnstormed on the memories, leaving a mass of unfinished, discarded works as well as moments of genius in a never-ending tour. Like Welles's *Touch of Evil* restored from its Cold War cuts, Dylan's Rolling Thunder Revue recordings and the all-but-forgotten *Renaldo and Clara* – out of time in their own time – may yet come to figure America's Great Recession.

3

ANTHONY DECURTIS

Bob Dylan as songwriter

Who expects what? I mean anybody that expects anything from me is just a
borderline case. Nobody with any kind of reality is going to expect anything
from me. I've already given them enough you know, what do they want from
me. You can't keep on depending on one person to give you everything.
Bob Dylan (1984), quoted in Williams, *1974–1986*, 275

If the songs are dreamed, it's like my voice is coming out of their dream.
Bob Dylan (1966), quoted in Shelton, *No Direction* 354

Does it need to be asserted that exploring Bob Dylan as a songwriter means
examining every aspect of who he is as an artist, a cultural figure, and a
human being? His songs are the very heart of the matter – the foundation on
which his aesthetic reputation rests and the fuel for the symbolic identities
and roles that he has at various points ambitiously sought, gotten entrapped
by, desperately attempted to escape, and manipulated to his own benefit. For
well over four decades now, the perception of Dylan as a shape-shifter has
at least as much to do with the type of song he has chosen to write as with his
sound, his look, his subjects, the quality of his voice and his attitude. With
Dylan, who so often invites references to Shakespeare, one conclusion is
inevitable: the song's the thing.

And as long as we're talking about Shakespeare, another remarkable
aspect of Dylan's songwriting is the "negative capability" it embodies – that
is, as Keats said referring to a quality of Shakespeare's work, "when a man is
capable of being in uncertainties, mysteries, doubts, without any irritable
reaching after fact and reason" (letter of December 21, 1817, quoted in Noyes
1211). That description could, of course, apply to every aspect of Dylan's
career, not just his songwriting. Still performing at an energetic pace, particularly for an artist of his age and stature; releasing new albums on a regular
basis; issuing and reissuing older material; writing a memoir; authorizing
films and a lengthy documentary; appearing in advertisements; hosting a
radio show, and occasionally doing interviews – all while maintaining an

impenetrable air of mystery – Dylan is the very definition of hidden in plain sight. He has perfected a version of himself that permits his being available virtually everywhere while letting very little of himself be known. It is a feat that would seem to be impossible in our media-drenched age, but he has accomplished it.

His songs are similarly ubiquitous and elusive. They introduce a multitude of characters and give expression to innumerable points of view. But it is very often impossible to know which, if any, of those views are his. Ultimately, as the "little neighbor boy" mutters "underneath his breath" after bearing out Frankie Lee's corpse in Dylan's enigmatic parable, "The Ballad of Frankie Lee and Judas Priest," "Nothing is revealed." At least about the writer of the songs themselves.

It is ultimately impossible to maintain that degree of mystery unless you, in some elemental way, remain a mystery to yourself – or, at least, your talent does. In a 1986 *Rolling Stone* interview with Kurt Loder, Dylan responded this way when asked if he felt that he had "tapped into the Zeitgeist" when he wrote his classic songs of the 1960s. "As I look back on it now, I am surprised that I came up with so many of them," Dylan said. "At the time it seemed like a natural thing to do. Now I can look back and see that I must have written those songs 'in the spirit,' you know? Like 'Desolation Row' – I was just thinkin' about that the other night. There's no logical way that you can arrive at lyrics like that. I don't know how it was done . . . It just came *through* me" (Loder 301).

Nearly twenty years later, Dylan answered in similar terms when Ed Bradley asked him about that same period in a "60 Minutes" interview. "I don't know how I got to write those songs," Dylan told him in that rare television appearance. "Those early songs were almost magically written" ("60 Minutes," December 7, 2004). Then, highly uncharacteristically, Dylan recited the extraordinary opening verse to "It's Alright, Ma (I'm Only Bleeding)":

> Darkness at the break of noon
> Shadows even the silver spoon
> The handmade blade, the child's balloon
> Eclipses both the sun and moon
> To understand you know too soon
> There is no sense in trying.

Perhaps because he quickly got fed up with others' poring over his words in search of the hidden meanings and messages they might impart, Dylan rarely cites his own lyrics. But in speaking to Bradley, he delivered his lines with a combination of matter-of-factness and pride. In his pronunciation, he even emphasized the Dylan-ness of those unnervingly repetitive five childlike rhymes – a conscious explosion of the stereotypical moon/June/spoon rhymes of Tin Pan Alley. (Characteristically, Dylan would reverse that process a few years later when he began exploring a lighter-hearted, more concise song-writing style, in opposition to the wild and whirling words of songs like "It's Alright, Ma." "That big fat moon is gonna shine like a spoon," he sings on "I'll Be Your Baby Tonight," from *John Wesley Harding*, and the tune's Tin Pan Alley sentiments are entirely unironic, an early effort to shed his Bardic identity.)

The look of detached confidence on Dylan's face as he spoke to Bradley conveyed beyond any doubt that he completely understood how unique and peerless those lyrics are. But again he confessed to having no idea how they were written. "Well, try to sit down and write something like that," he said after he finished his recitation, his voice filled with resignation but tart with challenge. "There's a magic to that, and it's not Siegfried and Roy kind of magic, you know? It's a different kind of a penetrating magic. And, you know, I did it. I did it at one time" ("60 Minutes," December 7, 2004). Asked it he could do it again, Dylan shook his head no. "You can't do something forever," he said. "I did it once, and I can do other things now. But, I can't do that."

In Dylan's case, such claims of not knowing how he wrote his best lyrics originate from issues far more complex than the usual artist's dodge that creativity is entirely a mystical – or, well, magical – process: "It just came *through* me." It's more than a result of the desire not to become self-conscious about technique – self-conscious, that is, to a degree that impedes untram-meled creativity, at least at the start of the writing process. With Dylan, ultimately, the issue is escaping expectations, wherever they might come from, even from within himself.

The relationship of Dylan's early songs to his later ones has been an issue he's been forced to confront – and to assert – since his move away from folk music to rock & roll (not that he ever completely left folk music behind) in 1965. That is to say it's been an issue ever since he can be said to have had an earlier style. As with many artists who become as iconic as Dylan has, a purist, prelapsarian view of their work develops, and the moment of the fall into commercialism or whatever shifts depending on which period of his music the observer likes best. Which isn't to say that all periods of Dylan's music are equally significant or accomplished. They are not. But the scene, possibly a dream sequence, in Todd Haynes's film *I'm Not There* in which a giggling Dylan shouts at a crucifix, "Do your earlier stuff!" perfectly cap-tures Dylan's own perception of the problem.

In one of its most intriguing manifestations, the issue arose as Dylan was working with producer Daniel Lanois on *Oh Mercy*, the 1989 album that was widely hailed as a return to form. In *Chronicles: Volume One*, the highly idiosyncratic memoir Dylan published in 2004 (it's really more like a long Dylan song than a nonfiction narrative), he writes that "Off and on during the time we were cutting 'Series of Dreams,' [Lanois would] say to me something like, 'We need songs like "Masters of War," "Girl From the North Country," or "With God on Our Side."' He began nagging at me, just about every other day, that we could sure use some songs like those. I nodded. I knew we could, but I felt like growling. I didn't have anything like those songs" (*Chronicles: Volume One* 195).

It's hard to imagine that many people would have the backbone to speak anything like those words to Dylan, let alone while he was making an album and demonstrating his new songs. It would also be fascinating to know what Lanois actually said, as opposed to what Dylan heard. Was Dylan interpreting Lanois's remarks, or was the producer really that direct?

Whatever the case, Lanois's willingness to push Dylan is precisely why *Oh Mercy* and *Time Out of Mind* (1997), the other album he produced for Dylan ten years later, are arguably the strongest albums Dylan has done since *Blood on the Tracks* in 1975, the one album that is the unquestioned equal of his 1960s masterpieces. (It should certainly be pointed out, however, that over the course of the past four decades Dylan has written dozens of songs that rank not only among his personal best, but among the best songs written during that era.)

It's telling that Lanois held up Dylan's older work to him as a standard – if, in fact, he did – and intriguing to think about what he was actually trying to get Dylan to do, what kind of song he was trying to get Dylan to write. "Series of Dreams," a decent enough, second-tier Dylan song, never made it onto *Oh Mercy* – whether because Lanois disliked it, or Dylan withheld it in a kind of spite is unknown. And Dylan also writes in *Chronicles: Volume One* that Lanois initially regarded "Everything Is Broken," one of Dylan's many catalogue songs ("Broken lines, broken strings / Broken threads, broken springs . . .") as "a throwaway" (*Chronicles: Volume One* 198).

Clearly, Lanois, as have so many of Dylan's collaborators, saw working with the singer as an opportunity to create an album that would be regarded as an aesthetic milestone, one that could stand proudly alongside the landmark work that Dylan had already done. What Lanois didn't understand, at least at first, is that Dylan makes no distinction between such legitimate desires on the part of his peers and the urging of recalcitrant fans to do his "old stuff." They are all expectations to be ignored, if not explicitly rejected.

The three songs from his past that Dylan recalls Lanois mentioning come squarely from the period when he was earning, if that's the appropriate term, his reputation as the "voice of his generation." All three songs are acoustic, and based on earlier folk melodies that Dylan transformed through his lyrics into thoroughly contemporary statements. Before starting work with Dylan on *Oh Mercy*, Lanois had produced the Neville Brothers' album *Yellow Moon* (1989), on which the Nevilles recorded "With God on our Side," along with "The Ballad of Hollis Brown," both of which had appeared on Dylan's 1963 album, *The Times They Are A-Changin'*. Lanois had even brought Dylan by to visit the sessions, and Dylan had been stunned by Aaron Neville's otherworldly interpretations of his songs.

At the 1963 Newport Folk Festival, Dylan had introduced a duet version of "With God on our Side" that he was about to do with Joan Baez by jokingly saying, "I thought I wrote this song." He went on to add that years before he had heard Liam Clancy sing the Irish ballad "The Patriot Game," "and it must have somewhere stayed in the back of my mind." Dominic Behan, who wrote "The Patriot Game" (which itself borrowed a melody from an older Irish folk song) accused Dylan of plagiarism (the song's thematic structure and some of its lyrics and tone are similar). For those reasons, "With God on our Side" became one of the early sites in the battle over the originality of Dylan's early work. The best of Dylan's various explanations for his borrowings is the simplest, and probably the most honest: "I did it because I like the melodies" ("Bob Dylan in His Own Words").

From Lanois's standpoint, that all three songs draw on traditional folk melodies is no doubt one of their strong points. Blending the traditional and the modern is his forte. While Dylan has been revered for "going electric" in 1965 and annihilating the claustrophobic aesthetic purity of the folk movement, his creating contemporary relevance for folk music was his first great achievement, one that, despite the easy breakdown of his career into "folk" and "rock" periods, has remained a significant part of his artistic repertoire. That reinvigoration of the folk tradition extends beyond the "finger-pointing" protest songs that established him as the so-called voice of his generation. It is most evident in "Girl from the North Country," which is hardly a political song, but a traditional English ballad that Dylan first encountered through the folksinger Martin Carthy, whose arrangement Dylan borrows. By the time of *Another Side of Bob Dylan* in 1964, Dylan had essentially re-imagined folk music in entirely personal terms. That turned out to be a prelude to his "going electric," but it essentially defined what would come to be enshrined as the singer–songwriter mode: deeply personal, intensely poetic songs performed in an identifiably folk (or folk-derived) acoustic style. That Dylan would later complain in his 1984 *Rolling*

Stone interview with Kurt Loder that contemporary folk singers didn't deserve that name because they all perform their own songs is just another of the many ironies of his unavoidable influence.

If not Dylan's most successful or best-known protest song, "Masters of War" is one of his harshest. In its vitriolic attack on arms manufacturers ("even Jesus could never forgive what you do," "I'll stand over your grave / Till I'm sure that you're dead") and uncompromising anti-war stance, the song epitomizes the sort of work that made Dylan a darling of the left in the early 1960s. Like many of even his most obvious protest songs, however, "Masters of War," which came out just seven months after the October 1962 Cuban Missile Crisis, has some unlikely elements. In the song, Dylan fixes his sights on a system that just two years before, former president Dwight D. Eisenhower, a general and war hero himself, had termed the "military–industrial complex." Rather than simply decrying the horrors of war, Dylan indicts the beneficiaries of an economic system that makes war profitable. For all its vitriol, it's a much broader and systemic critique than is typically offered in topical songs.

When Dylan later turned from political songwriting, he often said that such songs had become too easy for him to write. He had wanted to attract attention to himself as a songwriter, he claimed, and he knew exactly what his audience wanted to hear – and he gave it to them. Even allowing for Dylan's tendency to trivialize his own accomplishments as a means of avoiding expectations based on them, "Masters of War" bears out his own stated reasons for dismissing his socially conscious music. It, once again, borrows a traditional melody, and, for all its corrosive power, it flatters every aspect of his audience's assumptions about the world. It trades on contemporary anxieties about the Cold War and possible nuclear annihilation, as well as an activist generation's youthful righteousness.

Over the years, Dylan has performed the song on some significant occasions, notably at his 1990 concert at the United States Military Academy at West Point shortly after the launch of the Persian Gulf War, and on the Grammy television broadcast in 1991, when he received a Lifetime Achievement Award. On that latter occasion, his performance rendered the song unrecognizable, as did his concert performances of it around the same time. Both of those performances of the song enact the spectacle of Dylan cutting his meanings two ways. If you are opposed to the Gulf War, why are you playing at West Point? If you are so frustrated by being termed the voice of social protest, why would the one song you play before an international audience of a billion people as you are honored for your "Lifetime Achievement" be "Masters of War," a song that helped create that identity? And if you did choose to play it, why would you render it unrecognizable? Taken together, those actions and those questions summon the tensions at the heart of Dylan's relationship to his own work, particularly from his earliest period.

"With God on our Side," like "Masters of War," channels the anxieties of the Cold War years, but takes a withering look at American exceptionalism, the notion that God has a special historical plan for the United States. With a weary sarcasm, Dylan notes that that plan evidently included massacring American Indians and forming a strategic alliance with Germany after it slaughtered 6 million Jews. By the end of the song, his message is universal and pacifist, and delivered with staccato emphasis on its last five words: "If God's on our side, he'll stop the next war."

But, again, as always with Dylan, there is an aspect of the song that complicates its most obvious intentions. One verse raises an odd question, one different from the rhetorical questions that arise from the caustic historical analyses that drive the rest of the song. The verse runs like this: "In many a dark hour, I've been thinkin' about this: / That Jesus Christ was betrayed by a kiss. / But I can't think for you, you'll have to decide, / Whether Judas Iscariot had God on his side." While the song's very title moves it beyond history into the realm of metaphysics, this verse introduces issues that have little to do with the political or even moral points addressed in the rest of the song. In the broadest sense, it might be read to suggest that, just as America has betrayed its ideals – and, in its violence insulted the notion that God is on its side – Judas betrayed his declared love of and devotion to Jesus ("betrayed by a kiss") for greed, the biblical thirty pieces of silver.

But the verse can also be heard as revealing Dylan's inherent discomfort with absolute positions – sometimes even as he's taking them. At other moments he's reached for seemingly unforgivable figures and attempted to complicate or subvert what he perceived as his audience's one-dimensional view of them. One of these occurs in his song "Only a Pawn in Their Game" (also from *The Times They Are A-Changin'*), which addresses the 1963 murder of Mississippi activist Medgar Evers, one of the most heinous crimes of the Civil Rights era. Rather than castigate the killer – as it turns out, a ruthlessly violent Ku Klux Klan member whom it took three trials over the course of three decades to convict – Dylan focuses on the social and political conditions that create such men and make their crimes possible.

It's a bold step, but one that also can be seen as a refusal to share in the righteous condemnation of the killer. If the man who slayed Evers was "only a pawn" in a larger sociopolitical and class game, does that relieve him of responsibility for his actions? Other songs from this period – "Who Killed Davey Moore?" and "The Lonesome Death of Hattie Carroll," for example – employ a similar strategy, shifting the focus away from individuals to larger, but inevitably more abstract, social issues. If activists are often seeking to put a "human face" on political issues that can seem difficult to personalize, Dylan often does the opposite – moving the focus away from individual people and specific events, and pointing to larger social causes and meanings. "The answer is blowing in the wind," indeed.

Apart from his songwriting, Dylan took similar stands in interviews and public statements, all as part of a refusal to conform to viewpoints that his followers assumed he held. In a 1968 interview in *Sing Out!* with John Cohen and Happy Traum, for example, Dylan refuses to disavow support of the Vietnam War. He mentions "a certain painter," a friend of his, who, he says, is "all for the war. He's just about ready to go over there himself. And I can comprehend him." Traum is confounded, but Dylan insists, "I've known him a long time, he's a gentleman and I admire him, he's a friend of mine. People just have their own views. Anyway, how do you know I'm not, as you say, for the war?" (Cott 137).

Suggesting in 1968 that you might support the war would have forever damaged the counterculture credibility of just about anyone other than Dylan. By that point, however, Dylan had already become enough of a gnomic figure that his refusal to conform to progressive expectations might not have come as too much of a surprise. But three years earlier, in 1965, he made an even more dramatic statement in an interview in the *Los Angeles Free Press*. Discussing, yet again, why he had stopped writing protest songs, he said, "Like, I don't consider any elder generation guilty. I mean, they're having these trials at Nuremberg, right? Look at that and you can place it out. Cats say, 'I had to kill all those people or else they'd kill me.' Now, who's to try them for that? Who are these judges that have got the right to try a cat? How do you know they wouldn't do the same thing?" ("Bob Dylan In His Own Words.")

The best-known and most notorious of Dylan's rejections of left-wing orthodoxy occurred in December of 1963 when he delivered a speech at a National Emergency Civil Liberties Committee (NECLC) dinner honoring the Bill of Rights. The organization had chosen Dylan to receive its annual Tom Paine Award in recognition of the importance of his efforts in behalf of civil liberties. Honoring someone like Dylan was a departure for the organization, a conscious effort to recognize the younger generation of activists that was beginning to make its mark.

Dylan's acceptance speech opened with comments that insulted the guests at the dinner for being old ("I only wish that all you people who are sitting out here today or tonight weren't here, and I could see all kinds of faces with hair on their head"). And then, three weeks after the assassination of John Kennedy, Dylan declared, "I got to admit that the man who shot President

Kennedy, Lee Oswald, I don't know exactly . . . what he thought he was doing, but I got to admit honestly that I too, I saw some of myself in him . . . I don't think it could go that far. But I got to stand up and say I saw things that he felt, in me" ("Bob Dylan and the NECLC").

The outrage that Dylan's comments provoked – similar to what happened to outspoken critics of US policy like Bill Maher in the wake of the 9/11 attacks – caused him to respond at considerable length in a kind of prose poem to the NECLC. His remarks, characteristically, were alternately apologetic, defensive, confusing and irrelevant – once again, they were more like one of his songs than a statement. But they also revealed something about his state of mind, and the position that he would write from for the rest of his career: ". . . I am sick / so sick / at hearin 'we all share the blame' for every / church bombing, gun battle, mine disaster, / poverty explosion, an president killing that comes about."

As Dylan points out, it is braver and more difficult to interrogate your own relationship to the heinous events of your age than to shield yourself behind bromides like "we all share the blame." And, conversely, a comment like "if there's violence in the times then / there must be violence in me" provides a justification for the broad view he adopts in many of his protest songs, an understanding that condemning the individual who murdered Medgar Evers isn't enough, because an entire social structure helped make that act possible. Further, he understands that unless you recognize how you are implicated in and affected by those social forces, the righteousness of your protest is empty and, at least in part, self-serving. (Dylan seems to allude to his experience at the NECLC dinner in his emotionally tangled 1967 song "As I Walked Out One Morning.")

But Dylan makes an even more revealing point elsewhere in his response to the NECLC: "it is a fierce heavy feeling / thinkin something is expected of you / but you dont know what exactly it is . . . / it brings forth a wierd [sic] form of guilt." Obviously, the issue of expectations had already become significant for him, in his public and personal life as well as in his work as a songwriter. Even on *The Freewheelin' Bob Dylan*, the 1962 album that solidified Dylan's stature as a voice of protest, some signs indicated that he was already growing weary of that stance and that role. The album was released just three days after Dylan had turned twenty-two, and yet the song "Bob Dylan's Dream," the last song he recorded for the album, already imagined the breakages that would lie ahead in his life and work. Conjuring an image of himself among like-minded friends, he sings, "As easy it was to tell black from white, / It was all that easy to tell wrong from right. / And our choices were few and the thought never hit / That the one road we traveled would ever shatter and split."

While the lyrics overtly refer to the friends Dylan had made – and left behind – on the folk scene at the University of Minnesota, they also suggest the development of a world view that would soon not allow for the easy black-and-white certainties of the protest movement. The song's mood is a kind of anticipatory nostalgia, as if the world of such certainties had already passed and the singer was apprehensive about what lay ahead in the new, more complicated world he was beginning to envision.

That mood would alter completely the following year in "My Back Pages" on *Another Side of Bob Dylan*. The image of black-and-white absolutes recurs ("Lies that life is black and white / Spoke from my skull"), but this time Dylan is dismissing what he sees as the naïve stances of his real-life past, not one that he is summoning in a dream. He is not longing for the lost connections of his past, or the sense of community he no doubt felt for a time with his folk audience. Instead, he is moving forward with a new-found confidence – and a renewed sense of aesthetic vitality. "Ah, but I was so much older then," he concludes. "I'm younger than that now."

Bob Dylan's efforts to elude his audience's expectations reached their peak – or nadir – with his incomprehensible performance of "Masters of War" on the 1991 Grammy broadcast. His continual redefinition of his songs itself constitutes a form of songwriting – the compositional version of his so-called Never Ending Tour. At his best, he has treated his songs not as museum pieces but as living, breathing things, always subject to reinterpretation. Indeed, he had come to interpret his own work in the same way that anyone else might attempt to cover a "Dylan song," as nearly everybody else has.

But in reinterpreting his songs, Dylan didn't always enhance or deepen them. Particularly in the late 1980s and early 1990s, he often flattened their melodies, and his vocals – simultaneously garbled, arrhythmic and uncomprehendingly intense – rendered his lyrics indecipherable. He seemed to be displaying a contempt for his own work – and seeking to lose his audience. He had employed a similar strategy roughly two decades earlier with his much-derided 1970 double album, *Self Portrait*. Frustrated by obsessive fans who had camped out near his home in Woodstock and, later, in Greenwich Village, Dylan decided, "Well, fuck it. I wish these people would just *forget* about me. I wanna do something they *can't* possibly like, they *can't* relate to. They'll see it, and they'll listen, and they'll say, 'Well, let's go on to the next person. He ain't sayin' it no more. He ain't givin' us what we want,' you know? They'll go on to somebody else.' But the whole idea backfired. Because the album went out there, and the people said, '*This* ain't what we want,' and they got *more* resentful . . . And to me it was a *joke*" (Cott 301).

Having hit that bottom, however, Dylan began to rise again. Since the early 1990s, he has been in resurgence, a resurgence that started not with a return to his early songs, but a journey beyond them to songs in the folk tradition that inspired his early classics. Though some of the writing and arranging credits on both *Good as I Been to You* (1992) and *World Gone Wrong* (1993) have been disputed, neither album featured a single song written by Dylan himself, a first in his long career. Both albums consist exclusively of solo acoustic performances by Dylan, who accompanies himself on guitar and harmonica. They also provide a rare example of Dylan not feeling compelled to bolt in a new direction from one album to the next, even though *Good as I Been to You* was very well received, previously a sure indicator that Dylan would do anything rather than repeat it. Aptly, the album these two most resemble is *Bob Dylan*, the singer's 1961 debut, though even that release included two originals.

Recording folk and blues staples like "Sittin' on Top of the World," "Froggie Went A Courtin'," and "Stack A Lee" relieved Dylan of the pressure to meet his audience's expectations. The move worked to Dylan's advantage. While no one in the early 1990s would have expected Dylan to record an album of folk songs, whether he wrote them himself or not, his fans were delighted that he did. Dylan had made the image of a solo artist with a guitar and harmonica an indelible symbol of authenticity, and it excited his audience that he had once again assumed that role. From Dylan's standpoint, because the songs were not his own, he could not be held accountable for their "meaning" – though, ironically, his highly entertaining liner notes for *World Gone Wrong* offer vivid interpretations of all the songs on that album.

Perhaps most significantly, Dylan, now in his fifties, had claimed an identity that he found far more liberating than "voice of a generation" or anything that had come after that. His voice ragged, his guitar playing as raw and idiosyncratic as that of any of the artists whose work he was revisiting, his very role as an era-defining songwriter abandoned like a worn-out hobo sack, he had become like one of the old, broke-down bluesmen and folk itinerants who had been his early idols. The success of his youngest son Jakob's band, the Wallflowers, pushed Dylan further into the cultural margins, and he seemed comfortable there. Story after story in the media trumpeted tales of a generational changing of the guard, of the Wallflowers' young audience expressing surprise (and indifference) when told that Jakob's father was an important songwriter.

Also, the relatively brief time that Dylan had spent touring with the Grateful Dead had introduced him to a new, younger audience who viewed him in different terms from their parents' generation. They had less invested in his living up to any role he may once have played. They were curious about him and eager to hear him play the songs they had heard so much about, but they embraced his desire to rearrange them and loved that he played different sets every night. Whoever remained of Dylan's older audience had grown used to his ornery, unpredictable ways, and his younger audience knew and expected nothing different. Particularly after Jerry Garcia's death in 1995, the jam-band audience grew increasingly interested in Dylan.

Consequently, when Dylan began actively to write again, he not only had a contemporary identity that suited him, but an audience ready to hear what he had to say. On *Time Out of Mind* (1997), his first album of new songs in seven years, Dylan sang tunes like "Love Sick," "Not Dark Yet," and, most spectacularly, "Highlands" that did not attempt to pander to current trends, but cast him as a kind of ancient mariner, wandering amid the fragments of the shattered contemporary world and musing about his increasingly fragile relationship to it. That Dylan suffered a serious heart problem shortly before the album's release only added to the chilling whiff of mortality it gave off.

And, just as *Good as I Been to You* generated a companion piece in *World Gone Wrong*, *Time Out of Mind* has come to be seen as the first part of a trilogy with the two albums that have followed it, *"Love and Theft"* (2001) and *Modern Times* (2006). While stylistically distinct, the three albums all consist of songs whose main characters seem adrift in a world they barely recognize. Their touchstones are the musicians, musical styles, and values of a folkloric past, all made relevant by the sheer conviction with which they are evoked. Having dynamited the folk tradition when he went electric in 1965, Dylan repeatedly cast himself as part of that tradition in the 1990s. Folk musicians like Leadbelly and Woodie Guthrie "were free spirits who took chances," he insisted in one interview, "and I never wished to annul any of that spirit" (Cott 401).

In keeping with that spirit and tradition, Dylan redefined himself as a kind of traveling troubadour. The conventional wisdom of the music business in the 1980s and 1990s was that artists toured only to support new albums. Dylan not only rejected that thinking, he reversed it. "The world don't need any more songs," he asserted, and he performed often, whether he had a record release to promote or not (Cott 372).

As early as 1984 Dylan stated, "Yeah, well I'm just thankful I can play on stage and people will come and see me. Because I couldn't make it otherwise, I mean if I went out to play and nobody showed up, that would be the end of me. I wouldn't be making records I'll tell you that. I only make records because people see me live. So as long as they're coming along to see me live I'll just make some more records"(Cott 324).

It is perhaps inevitable that Dylan's three most recent albums, like his folk classics from the early 1960s, have been taken to task for their borrowings from such wildly varied sources as Junichi Saga's *Confessions of a Yakuza*, an oral history of a Japanese gangster, and the little-known work of the nineteenth-century American poet Henry Timrod. Writing about Dylan's alleged plagiarism in the *New York Times* in 2006, singer–songwriter Suzanne Vega argued that, "He's never pretended to be an academic, or even a nice guy. He is more likely to present himself as, well, a thief. Renegade, outlaw, artist. That's why we are passionate about him" (Vega).

In that sense, Dylan's songwriting is something that he enacts as much on stage as in the studio, as much in the songs of the past that he covers as in a song he's written that he reinvents. His body of work is unrivaled, but its edges are sharp and rough with wear. As highly refined, endlessly suggestive and intellectually captivating as they often are, his songs are built for performance and interpretation. They are songs that demand, as in the tradition in which Dylan began, that voices, new and old, rise up and sing.

4

ALAN LIGHT

Bob Dylan as performer

In December of 1965, Bob Dylan gave a press conference in San Francisco. It was a prime example of his hyperspeed, evasive jousting with the media at the time. "How do you explain your attraction?" he was asked at one point in this curious televised event, to which he responded, "Attraction to what?" But Dylan, then 25 years old and in the midst of the historic concert tour that found him getting booed around the world for playing with an amplified rock band, gave a serious answer when someone inquired about whether he preferred playing live or making records. "Concerts are much more fun than they used to be," he said, "[but] the albums are the most important. It's all concrete, it's very concise, and it's easy to hear the words and everything" (*Dylan Speaks*).

Several months later, frayed and ravaged from the tour (and from the requirements and expectations involved in being Bob Dylan), the singer wrecked his motorcycle in Woodstock, New York, and while the severity of his injuries has never been verified, it provided him with the necessary justification for getting off the road. It would be eight years until he went back on tour – and so, at the peak of his popularity and influence, it seemed certain that Bob Dylan would be defined almost entirely as a recording artist.

Forty years later, though, things didn't work out that way. After an ambivalent and erratic approach to live performance in the 1970s and '80s, Dylan embraced the touring life whole-heartedly, connecting himself directly back to the troubadour tradition from which he sprang. Since beginning the journey often referred to as the Never Ending Tour in 1988, he has played over a hundred shows a year, every year: he has now passed the 2,000-concert mark during this era. Dylan sightings were once as rare as those of the Loch Ness Monster. Now, he can be found on stage at state fairs, corporate functions – anywhere with an audience is apparently fine by him.

Some of these appearances have been astonishing, revelatory, while some have been painfully awful. Most significant, though, is the way in which this dedication to touring has largely redefined Dylan and his legacy. While obviously his unparalleled body of recorded music will live on forever, he has gone to great lengths to recreate himself as, first and foremost, a performing artist. He is not usually thought of as a showman or an on-stage force on a par with the Who or Bruce Springsteen. But it is through his work in front of an audience that much of his finest music has been made and that much of his story can best be told.

"This is Dylan's true magic," wrote Sam Shepard of a stop on the 1976 Rolling Thunder Revue tour. "Leave aside his lyrical genius for a second and just watch this transformation of energy which he carries...He's infused the room with a high feeling of life-giving excitement. It's not the kind of energy that drives people off the deep end but the kind that brings courage and hope and above all brings life pounding into the foreground" (32).

Almost fifty years into a career unlike any other, Bob Dylan is a legend, a hero, a mystery. He is also a working musician. "A lot of people don't like the road, but to me it's as natural as breathing," Dylan told the *New York Times* in 1997. "I do it because I'm driven to do it...I'm mortified to be on the stage, but then again, it's the only place where I'm happy. It's the only place where you can be who you want to be. You can't be who you want to be in daily life" (Hasted 110).

First, a word about Dylan's bad nights. It may seem an odd place to start, but at this point, numerous second- and third-generation Dylan fans have trooped off excitedly to see their idol, only to witness a lackluster, mumbly performance and conclude that his best days are behind him. (My wife attended a notoriously dreadful New York City show in the early 1990s, and it took me many years to convince her to give him another shot.) In fact, if you put a bunch of diehard Dylan fans together, the conversation will quickly turn to comparing notes on the worst show they attended. It's a badge of honor, to have sat through a bad night – or two, or a dozen – and keep going back, only to be reminded sooner or later of why such commitment is worthwhile. "You get what Bob gives you," Ringo Starr recently said. "The last time I saw him, it was hard to recognize the songs. But the time before, he was clear as a bell" (Schou).

Dylan has always made it clear that he considers his songs to be living, breathing things, and that the chance to continually reengage and reexplore his material is what excites him the most. "There's always new things to discover when you're playing live," he said in 1989. "It might be the same song, but you find different things to do within that song which you didn't think about the night before. It depends on how your brain is hooked up to your hand and how your mind is hooked up to your mouth." Ten years (and a thousand or so shows) later, he added that "Once the architecture is in place, a song can be done in an endless amount of ways. That's what keeps my current live shows unadulterated" (Heylin, *Behind the Shades* 682).

Most critical to Dylan, it seems, is demonstrating that his songs aren't permanently fixed museum pieces. Never comfortable with the process in the recording studio to begin with, he has always argued that the album versions just happen to be what got caught on one particular day. So it's no surprise that he feels a need to consider his writing anew every time he performs – sometimes reaching new depths or finding new meaning, sometimes coming up with nothing at all. As Paul Williams, whose multi-volume *Bob Dylan: Performing Artist* series is easily the definitive study of Dylan's live work, once wrote, "every night, whether he is in good form or bad form, he says, in effect, 'Think again.'"

So where does this leave a casual fan or a newcomer, who just sat through ninety minutes of a 60-something-year-old man wheezing through unrecognizable renditions of some of the greatest songs ever written? First, remember that one of the reasons you love Bob Dylan is for his unpredictability; if it's not, you're setting yourself up for disappointment. And second, you can be pretty certain that he'll be back in the area sometime soon – and that he keeps his ticket prices relatively low.

Tracing Dylan's evolution from a wary but brilliant live performer to a revered road warrior isn't especially hard, since his performing career is as well-documented as that of any other musician, save possibly his comrades in the Grateful Dead. There have been ten or so official live albums – from such unfortunate, haphazard releases as 1984's *Real Live* to the thoughtfully curated "Bootleg Series," overseen by Dylan's manager, Jeff Rosen – plus appearances on albums commemorating various all-star galas and events, and a handful of concert videos and DVDs. All of that, of course, is on top of a mammoth collection of bootleg recordings, which seem to have captured every moment that Bob Dylan has appeared in public, often more effectively than the authorized albums were able to. For the purposes of this chapter, I'm going to try to avoid the bootleg universe – it's an endless and addictive rabbit hole to go down, but virtually impossible to address in any comprehensive manner. (Also, Dylan himself has always expressed hostility toward bootlegs, so the ethical questions they raise are entirely in your own court.)

Though scattered recordings as far back as 1959 have been released, the earliest long-form representation of Dylan in front of an audience is the *Live at the Gaslight, 1962* album, which was released in 2005 in conjunction with the publication of his *Chronicles: Volume One* memoir. Likely taped in October across several sets at the prototypical Greenwich Village folk club, these ten songs were recorded between the release of his 1961 debut, *Bob Dylan*, and his 1963 breakthrough *The Freewheelin' Bob Dylan*. It mixes three of his new, original compositions – most notably, his early masterpiece "A Hard Rain's A-Gonna Fall" – with seven traditional songs, such as "Barbara Allen" and "Cocaine."

In *Chronicles: Volume One*, Dylan writes that the Gaslight was "a cryptic club – had a dominant presence on the street, more prestige than anyplace else" (15). But what blazes through the album is Dylan's absolute confidence and self-assurance; no sense of intimidation or uncertainty is perceptible. And why should there be? He was already playing concert halls at this point, had released an album (granted, a commercial disaster) on the country's leading record label, and had blown past the dues-paying stage of playing clubs at lightning speed.

If the Gaslight set reveals the young singer on the brink of making the leap from gifted student and interpreter of folk songs to a unique and creative voice of his own, the six-song *Live at Carnegie Hall 1963* EP captures the pinnacle of Dylan's protest phase, full of what he later called such "finger-pointing songs" as "Ballad of Hollis Brown" and "With God on our Side." In turn, the two-disc *Live 1964: Concert at Philharmonic Hall* reveals how quickly he transcended such material, as he unveiled more abstract, mystic works like "Gates of Eden" and "Mr. Tambourine Man." As his songs went from setting the standard in established folk forms to breaking entirely new ground, Dylan knew that he had to lead listeners to his destination. He began to draw out his lines and over-enunciate on stage – listening now, with his latter-day mumble-growl lodged in our heads, it sometimes sounds almost uncomfortably precise, until you remember how unprecedented this kind of extended, non-linear songwriting really was.

The best one-stop demonstration of what was happening during these years is the 2007 DVD *The Other Side of the Mirror: Live at the Newport Folk Festival 1963–1965*. In the earliest footage, Dylan is clearly folk music's Golden Child – surrounded by Doc Watson and Clarence Ashley, duetting with the scene's princess (and his champion/patron/lover) Joan Baez, ultimately closing the festival locking hands with Baez, Pete Seeger, the Freedom Singers, and Peter, Paul, and Mary for a triumphant version of "Blowin' in the Wind." His political writing – "Who Killed Davey Moore?," "Only a Pawn in Their Game" – is delivered earnestly, passionately, by this new hero of the old guard.

The following year, there's nothing eager to please about Bob Dylan's appearance at Newport. He's the reigning superstar, and he knows exactly how much he is capable of blowing everyone's mind. The majestic "Chimes of Freedom" tears the place apart. His awkward charm was hardening into a stylish and devastating cool. As the DVD illustrates, there was already no one in his league.

And then came the Newport Folk Festival of 1965.

It is the stuff of myth, impossible now to truly imagine. Today, it feels like when Dylan took the stage on July 25, 1965, clad in a leather jacket and backed by the Paul Butterfield Blues Band (without Butterfield), the ground shook and the heavens split asunder. The depiction of the scene in Todd Haynes's 2007 film *I'm Not There*, in which Cate Blanchett's Dylan character and his bandmates literally open machine-gun fire on the crowd, may seem heavy-handed, but it also represents precisely the way history remembers this first time the folksinging icon presented himself with full rock & roll accompaniment.

Does anyone really know what happened? Was the audience booing with scorn and hatred, or because the sound mix was bad and the set only fifteen minutes long? Did Pete Seeger actually grab an ax and threaten to cut the electrical cables? When Dylan returned to the stage and played a biting, acoustic rendition of "It's All Over Now, Baby Blue," was it an act of deference or defiance? What matters now is not the performance but its impact, which was to draw a line in the sand and proclaim a new era. The footage of "Maggie's Farm" and "Like a Rolling Stone" on the *Mirror* DVD reveal a manic, rushed intensity, a sound dominated by the chaotic splatter of guitarist Mike Bloomfield's riveting fills and solos. Watching this document, it seems that all the interpretations are true, that excitement, confusion, frustration, betrayal, inspiration are all filling the Newport air.

Lost in the conventional telling of the story is the fact that Dylan didn't just parachute in and tear the heads off the festivalgoers – the day before, he participated in the usual songwriting workshops, playing solo versions of some of his new songs just as he had in previous years. Furthermore, how shocking could the band really have been? He had already released the half-electric *Bringing It All Back Home* album, and "Like a Rolling Stone," from the flawless, fully rocked-up *Highway 61 Revisited*, was a huge radio hit.

Regardless, the gauntlet had been thrown down, and the concerts that followed often turned into pitched battles with the audiences. So much has been written about the tour (which went first across America, then on to Europe) with backing provided, for the first time, by the group soon to be known as the Band, it's hard to add anything to the discussion. The music, definitively captured at the legendary Manchester show on May 17, 1966 that was finally released in 1998 as *Live 1966: The "Royal Albert Hall" Concert*, was simply some of the most thrilling, exhilarating rock & roll ever created. The opening, acoustic half of the show is easy to overlook in the drama of the moment, but the razor-sharp delivery of "Visions of Johanna" and "Desolation Row" is stunning – the perfect jab to set up the knock-out punch that followed.

How hostile was the response to the searing, daredevil electric half of these shows? Bad enough that Band drummer Levon Helm bailed out partway through the US part of the tour. Bad enough that the Dylan visible at the end of Martin Scorsese's magnificent documentary *No Direction Home*, as the European dates are ending, is pale and waxy, palpably at the end of his rope. Baiting the press, hanging a gigantic American flag behind the stage in France, and racing through the days on a steady diet of drugs certainly didn't help matters. But the tension and pressure of creating groundbreaking art while trading the shackles of being perceived as a political leader for the madness of being taken for a seer, a divine truth-teller, had become impossible.

Soon after the tour concluded came the motorcycle accident. Dylan would appear live just three times in the next seven-plus years: at a memorial concert for Woody Guthrie in 1968, playing knockabout versions of three Guthrie songs backed by the Band at Carnegie Hall; in a lackluster set at the 1969 Isle of Wight festival; and at 1971's Concert for Bangladesh, the first all-star benefit rock concert, at which he delivered a heartfelt, old-school acoustic set. He continued to release albums – from the cryptic, haunting *John Wesley Harding* to the tossed-off *Self-Portrait* – but other than the two hours of those three appearances, there was no indication that he had plans to spend any more time on stage.

During Dylan's years at home, the scale of the rock & roll business changed. The Woodstock Festival of 1969 illustrated the size of the new rock marketplace. Tours were booked into bigger venues, ticket prices went up. In the meantime, the Band went from being an incomparable backing group to stars in their own right, even landing on the cover of *Time* magazine. By 1973, the opportunity for a tour that reunited Dylan and the Band was simply too big to resist. They bashed out the underrated *Planet Waves* album to warm up, and announced that they would play forty concerts in twenty-five cities in January and February of 1974.

Tickets were sold through a mail-order lottery, and it is estimated that 4 percent of the American population applied for seats. Promoter Bill Graham assembled the most ambitious, most luxurious tour ever, with the musicians flying between cities on their own tricked-out private plane. As tour publicist Paul Wasserman said, "the Dylan tour that year was like Jesus coming back" (Graham and Greenfield 358).

Unfortunately, according to Band drummer Levon Helm, they "felt unready" at the opening date in Chicago, and never did muster much enthusiasm for these shows. The evidence on the *Before the Flood* album – which was recorded at the final shows in Los Angeles, and was actually Dylan's first-ever official live release – reveals an adequate, occasionally top-notch set, and bootlegs don't offer many other conclusions. The opening sprint through a roaring recast of "Most Likely You Go Your Way (And I'll Go Mine)" is actually the highlight, along with a version of "All Along the Watchtower" inspired by Jimi Hendrix's firestorm cover. But, as Helm put it, "I sometimes had a funny sensation: that we were acting out the roles of Bob Dylan and the Band, and the audience was paying to see what they'd missed many years before ... The tour was damn good for our pocketbooks, but it just wasn't a very passionate trip for any of us" (Helm and Davis 248).

The 1974 tour, playing out in counterpoint to the Watergate hearings, truly ushered Dylan into the 1970s. There was too much money and not enough soul. Dylan, who would later dismiss the performances as "just full-out power," probably nailed it best when he said that "the problem was that everyone had his own idea of what the tour was about" (Heylin, *Behind the Shades* 364).

The tour also overlapped with the demise of Dylan's marriage to Sara Lowndes. It was devastating personally, but it also led to a creative resurgence with the magnificent *Blood on the Tracks* and *Desire* albums. If *Blood on the Tracks* saw Dylan go deeply into himself, *Desire* took him back out into the artistic community – most of it was written nose-to-nose with playwright Jacques Levy and recorded with a band hastily assembled from struggling Village combos. Fueled by the cause of boxer Rubin "Hurricane" Carter, who had been jailed on a questionable murder charge, and indirectly inspired by the impending American Bicentennial, Dylan quickly decided to get back in motion, but on very different terms from the 1974 spectacle. As soon as the *Desire* sessions were finished, he corralled the band and added guests and friends including Roger McGuinn, Allen Ginsberg, and Joan Baez, gathered them up into buses, and booked the whole package into small New England theaters on a moment's notice. The impromptu, improvised tour, closer to a traveling circus or medicine show than a series of rock concerts, was dubbed the "Rolling Thunder Revue"; Dylan also decided to film all the goings-on for a film titled *Renaldo and Clara*.

The recordings taken from the Worcester, Cambridge, Boston, and Montreal stops and stitched into the *Live 1975: The Rolling Thunder Revue* album are representative, and superb (though, at risk of overplaying the bootleg card, they aren't the tour's best performances). Dylan was simply on fire for these shows, fully inhabiting and reconfiguring the songs from *Desire* – which hadn't even been released yet – and digging hard into his classic material. The allegorical saga "Isis" took on a roiling, preacherly fervor (the version from Montreal on the *Biograph* collection is definitive). He sang with a sense of purpose that was every bit the equal of the 1965/66 tours, and the band, sloppy and makeshift though it may have been, fit the mood perfectly.

The first part of the Rolling Thunder tour ended triumphantly. But the costs from mounting these complicated shows, from carrying a large entourage, and from filming dozens of hours of the proceedings, all kept rising, and it was decided to take the tour west, and into larger venues, to help offset the costs. The attitude was vastly different on the second half of the Rolling Thunder stops – as signified by Dylan's on stage headgear, which shifted from a theatrical, oversize white hat to a battle-ready *keffiyah*. (Years later, I interviewed Joan Baez at the South by Southwest festival, and a member of the audience said he had seen her on the Rolling Thunder tour. "Oh, yeah?" she said. "One of the funny hat shows or one of the turban shows?")

Dylan was exhausted, trying to keep the movie together, losing his final struggle to hang on to his wife. For another cash infusion, the stop at Fort Collins, Colorado, was shot for telecast on NBC and recorded for a live album – which inevitably meant there were downpours whipping the outdoor stage that night. The results, released as *Hard Rain*, are usually dismissed as messy and wildly uneven, but the emotions Dylan was wrestling with make for some brutally compelling music. He shouts like a man at the bottom of a well, sacrificing nuance for raw fury. "I Threw It All Away" is stripped of its pensive tenderness and turned into a yowl of regret. "Shelter from the Storm" removes any hint of empathy and gratitude, and becomes a raging, slashing stomp. It's not easy, but it's one of the great performances of Dylan's career.

When *Renaldo and Clara* came out in January of 1978, it was massacred by the critics and ignored by moviegoers. Dylan's divorce was finalized, he was locked in a custody battle, his finances were in chaos. He wasn't even able to help "Hurricane" Carter get out of jail. In the previous few years, he had made some of the finest music, and played some of the strongest shows, of his career, but he had little to show for it.

The next sound in Dylan's head required a different kind of musical configuration. The obscure, intriguing, frustrating songs that would become the *Street Legal* album were recorded with a larger and more fleshed-out ensemble – horns (featuring legendary saxophonist Steve Douglas, later one of the few sidemen inducted into the Rock & Roll Hall of Fame), a big organ sound, and a female vocal trio singing background parts. The whole gang rehearsed and recorded in a cavernous Los Angeles warehouse, and the sessions rolled directly into warm-ups for the biggest international tour of Dylan's career.

The *Street Legal* material made up a significant bit of these lengthy shows, for better and worse. The rest of the set found Dylan once again dramatically reworking his back catalogue to fit the big-band set-up. The results were occasionally interesting (a reggae-fied rendition of "Don't Think Twice, It's All right"), but more often turgid and bloated. Some wrote that the spotlight given to saxophonist Douglas was a response to the rise of Bruce Springsteen, the primary inheritor of Dylan's mantle as American rock icon. The feeling of these arrangements, however, was closer to latter-day Elvis (whose death in 1977 shook Dylan badly and interrupted the writing of the *Street Legal* songs) or even Neil Diamond (whose manager, Jerry Weintraub, was working with Dylan at the time).

Most notably, the 1978 tour returned Dylan to the global stage. Though the US dates were greeted with mixed reviews, and the limp *At Budokan* album, recorded at one of the 115-date tour's earliest stops, was quickly dismissed, critics in the UK gave him glowing notices. "The Greatest Concert I Have Ever Seen" said the front of one of London's tabloids. To be fair, as the juggernaut (dubbed "the Alimony Tour" by some insiders, "the Vegas Tour" by various observers) rolled on from arena to arena, the band was better able to navigate the older songs, and Dylan was sometimes able to transcend the musical limitations with the force of his vocals. But mostly, he was too locked into the demands of the bulky band to take flight.

He concluded this jaunt exhausted, but already his mind was elsewhere. Dylan was still battered by his divorce and facing a spiritual crisis. Several of his musicians and collaborators, including a new girlfriend, Mary Alice Artes (credited as "Queen Bee" on *Street Legal*) led him to the Vineyard Fellowship congregation in Tarzana, California. The chronology of his spiritual awakening gets a bit hazy, but by this time he had already started wearing a cross around his neck, and had been soundchecking for the final stops on the tour with new songs including "Slow Train Coming."

In due time, though he later denied using the term, Bob Dylan, born Robert Allen Zimmerman, had been born again. He was deep in Bible study, and writing songs addressing his newfound faith. The resulting album, *Slow Train Coming*, had the most polished sound Dylan ever captured in the studio, featuring Dire Straits guitarist Mark Knopfler, and the sly "Gotta Serve Somebody" even gave him a hit single. But the messages of the album, declarations of his Christian principles and warnings to non-believers, were seriously freaking out Dylan's fans.

In retrospect, the move was linear, if not necessarily a logical progression. If the overarching project of Dylan's career has been the examination of American musical history – by this time he had already worked in the folk, blues, country, and rock styles – perhaps it was inevitable that the other great tradition, gospel music, would be something he would need to explore. The sound of *Street Legal*, so heavy on the female back-up trio, was already getting closer to a gospel sound. And this wasn't something that could be isolated to the recording studio; gospel is a music that truly lives in performance, in communion with an audience.

In November of 1979, Dylan began an American theater tour with fourteen nights at the Warfield in San Francisco. He played no familiar songs, only new, Christian-themed material. Fourteen years after Newport, he had put himself back in battle with his followers. Some fans protested, some walked out, others were won over by the passion and conviction of his delivery. The next four nights, in Santa Monica, California, were especially warm and celebratory – whatever one thinks of the content of these songs, there is no question that Dylan and his tight little band were making some glorious music. (It is the major omission of the "Bootleg Series" that none of the gospel-era shows have been released, though it's certainly easy to understand why revisiting this period may not be a priority for Columbia Records.)

As the tour went on, though, Dylan began to lecture and scold the audiences more, and the crowds grew more vocally hostile. He delivered lengthy Armageddon scenarios and homophobic rants. The joy of the first few shows gave way to a heated crusade. Dylan recorded some of the new songs he was playing on stage for the *Saved* album, which had more of a revivalist feeling and sank like a stone. Almost one year to the day after kicking off the gospel tour, he returned to the Warfield. This time, he mixed in some new songs that didn't have the evangelical focus of his recent work, and even played a handful of his older hits.

His third album in less than three years, *Shot of Love* balanced biblical themes, both more and less strident, with such secular lyrics as "Lenny Bruce." It was a mixed bag, and it sounded like it had been recorded inside a cardboard box, but it inspired a fine set of shows across the US and Europe. Backed by a band of studio aces, and reuniting Dylan with organist Al Kooper for part of the tour (and even guitarist Michael Bloomfield for a couple of shows, his final appearances before his death), the late 1980/early 1981 shows were inventive and exciting, if sometimes a bit overlong and sprawling. In what had become a familiar pattern, the performances also ran out of steam as the tour went on.

The gospel era had greatly reduced Dylan's fan base. He had gone from selling out arenas on the big-band tour to playing less-than-full theaters a mere three years later. And yet again, the recorded evidence from this period leaves us with only the worst examples of his work. But it set the tone for the decade that followed – the 1980s would truly be the most difficult years of Dylan's career.

After closing out the *Shot of Love* dates, Dylan stayed off the road for three years, his longest respite since the 1966–1974 "retirement." He was photographed in Jerusalem at his son's bar mitzvah and was hanging out with a sect of Hasidic Jews – clearly, his spiritual identity continued to metamorphosize. He was uncertain of the direction he wanted his next album to take, and after considering producers from Frank Zappa to David Bowie, settled on Mark Knopfler, so closely associated with the sound of *Slow Train Coming*, for the album that would become *Infidels*.

The record was full of apocalyptic visions and mysterious images. It was powerful, if a bit out of focus, and widely hailed as a return to form. The sound was rooted in the play between the guitar leads of Knopfler and former Rolling Stone Mick Taylor and the reggae rhythm section of Sly Dunbar and Robbie Shakespeare. The live debut of this material, though, was presented far differently.

Dylan had been checking out such punk bands as the Clash and X, and he invited members of the LA groups the Plugz and the Cruzados to rehearse at his Malibu home. To promote the new album, he went on *Late Night with David Letterman* backed by a scruffy trio, blasting through two songs from *Infidels* and a furious version of Sonny Boy Williamson's "Don't Start Me Talking." The performance is a hoot, with the young rockers hanging on for dear life, visibly unsure where the fired-up Dylan is headed (a quick trip to YouTube is well worth it for these clips).

Unfortunately, this unexpected new direction was not to last. Promoter Bill Graham offered Dylan a tour of European stadiums, and Dylan turned to Mick Taylor to assemble a thoroughly professional, uninspiring band. The 1984 shows played to the biggest audiences of Dylan's career, but amounted to little more than a dull walk through his greatest hits, as heard on the entirely unnecessary *Real Live* album.

The week after the release of his next album, *Empire Burlesque*, in July of 1985, Dylan was given an even bigger spotlight when he closed the Live Aid concert in Philadelphia. Backed by Keith Richards and Ron Wood, the three-song set was a trainwreck; the musicians claimed they couldn't hear themselves, and that the all-star choir was rehearsing for the "We Are the World" grand finale while they were on stage. "When the Ship Comes In" also seemed a questionable choice for this occasion (most likely, Dylan wanted to sing the line "The whole wide world is watching," but the climax is the vindictive "Then they'll raise their hands, sayin' we'll meet all your demands / But we'll shout from the bow your days are numbered"). Dylan's biggest impact came from a remark suggesting that we should also pay some attention to the plight of the American farmer, which pissed off the Live Aid organizers, but led Willie Nelson and others to spearhead the creation of the Farm Aid organization.

Dylan played the inaugural Farm Aid show backed by Tom Petty and the Heartbreakers – a tough, rocking set that would kick off the next phase of his touring. A worldwide, co-headlining excursion followed, but the format, which alternated mini-sets by Dylan and Petty, with the Heartbreakers backing for the duration, proved unwieldy. In *Chronicles: Volume One*, Dylan writes that on this tour, he "had no connection to any kind of inspiration," that "my own songs had become strangers to me...I was no longer capable of doing anything radically creative with them. It was like carrying a package of heavy rotting meat" (148).

During breaks in the Petty tour, he also did some dates with the Grateful Dead. He writes that, feeling frustrated during rehearsals with the Dead, he took a walk in their Marin County town and came across a singer in a jazz club whose voice "brought me sharply back to myself" (*Chronicles: Volume One* 150). Any new inspiration he found, though, is far from evident in the shows he played with Jerry Garcia & Company, captured at an especially low point on the abysmal *Dylan & the Dead* live album.

In 1988, George Harrison approached Dylan and Petty about joining forces, along with Roy Orbison and Jeff Lynne, for the Traveling Wilburys project. The high-spirited album put Dylan back in the Top Ten while he was simultaneously selling out stadiums with the Dead. Harrison apparently wanted to play live with the Wilburys – "We talked about doing a tour most every day," says Petty, "but by the time we sobered up, we didn't want to do it anymore" (Light).

Instead, Dylan and Petty went back on the road. The set list had expanded, and Dylan was feeling more engaged with the material. But one night in Switzerland, he says, he opened his mouth to sing and nothing came out. Seeking a way to get through the show, a phrase came into his head – "I'm determined to stand whether God will deliver me or not" (*Williams, 1986–1990* 88). And just like that, if our man is to be believed, he decided to really get back in the game. He devised a plan to start touring constantly, and to return to the same markets repeatedly to rebuild his audience. And so, in 1988, the Never Ending Tour began.

Dylan says that there was a Never Ending Tour, but that it ended. "That one's long gone," he wrote in the liner notes to 1993's *World Gone Wrong* album, proceeding to list such other go-rounds as the "Principles of Action Tour" and the "Money Never Runs Out Tour." By any name, though, the reality is that Dylan has stayed on the road steadily since June, 1988 – including 1997, the year of his near-fatal lung infection – with no apparent plans to stop. His explanation is purely pragmatic. "I simply work a certain number of days each year, which puts me in the category of someone who makes their living by a trade," he told Alan Jackson of the London *Times* in 1997. "The fact is, continuous touring is less of a hardship. You don't have to keep assembling and rehearsing a new team. There's less upheaval and dislocation in your life" (*Dylan Speaks* 128). The earliest shows, backed by a trio led by former *Saturday Night Live* guitar-slinger G. E. Smith, were rough and spiky affairs. The punkish blasts through the Dylan catalogue were exciting and energized. The release of *Oh Mercy* in 1989, his strongest and most realized album at least since *Infidels*, added to a sense that Dylan was truly a vital force again.

But quickly, the "upheaval and dislocation" flared up. Smith parted ways with the band, leading to a spate of scattershot, under-rehearsed shows with various replacement guitarists in the early 1990s. Dylan's next album, *Under the Red Sky*, was a mess. Word was that Dylan was drinking excessively (which he denied), and he took to appearing on stage with the hood of a cheap sweatshirt pulled over his head. There were still exceptional nights; in January of 1990, he played his first club show in decades at Toad's Place in New Haven, and performed fifty songs over four hours, taking requests and generally acting playful and charming.

In 1992 and 1993, Dylan recorded a pair of albums, *Good as I Been to You* and *World Gone Wrong*, that featured him, alone, playing traditional folk, country, and blues songs. The discs had zero commercial impact, but they seemed to refocus his sense of purpose. He settled into a more consistent band line-up, anchored by bass player Tony Garnier (who joined in 1989 and has been there ever since, making him easily Dylan's longest-running associate ever). A remarkable set of mostly acoustic shows at New York's Supper Club, featuring the traditional songs, was filmed but never released: another document that we can only hope will see light of day.

Dylan released no new compositions between 1989 and 1997, and no new music at all for four years after *World Gone Wrong*, but his live shows were gaining steam again. By the time the shockingly first-rate *Time Out of Mind* came out in 1997, he was consistently attaining peaks in concert that seemed implausible a few years before. The new songs, which fully absorbed and then transformed the blues explored on the previous two albums, were particularly strong live vehicles. It felt as if Dylan's whole career had led up to these shows – he was striking a perfect balance between unfamiliar and classic material, satisfying new and old fans, honoring both the history he revered and the innovation he required.

The band reached its zenith around the turn of the century, with guitarists Larry Campbell and Charlie Sexton flanking Dylan and in masterful command of his catalogue. When Dylan changed drummers, from David Kemper to George Recile, things only got hotter on stage. This line-up (attired in matching cowboy-themed uniforms) deserves to be immortalized on record, though there are satisfying scraps to be found: a series of Japanese singles included almost an album's worth of bonus live material, and the soundtrack to Dylan's bonkers 2003 film *Masked and Anonymous* has five tracks cut live on a soundstage by this band in its prime.

Dylan was spending more time at the keyboards in concert, until, in 2003, he began leading the entire show from this seat. No explanation was given for the change, and one had to wonder if there was a physical reason – it couldn't be easy for a 63-year-old man to hold a guitar all night for a third of the year. Sexton left the band, then Campbell, and all of these changes combined to make the shows a bit less powerful. Nor were the songs from 2006's *Modern Times* quite up to the standard of *Time out of Mind* or its comparably spectacular follow-up, 2001's *"Love and Theft"*. But in 2007, Dylan started to pick up the guitar again, for at least the first few songs of each show, and if he and his current band don't fully match the intensity of his performances a few years earlier, he's still out there kicking, night after night.

Can he keep going forever? Will he live out the sentiment of 1962's "Let Me Die in My Footsteps," and just stay on the road until his time runs out? With Bob Dylan, there's no way to know, of course – though he would probably point out that B. B. King and Chuck Berry and George Jones are all still on the circuit. The better question, though, is if he were to stop, what else would he do?

"When I [have been] touring," Dylan once said, "it [has been] my line of work, to go out there and deliver those songs. You must accept that in some way. There's very little you can do about it. The only other thing to do is not to do it" (Heylin, *Behind the Shades* 642).

5

MARTIN JACOBI

Bob Dylan and collaboration

In this chapter I want to expand on the conventional meaning of "collaboration" to look at how Bob Dylan's use of musical, historical, and other cultural influences helped to shape him as a performer. This expansion will take two forms: the first follows a commonly accepted argument in literary theory, that works of art are the result not of individual artists working in isolation but rather the result of the collaboration of artists with their various historical, social, and personal influences; the second uses performance-studies theory to claim that artists remake themselves and create (perceptions of) reality through their performances, including live as well as recorded or written performances.

Dylan has never been forthcoming about or particularly appreciative, publicly at least, of any collaborative help he has received, yet the help has sometimes been substantial. The initial assistance provided by Joan Baez goes generally unacknowledged by Dylan even though she provided him with the exposure and audiences he needed to start his career. Dylan also has downplayed the influence of Harry Smith's *Anthology of American Folk Music*, contending that many people had listened to it but also to many other songs, that his transient lifestyle at the time did not allow him to spend a great deal of time listening to any album, and that he and other young musicians preferred to hear these and other songs done live in the Village and elsewhere (Gilmore). Further, about the assistance he received from the producer Daniel Lanois on his Grammy-winning *Time Out of Mind* Dylan has said that he is "no great fan of the swamp sound" associated with this producer and, more generally, he tells Jonathan Lethem, "I felt like I've always produced my own records anyway, except I just had someone there in the way. I feel like nobody's gonna know how I should sound except me anyway, nobody knows what they want out of players except me, nobody can tell a player what he's doing wrong, nobody can find a player who can play but he's not playing, like I can. I can do that in my sleep" (Lethem 76). Finally, the two artists who, according to Dylan, figure most prominently in his comeback in the 1990s are Lonnie Johnson and an unnamed "old jazz singer" in San Rafael, California. Johnson's assistance has to do with a style of guitar playing taught to Dylan in "the early 60s" (*Chronicles: Volume One* 157), but Dylan never clearly explains the technique. Dylan heard the jazz singer in San Rafael, he tells us, after he had left a practice session with the Dead and was contemplating retirement. As Dylan listened to him, he says that "without warning, it was like the guy had an open window into my soul. It was like he was saying, 'You should do it this way' " (150) – although it is not clear what "this way" is. Apparently, although Dylan is once again unclear, it was the old jazz singer who came to his rescue in Locarno, Switzerland, when he was playing with Tom Petty and the Heartbreakers and suddenly found himself unable to sing at all; as he says, he "conjured up some different type of mechanism to jump-start the other techniques that weren't working" (153). Since Johnson died in 1970 and since no one except Dylan knows just who that old jazz singer is, it seems fair to say that Dylan's vagueness here helps to perpetuate the sense that he is *sui generis* by limiting his acknowledgments of collaborative assistance.

When Dylan began his professional career in New York in 1961 he occasionally performed with other musicians but in effect he was a solo act. After he went electric in 1965, he was the headliner, who could change his backing groups and still draw the crowds. He has also written almost all of his own music and lyrics, and now he even produces his own albums. Yet if Dylan was simply or even primarily a solo act, this book would not include this chapter. Dylan has co-written a number of songs, with the most important collaboration being with Jacques Levy, who co-wrote with Dylan all the songs on *Desire* with the exceptions of "Sara" and "One More Cup of Coffee." Other collaborators include Robert Hunter, the lyricist for the Grateful Dead, who co-wrote two songs from *Down in the Groove*, "Silvio" and "The Ugliest Girl in the World." On *Knocked out Loaded*, Tom Petty co-wrote "Got Your Mind Made Up," Carole Bayer Sager co-wrote "Under Your Spell," and the playwright Sam Shepard co-wrote "Brownsville Girl." "Saved" was co-authored with bass player Tim Drummond, and George Harrison was co-author for "I'd Have You Anytime." A number of the songs recorded at Big Pink were co-authored, with, for instance, "This Wheel's on Fire" written with Rick Danko and "Tears of Rage" written with Richard Manuel.

Dylan has also worked with a variety of producers to create his albums. A list of important producers would have to include Daniel Lanois, who worked with Dylan on *Under the Red Sky* and *Time Out of Mind*; Robert Johnston, who produced *Highway 61 Revisited*, *Bringing It All Back Home*, and *Blonde on Blonde*; John Hammond, who produced Dylan's first two albums and introduced him to the music of Delta bluesman Robert Johnson; and Dylan's brother, David Zimmerman, who fundamentally reworked *Blood on the Tracks*.

Of course, Dylan has played on stage and in the studio with a vast number of musicians, although it is perhaps useful to begin by noting the music giants with whom he did *not* play. He did not play with Woody Guthrie, because by the time Dylan came to New York the folk icon was in the late stages of Huntington's disease, unable to play. He never played with Elvis Presley, because Colonel Tom Parker turned down Dylan's overture in 1970 (Sounes 240). He did not play or sing with Frank Sinatra although he did sing "Restless Farewell" at Ol' Blue Eyes's 80th birthday celebration, and he has not yet played with Little Richard, although as a youth in Hibbing, Minnesota he identified in his high school yearbook his ambition to become a member of Little Richard's band. He has not played with Jerry Lee Lewis who loudly and aggressively refused Dylan's offer (Sounes 240), he did not play, at least publicly, with John Lennon nor has he played publicly with Paul McCartney, although Dylan and the Beatles influenced each other's music.

He has played, however, with George Harrison – in the Traveling Wilburys (which also included Tom Petty, Jeff Lynne, and Roy Orbison) and at the Concert for Bangladesh – and with Ringo Starr at the Concert for Bangladesh and on *Under the Red Sky*. He has performed with the Rolling Stones on stage and with various members of this band on stage and on his albums, with the Grateful Dead and with Tom Petty and the Heartbreakers, and with such stars as Bruce Springsteen, Eric Clapton, and Carlos Santana, with Van Morrison, Paul Simon, and Bono, and with Mark Knopfler (who also produced some of Dylan's work), Leon Russell, Joni Mitchell, and Johnny Cash. He played with Mike Bloomfield and Al Kooper both at the Newport Folk Festival when he first went electric at a public performance, as well as on the song *Rolling Stone* magazine calls the greatest rock & roll song of all time, "Like a Rolling Stone," and of course he has played with Joan Baez and with the Band.

Dylan's folk music career began in the Twin Cities, and during his apprenticeship in Greenwich Village in the summer of 1961 he performed at various venues with Paul Clayton, Tom Paxton, Dave Van Ronk (from whom Dylan took, without permission, Van Ronk's arrangement of "House of the Rising Sun"), Jack Elliott, Judy Collins, and Phil Ochs. On July 29 of that year he played at the Riverside Church with Jack Elliot (where he met Suze Rotolo, who introduced him to Rimbaud and Verlaine, to Brecht, and to the importance of the Civil Rights movement). He traveled to Boston where he played a few songs with Carolyn Hester and learned from Eric von

Schmidt "Baby Let Me Follow You Down," which was to appear on his first album. As he became more of a star, Dylan took the stage with a number of important folk singers, including, at the Newport Folk Festival, Joan Baez and the by-now popular Peter, Paul, and Mary; in Greenwood, Mississippi, with Pete Seeger, Len Chandler, the Student Nonviolent Coordinating Committee (SNCC) Freedom Singers; and at the march on Washington in 1963 with Baez, Odetta, Harry Belafonte, and Peter, Paul, and Mary.

Dylan had met Joan Baez while playing the folk clubs in New York, and they began playing together, with Baez introducing the relatively unknown Dylan to her large audiences. They performed off and on together until Dylan went electric. When Dylan went on tour in 1965 to England, Baez accompanied him, but he did not invite her on stage despite her earlier invitations to him. She appeared briefly during the Rolling Thunder Revue tour in 1975, but for all practical purposes their collaboration was finished during this tour in 1965. Many observers of the folk scene in the early 1960s believe that the collaboration benefited Dylan enormously, since Baez was a huge star and he was barely known. Further, although Dylan claims that there are little to no autobiographical references in his work, Dylanologists claim that a number of songs, from his first electric albums, are inspired by or otherwise "about" Baez, which is to say that his collaboration with Baez influenced his songwriting, although it does not seem to have influenced to any appreciable extent his stage performance.

As the personal and professional relationship with Baez was ending, Dylan had been developing a brief but very productive collaboration with Mike Bloomfield and Al Kooper, which presaged a number of other near, future, and ill-fitted collaborations. Both played with Dylan at the 1965 Newport Folk Festival and on *Highway 61 Revisited*, and both played intermittently with Dylan for a number of years. But perhaps just as productive a collaboration began after his initial work with Bloomfield and Kooper, with the Hawks, who would later become the Band: Robbie Robertson, Levon Helm, Garth Hudson, Rick Danko, and Richard Manuel. If Dylan began his rock career with Kooper and Bloomfield, he refined it with the Band.

After completing *Highway 61*, Dylan had asked Bloomfield, Kooper, and John Sebastian to join him in a touring band, but both Bloomfield and Sebastian turned him down. Given the careers of these men over the ensuing years, one wonders what that band would have been like – perhaps the first super group, before Blind Faith, Cream, or Crosby, Stills, Nash, and Young. But, as Chris Rowley contends, they were "strong stylists with reputations of their own [and] they had strong egos" (84), and at least Bloomfield's and Kooper's creativity was profuse, varied, and increasingly directed toward their own projects. Bloomfield was to go on to play with the Paul Butterfield

Blues Band and formed Electric Flag, and Sebastian would lead the Lovin' Spoonful and go on to a relatively successful solo career. Kooper would form and play with the Blues Project and with Blood, Sweat, and Tears, and, along with Bloomfield and Steven Stills, he recorded the album, *Super Session*.

Without Kooper and Bloomfield, Dylan turned to the Hawks. He did play with Kooper and with two members of the Hawks – Robbie Robertson and Levon Helm – at Forest Hills, NY and the Hollywood Bowl, and after these performances he hired the rest of the band. Together, Dylan and the Hawks went on a tour that Sounes calls "one of the most important of his career, and one of the truly historic tours in popular music" (191), which lasted from late September of 1965 to the summer of 1966 (with Levon Helm off the tour for a time). This tour was important primarily because it brought the electric Dylan to the world, but also because on it Dylan greatly enhanced his ability to play with a supporting band.

In May of 1966, while the tour was still running, Dylan did record, with Al Kooper and the Hawks on early sessions, and with Nashville professionals on most of the later sessions, *Blonde on Blonde*, but he continued touring with the Hawks until his motorcycle accident in July of 1966. Some time later, after the Hawks had become the Band and had achieved great success on their own, they played with Dylan at impromptu sessions in the basement of the Band's house, Big Pink (with the result a huge number of bootleg tapes and *The Basement Tapes*; on many songs, according to Levon Helm, Richard Manuel collaborated with Dylan [Smith 147]). They also played together on a 1974 tour, which brought about *Before the Flood* and was the first rock & roll tour to use primarily big stadiums.

Dylan's next significant collaborative venture was with the Rolling Thunder Revue. After his divorce from Sara Lowndes Dylan, he gathered a number of performers, as well as the poet Allen Ginsberg and the playwright Sam Shepard, and toured twice in the span of less than two years. Dylan's collaborators included the musicians who had just played on *Desire*, and also Joni Mitchell, Roger McGuinn, Joan Baez, and a number of others. In many ways, this tour was the first inkling many fans had that Dylan was a different kind of performer, with an interest in more than the standard approach to rock concerts. He was to some extent playing to the cameras, for he was taping the performances for a documentary, which would become *Renaldo and Clara*. He also worked with Shepard on a script, and he acted in a number of skits off stage, including a couple with Ginsburg. He had performed a small part in Sam Peckinpah's *Pat Garrett and Billy the Kid*, but his live performances on Rolling Thunder and his *Renaldo and Clara* performance, so far as collaboration is concerned, seemed to feed off a vibrancy on the stage that he has rarely repeated.

In 1987, some years after Rolling Thunder, Dylan did play some tour dates with the Grateful Dead. He was not an impressive addition to the Dead's show, and Sounes contends that because of heavy drinking he couldn't play in the right key or even remember his own songs (379). Dylan also was playing at this time with Tom Petty and the Heartbreakers, and many commentators feel that Dylan had entered a fallow creative period. To be sure, his albums were much less well received than anything he had done to that time, and it is possible that he felt that by collaborating with this accomplished band he might be re-energized. Two years later, in 1989, Dylan asked to join the Dead but was turned down (Sounes 380). In addition to observations that he might simply have been exhausted by being the stage presence that he was, just to have asked to join implies that Dylan wanted this collaborative opportunity either because he had already felt the benefits or because he thought he could foresee them; yet, as Sounes observes, correctly I believe, Dylan "was such a powerful musical presence that he would alter any band out of all recognition – The Grateful Dead, for instance, would simply have become his backing group" (380). (In 1995 he opened for the Dead three times, shortly before Jerry Garcia's death.) Thus, while the collaboration might have been able to re-energize him, it might also have harmed the popularity and creativity of the Dead.

Dylan has been touring nearly continuously (on what is sometimes called the Never Ending Tour) since 1988, with various combinations of band members. However, rather than collaborators of the importance of Kooper or Bloomfield or the Band, these musicians serve as backing groups, albeit in the iterations I have heard, very tight ones.

I want to turn now to a broader analysis of collaboration, one that includes influences on Dylan's craft from those inside and outside of the world of music. One of the most significant musical influences was Woody Guthrie, of whom Dylan became aware while in Minneapolis. Dylan says about this time that "Woody's songs were having a big effect on me, an influence on every move I made, what I ate and how I dressed, who I wanted to know, who I didn't" (*Chronicles: Volume One* 247). Marqusee says that "Dylan took more from Guthrie than an image and an accent. In Guthrie's work, Dylan found a creative fusion of humor and rage, a wanderlust that was both individualist and populist, and, most importantly, a folksinging model of honesty and commitment" (20).

Dylan mentions that he was also influenced by the acetate recording of Robert Johnson, loaned to him by John Hammond, and he mentions the "free association that [Johnson] used, the sparkling allegories, big-assed truths wrapped in the hard shell of nonsensical abstraction" (*Chronicles: Volume One* 285). I've already mentioned the influence Dylan claims from

Lonnie Johnson and the old jazz singer in San Rafael, and in *Chronicles: Volume One* he says that from the Clancy Brothers he "grasped the idea of what kind of songs I wanted to write, I just didn't know how to do it yet" (84). He was also "greatly influenced" by Dave Van Ronk (262) and Robert Shelton claims that, after hearing Buddy Holly, Dylan "began to imitate Holly's sweet, naïve, almost childlike voice. The vocal quality of many of Dylan's recordings shows his debt to Holly" (*No Direction Home* 53).

Another significant influence was Bertholt Brecht, to whose songs Rotolo had introduced him. Dylan claims that after hearing "Pirate Jenny" he "took the song apart" and saw its "form, the free verse association, the structure and disregard for the known certainty of melodic pattern." He "wanted to figure out how to manipulate and control this particular structure and form" and claims that if he had never heard the song "it might not have dawned on me to write" such canonical songs as "It's Alright Ma (I'm Only Bleeding)," "Mr. Tambourine Man," and "Only a Pawn in Their Game" (*Chronicles: Volume One* 275, 276, 287–288). Jason Zinoman says, following an argument developed by Esther Harcourt, that Brecht's influence is "the missing piece of the answer to the much-debated question of why Mr. Dylan moved away from the folk and protest scenes in the early 60s (Zinoman AR 7)."

While Zinoman does not identify the other pieces of this answer, it is possible that Allen Ginsberg was one of those pieces – a poet who, according to Rowley, also influenced Dylan's reading of American poetry (84) and who, according to Richard Hishmeh, provided Dylan with cover to move from folk singer to "the poet laureate of rock & roll." After all, folk purists "would find it much more difficult to reject a rock icon who held court with poets and, through such allegiances, became a poet himself" (398). Rotolo, besides introducing Dylan to Brecht, also encouraged him to read the French symbolist poets, and in *Chronicles: Volume One* Dylan places on his reading list (prior to meeting Ginsberg) the English Romantic poets Byron, Shelley, and Coleridge, as well as the American poets Longfellow, Poe, and Whitman – all of which suggests that while he was in the midst of his folk stage he was in fact preparing to become rock's poet laureate.

He claims among his list of Greenwich Village readings Milton's "Massacre in Piedmont" and Thucydides, which he says "tells about how human nature is always the enemy of anything superior. Thucydides writes about how words in his time have changed from their ordinary meaning, how actions and opinions can be altered in the blink of an eye. It's like nothing has changed from his time to mine" (*Chronicles: Volume One* 36). During this time Dylan also read Carl von Clausewitz, who showed him that "There isn't any moral order" and "Morality has nothing to do with politics" (44). Dylan has long read newspapers from the Civil War, and it is also clear that he has "collaborated" with current events in writing his songs – whether he picked up his information from current newspapers or elsewhere. For instance, Noel Stookey (later changing his name to Paul as a member of Peter, Paul, and Mary) once gave Dylan a newspaper item and suggested that Dylan might think about it for a song, with the result being "Talking Bear Mountain Picnic Massacre Blues" (Sounes 94); songs about various contemporary figures – such as Medgar Evers, Emmett Till, Hattie Carroll, and Rubin "Hurricane" Carter – also point to Dylan's collaboration with the events of the day.

James Dunlap mentions Ralph Waldo Emerson and John Steinbeck as influences and Allan Simmons contends that Dylan's "Black Diamond Bay" is inspired by his reading of Joseph Conrad's *Victory* (106). Simmons's evidence is compelling but so is his warning that "once one begins to listen for echoes of Conrad in Dylan, one begins to hear them everywhere," leading to the suspicion that one is, in fact, imposing the correlation that one seeks: "Some coincidences clearly strain credibility" (107–108). Simmons's warning might well be heeded by a number of Dylanologists, including Michael Karwowski, whose claims concerning *Blonde on Blonde* to my mind seem truly bizarre – for instance, that the "blondes" of the title "represent two of the horses of Revelations" and that the "Catholic Church, in fact, is the subject of the song 'Sad-eyed Lady of the Lowlands'" (168). Similarly, David Yaffe says that Christopher Ricks "links Dylan to languages that Dylan doesn't necessarily know, books he hasn't necessarily read, and a systematic biblical schema of allusions to the seven deadly sins that would have more to do with Dante's terza rima than with the lyrics of 'Sad-Eyed Lady of the Lowlands.'"

As a number of commentators have pointed out, Dylan's influences include some he does not mention, even when the evidence seems irrefutable. That is, while Simmons says that "Dylan is obviously not retelling Conrad's tale but using it as a springboard for his own creative purposes" (106), some critics say that Dylan is not so much retelling certain stories, or for that matter thinking about certain songs, as he is plagiarizing them.

These charges, particularly the more recent ones, are well known to Dylan fans. Sounes claims that songs on *Time Out of Mind* contain "phrases that Bob had picked magpielike from songs on the Harry Smith *Anthology*, as well as records by Fats Domino and Jimmie Rogers" (416). Of "*Love and Theft*" David Yaffe states that the title apparently comes from "Eric Lott's landmark 1993 study of blackface minstrelsy," a claim that Sean Wilentz sees as reasonable, and Wilentz goes on to point out that individual songs have titles and lyrics lifted from, among others, Robert Johnson and Charley

Patton, and that Dylan has "lifted what he pleases from the last century's great American songbook." Further, as Smith and many others have pointed out, apparently Dylan also used portions of Junichi Saga's *Confessions of a Yakuza* for songs on this album (9). And as regards *Modern Times*, Dylan has been accused of plagiarizing the work of an ante-bellum Southern poet, Henry Timrod, whom Dylan may have encountered in his reading of Civil War-era newspapers.

Accusations about his "plagiarism" go back as far as his early days in New York. "Blowin' in the Wind" takes its melody from "No More Auction Block," "Song for Woody" from Guthrie's own "1913 Massacre," and "Masters of War" from Jean Ritchie's arrangement of "Fair Nottamun Town." Actually, the list of Dylan's early songs with "stolen" melodies is quite extensive, including "Ballad of Emmett Till," "Girl from the North Country," "With God on our Side," and "Lonesome Death of Hattie Carroll," to name but a few.

The defenses mounted on Dylan's behalf are also extensive. For instance, Jon Pareles claims that in *"Love and Theft"* Dylan "was simply doing what he has always done: writing songs that are information collages. Allusions and memories, fragments of dialogue and nuggets of tradition have always been part of Mr. Dylan's songs, all stitched together like crazy quilts" ("Plagiarism in Dylan" B7). Of his appropriation of Guthrie's melody, Sounes observes that since Guthrie himself appropriated melodies, there "was no ethical lapse" on Dylan's part (82). Suzanne Vega doubts that Dylan appropriated Timrod's words "on purpose," preferring to imagine that his immersion in the "times and texts of the Civil War" led to a "completely unconscious" use of the material, and claiming that we are passionate about Dylan *because* he presents himself as "well, a thief. Renegade, outlaw, artist." However, regarding Sounes's justification I can hear my parents telling me that "two wrongs do not make a right," and, regarding Vega's justification, I am not sure that we should approve of a thief's action because we *like* that thief. To my mind Wilentz's defense is more persuasive: he says that "Dylan is a minstrel, filching other people's diction and mannerisms and melodies and lyrics and transforming them and making them his own, a form of larceny that is as American as apple pie," and I am more persuaded still by Robert Polito's observation that given the debate over Dylan's songwriting ethics we "might not guess that we've just lived through some two and a half decades of hip-hop sampling, not to mention a century of Modernism."

However, I am old enough to remember that George Harrison lost a case to Bright Lights Music for "filching" or "sampling" the melody from "He's So Fine" for his own "My Sweet Lord," so at least technically I would differentiate between taking copyrighted material and taking material no longer or never under copyright protection. I also know, from Richard Posner, that the legal term for "unconscious" plagiarism is "cryptomenesia," but while Posner claims that such an action is a "sin of neglect rather than of intention and, therefore, less blameworthy" (97), he does not claim that it is legal.

I do not wish either to condemn or to exonerate Dylan regarding the charges of plagiarism. Instead, I want to close with an argument that if it does not either condemn or exonerate at least might explain why Dylan has been able to "get away with" his various samplings. The argument is grounded in performance studies, and it is this: Dylan's use of other people's material – titles from books, images or even phrases and clauses of another's poetry – is in fact a reconceptualization, a reinterpretation of that material. Performance-studies theorists observe how a performance does not simply reflect reality but rather creates it, grounding their contention on J. L. Austin's observations regarding performative language – that when a jury tells a defendant, "You're guilty," or a justice of the peace says to a couple "I now pronounce you husband and wife," reality changes for those audiences. Dwight Conquergood, quoting M. M. Bakhtin, says, "It is not experience that organizes expression, but the other way around – expression organizes experience. Expression is what first gives experience its form and specificity of direction" (58). Thus, as Gilmore claims, each time Dylan performs a song it is "a new moment and creation, a new possibility... [and] night after night he takes us to unfamiliar and transfixing understandings of what we once thought we knew so well" (58).

This argument is continued in Della Pollack's contention that repetition serves to "repeat with a vengeance, making repetition stumble, stutter... thus at least promising repetition with a difference" (92). Pollack observes that in a performance "the self is not simply put forward but... is reworked in its enunciation" (87), and reworked in the process of re-creation for and by the audience. D. Soyina Madison and Judith Hamera agree, claiming that such repetitions lead to an understanding of people and performances as "socially determined, [which] opens the possibility of alternative performatives and alternative ways of being" (xviii). We can thus say that Dylan, through his performances on stage but also in interviews and otherwise before the media, has been creating the persona of "Bob Dylan," a persona of a performer who in fact publicly constructs this persona, saying that he grew up in the circus and was an orphan from an early age, saying that he paid little attention to Smith's *Anthology* but was bowled over by an old jazz singer just in time to save his career – in effect telling stores about himself that may or may not have any corroboration.

Further, one can consider how Dylan "collaborates" with his previous selves when he performs. In late September of 2007 I saw a Dylan show in Clemson, South Carolina, and while I cannot remember if he did "John Brown" at the first Dylan concert I attended, sometime in the mid-1960s after he had gone electric, if he had performed it at the concert I have no doubt that it would have been markedly different from the song's performance in Clemson. I had heard him perform "All Along the Watchtower" in Atlanta in 2002 and it was nothing like either the acoustic performance on *John Wesley Harding* or the electric performance done for an encore in Clemson. In a very real way Dylan collaborates with a particular context and a particular audience, and in effect with his previous selves. Following Pollack, it can be said that the iterations of these songs in effect create a new reality – with a different musician and different songs.

To make this argument is not to say that Dylan is thereby off the hook on a charge of plagiarism if he performs someone else's material and calls it his own – if for no other reason than the law does not recognize such an argument. But the claim does offer a possible reason for why Dylan has not been so accused, because in a fundamental way he has performed a different song, one that has become *his* song. In any event, to stretch my expansion of "collaboration" to the breaking point, it is the case that Dylan collaborates not only with those consciously aware of the collaboration but with musicians, artists, and others long dead or otherwise unaware of this collaboration, and that he also collaborates with previous iterations of "Bob Dylan." On this last point, it seems fair to say that, in addition to his revolutionary addition of meaningful lyrics to rock music, Dylan has shown a revolutionary approach to collaboration.

6

BARBARA O'DAIR

Bob Dylan and gender politics

I was 12 when I heard "Lay, Lady, Lay." *Bob Dylan's Greatest Hits, Vol. 2* had just been released and "Lady" saturated the air. I played it over and over in my neighbor's basement, and sank into my first real swoon. "His clothes are dirty but his hands are clean / And you're the best thing that he's ever seen . . ." This man with dirty clothes and clean hands was, in my dreams, Bob Dylan.

Romance novels and their fluttering women who needed a rough man's touch and soap operas, in which bad-girl Veronicas competed with good-girl Bettys, left me cold. Those mass-media depictions of women seemed narrow and outdated next to the powerful and exciting promise of feminism and sexual liberation. Strange, then, that the conventional gender dynamic on "Lay, Lady, Lay" clicked with my nascent sexuality; for me, Dylan was the one to crack open the door.

Once I was hooked, I pored over the history of this tousled, sensitive man–boy. I hung on every tawdry tale in Tony Scaduto's 1971 Dylan biography. A more nuanced picture of him emerged from repeated listenings to *Bringing It All Back Home, Highway 61 Revisited*, and *Blonde on Blonde*, as his point of view alternated between wounded lover and acerbic appraiser. Eventually, his protest songs and poetic excursions displaced my lust, and I came to love him for his mind. Still, when I'd hear, "Whatever colors you have in your mind / I'll show them to you and you'll see them shine," I knew Dylan held out a key to my creativity, and a promise. He would introduce me to the world of art and grownups and he would escort me into it, loving me for who I was, in my essence.

The man on "Lay, Lady, Lay" is commanding and kind, benevolently paternalistic. The song, from 1969's *Nashville Skyline*, conjures both strength and vulnerability. Critic Richard Goldstein wrote in the *Nation* in 2006 that Dylan's "love songs . . . bask in feminine submission." That's not entirely true. "Lay across my big brass bed" is more tender than aggressive.

What's truly interesting is how the combination of these effects gives the song its mesmerizing power.

Almost thirty years after *Nashville Skyline*, Dylan released *Time Out of Mind*. In a raw and rattling voice, he rues lost love in a badly lit bar: "You left me standing in the doorway crying / Suffering like a fool." Gone is the courtly confidence or know-it-all sneer of earlier songs: he's love-sick. While downbeat and stark, *Time Out of Mind* stands out as an engaged and personal album. Naturally, then, its fans were moved to speculation: Who broke his heart? Was he dying?

Dylan, in fact, had been diagnosed with pericarditis, a heart infection that makes breathing difficult, and which laid him up for six months or so. But the songs for *Time* had already been written and recorded when he fell ill. Still, some listeners persisted in reading his illness into the work and its seeming preoccupation with death. On the other hand, critic Robert Christgau dismissed the idea that the album was inspired by Dylan's health or, indeed, that death is its overriding theme. Linking time to death, of course, remains a rich aesthetic choice. It reverberates in the bleak humor of Samuel Beckett and the grace and gloom of Cormac McCarthy. Need we read their private lives into their despairing landscapes? *Time Out of Mind* snakes across similar terrain.

Dylan, though, puts a woman at the center of it all. Has she pushed him to the edge of darkness? She might've saved him, but she didn't: no shelter from the storm. And it seems she was his last hope.

When he offers us a woman his lyrics have given too much power, however, we know we'll see him take it away. He may throw out a joke to turn the whole thing on its head, deflecting any emotional disarray the lyrics have revealed, and pleading ignorance as to his meaning. In the last and very long track on *Time*, he tries on the guise of an ignoramus who aims to win a dame he'll never understand: "She says 'You don't read women authors do ya?' / I said 'You're way wrong' / She says, 'Which ones have you read then?' / I say, 'Read Erica Jong . . .' "

Erica Jong. Now *that's* funny, plucking that name out of the air for a rhyme. Perhaps he even *believes* she's a cutting-edge feminist writer – no matter that *Fear of Flying* was published in 1973. We'll never know. But Dylan isn't one for -isms. Nor will he probe his own work for us; discourse and self-analysis are not his bag. He told a journalist in 1985, "I've never read Freud. I've never been attracted to anything he has said, and I think he's started a lot of nonsense with psychiatry and that business."

Dylan's tricks cover his wounds with humor that distracts and diffuses. As with the Great Houdini, his creative acts depend on his ability to slip any bonds. In Martin Scorsese's 2005 Dylan documentary, *No Direction Home*,

Joan Baez told a story about Dylan visiting her in Carmel, California, in 1963:

> He would always say: "Read this." And I wouldn't understand the thing at all. But I loved it. So I would think: "Okay, I'm going to figure this one out." So I read through it. And I gave back my interpretation of what I thought it was about. He said: "Ah, that's pretty fuckin' good. Do you know, 20 years from now, all these people, all these assholes, are going to be writing about all the shit I do. I don't know what the fuck it's about . . ."

Nevertheless, it would be delightful to hear his rationale for selling a song from *Time Out of Mind* to Victoria's Secret in 2004. Dylan not only sold "Love Sick" to the lingerie company for a TV commercial but he agreed to appear in it. It goes like this: a dark stranger, wearing a pencil-thin mustache on his deeply creased face, enters a Venetian palazzo and encounters an "angel," waiting, who then promenades on a pedestal and strikes suggestive poses before him. Barely legal, she parades in pale blue lingerie, a pair of oversized snow-white wings rising from her back, offsetting her luscious lips and locks. The man tosses down his hat, and squints up at this angel of eternal life, who will remain forever young in a dying city. It's a parody of Thomas Mann's *Death in Venice*: an overheated melodrama in two minutes, in which our aging hero confronts the allure of youth – and broods. In this prank, Dylan pokes fun at those who carried on about his death wish, telling us that, again, the joke's on us.

Many Dylan songs roil with scenarios of power, gender, and sex. Early lyrics showcase women characters who often exercise power from within their traditional roles. Dylan limns a well-worn male–female dynamic in "Don't Think Twice, It's All Right," where, in the guise of a needy girlfriend, the woman really just wants to change him: "I once loved a woman, a child I'm told / I gave her my heart but she wanted my soul / But don't think twice, it's all right . . ."

Another type is inscrutable, unattainable or elusive – her gown whisks the floor as she disappears behind a door. "I waited for you when you hated me . . . / When you knew I had some other place to be . . . / Now, where are you tonight, sweet Marie?" ("Absolutely Sweet Marie," *Blonde on Blonde*, 1966). There's the spoiled libertine ("Leopard-Skin Pill-Box Hat"), and the operator who gets her comeuppance ("Like a Rolling Stone"). "Visions of Johanna" has a goddess at its center; the ordinary woman closer to the singer is just "all right." "Johanna" is not there, thus coveted. (Of course, once he gets her, he'll be gone, which she probably knows. He's just in it for the chase.) On "All I Really Want to Do," he assures her of his good intentions, insisting that he doesn't want to possess her as he tries to coax her out of her hiding place. (He sounds as convincing as a cop wooing a criminal.) Ten years later, he famously morphs a character into a ministering mother figure (who quite possibly offers homemade soup and her bed): "I came in from the wilderness, a creature void of form / 'Come in,' she said, 'I'll give you shelter from the storm' " ("Shelter from the Storm," *Blood on the Tracks*, 1975).

Dylan also has a vast collection of male outsiders from which to try on images. One that fits him nicely is the solo cowboy with a squint and a code of ethics all his own. Playing dress-up has produced rich material; the game of match-up between lyrics and life is something else, potentially boiling out the energy in the songs. "Johanna" may or may not be "about" his former lover and collaborator Joan Baez. We're told Dylan threw her over once she'd opened doors for him in New York, but in song he worships Johanna – or at least her memory. It sounds like Edie Sedgwick is the trigger for "Leopard-Skin Pill-Box Hat" – and "Just Like a Woman," and "Like a Rolling Stone." Women in these songs are dominated or dismissed in a masterly way – in both senses of the word.

One set of love-and-betrayal songs – "Sad-Eyed Lady of the Lowlands," "Sara," and "Idiot Wind" – spans a ten-year-period, addressing a woman that bears a resemblance to his now ex-wife Sara Lowndes. Together, the songs click through a kaleidoscope of images – from Madonna ("With your silhouette when the sunlight dims / Into your eyes where the moonlight swims," "Sad-Eyed Lady of the Lowlands," *Blonde on Blonde*, 1966); to sphinx ("Sara, oh Sara / Scorpio Sphinx in a calico dress," "Sara," *Desire*, 1976); to demon ("Idiot wind, blowing every time you move your teeth / You're an idiot, babe / It's a wonder that you still know how to breathe," "Idiot Wind," *Blood on the Tracks*, 1975). When "Idiot Wind" was released, its naked contempt was embarrassing, but now I hear the end of the song: "We're idiots, babe / It's a wonder we can even feed ourselves," words by which Dylan opens the reach of the song to include its speaker, and maybe the rest of us, too.

These songs of romantic entanglement and bitterness hit real if not true notes. We don't know – and why should we care? – to what degree Dylan carries on this way behind closed doors. While his rumored extramarital affairs may or may not have unraveled his first marriage – and thus "Idiot Wind" is despicably blaming the victim – this kind of biographical sleuthing will never yield the meaning we might want. The raucous energy, wicked bite, playful fancies, and emotional yearning in his best songs have a life force all their own.

Dylan couldn't have said it clearer when he told Scott Cohen in an interview for *Spin* in 1985:

> Sometimes the "you" in my songs is me talking to me. Other times I can be talking to somebody else. If I'm talking to me in a song, I'm not going to drop everything and say, all right, now I'm talking to you. It's up to you to figure out who's who. A lot of times it's "you" talking to "you." The "I," like in "I and I," also changes. It could be I, or it could be the "I" who created me. And also, it could be another person who's saying "I." When I say "I" right now, I don't know who I'm talking about. (Cohen 40)

As in dreams, we project versions of ourselves into the art we make. "I want some real good woman to do just what I say" ("Thunder on the Mountain," *Modern Times*, 2006). Dylan is acting here despite the fact that Richard Goldstein wrote in the *Nation* (May 15, 2006) that "hostility to women is a recurring motif in Dylan's songs ... I don't claim that Dylan is determined by machismo ... but I will say that he reaches many men of a certain age and status on precisely these grounds." I always heard this as a limitation of his generation: the next line he sings is, "Everybody got to wonder what's the matter with this cruel world today."

One can say easily that Dylan is not a charter member of the Enlightened Machismo club, the one that includes Bruce Springsteen, John Lennon, Bono, and Eddie Vedder. He more likely makes the fourth for bridge with Neil Young, Leonard Cohen, and Lou Reed, pre-feminist men who are just as confused by their own roles in the free world as they are by the women who surround them. In their 1995 book, *The Sex Revolts: Gender, Rebellion and Rock 'n' Roll*, Simon Reynolds and Joy Press write that anti-sexual punk music looked to the "hyper-macho, misogynist white blues of the '60s" for lessons –"[Punks] learned how to express their rejection of society from songs about rejecting women" (24). With Dylan, it was perhaps the other way around: after folk, his anti-establishment reputation was cemented by his put-down songs about women.

In 1965, when "Like a Rolling Stone" is released, Dylan officially becomes the angry young man of the counterculture – the first punk, if not the first rebel, with a cause that is not exactly known. "Ballad of a Thin Man" addresses an establishment figure adrift in a new world: "Because something is happening here / But you don't know what it is / Do you, Mister Jones?" In "Like a Rolling Stone," it's a youth, presumably female, who is as lost and unmoored as Jones: "Now you don't talk so loud / Now you don't seem so proud / About having to be scrounging for your next meal."

"Ballad of a Thin Man" was purportedly aimed at pop critics who didn't "get" Dylan and stood in for the establishment; "Rolling Stone" seemed to target privileged young ladies on the scene, quite a lot like heiress and social butterfly Edie Sedgwick. The song has always sounded gender non-specific, though; one could substitute a Dylan rival or former friend for this little girl lost who inspires such ire. Dylan has made a career skewering poseurs and frauds, even as he works his own masquerade. Some of our most exciting music walks the line between taking potshots at the powerful and being thoroughly liberating. In fact, caustic artists like Elvis Costello or Eminem can make women their targets in songs that are nonetheless moving to both men and women.

What is this strange phenomenon of women relating to so-called misogynistic material? Critic Karen Durbin put the dilemma into perspective. On the occasion of her accompanying the Rolling Stones on tour in 1975, she wrote, "It's their complexity, their capacity for paradox, that makes them great ... I have an impulse to clean them up, make them tidy and undisturbing. But it's only the disturbing artists who are important, who fire our imaginations so that their art gives rise to our own" (9). Critic Robert Christgau probed an equally difficult idea when he wrote in 1970, in an article entitled "Look at that Stupid Girl" in the *Village Voice*: "Even if the energy of rock is nothing more than sublimated (or not so sublimated) machismo, such machismo can be a step on the way out, a naïve reaction against apparent sources of oppression, and in that way it is beautiful."

These provocative ideas are useful and encouraging. If machismo can have rebellious radiance, as I read Christgau's meaning, girls, too, can use this transgressive energy to assert themselves. Some of them like Lucinda Williams, Cat Power, and Polly Jean Harvey make searing music that often transcends gender. When Cate Blanchett plays the androgynous Dylan of the 1960s in Todd Haynes's 2007 film, *I'm Not There*, she points up Dylan's perhaps fleeting gender-bending tendencies as part of an artistic strategy. In the same way, Dylan uses macho stereotypes for a good story. His shapeshifting offers him greater aesthetic freedom (not to mention protection from unwanted personal scrutiny).

It's hard to recall just what was offensive in "Just Like a Woman" – ". . . you ache just like a woman / But you break just like a little girl" – unless it was the combination of its potency and its ambiguity. Am I being insulted here, or what? It's a catchy sentiment, or maybe just another put-down in the guise of wise. Women have objected to lines like "you fake just like a woman," a charge that claims Dylan has swept all women into the category of devious manipulator. But then comes the line that reveals shame and vulnerability: "Please don't let on that you knew me when / I was hungry and it was your world."

In many of his love songs, Dylan bobs and weaves, both eluding inter-pretation and accurately portraying the fickleness of roles within relation-ships. In all, don't expect Dylan to follow a well-marked path, which is why his work stays rich and relevant. Critic Ellen Willis wrote in 1967 that in the same way Dylan had broken the strictures of folk music at Newport Folk Festival in 1965, he returned to folk with the "backward-looking" plainspokenness of *John Wesley Harding*, again defying expectations.

Dylan's attitude toward women can be similarly backward looking: As a rebel himself, he might appreciate their power grabs; as a man of his generation, he's bewildered by women who stake their claims, efforts that threaten a quick-change artist who depends on the Other to stay in a fixed role. Every chameleon needs his rock.

7

R. CLIFTON SPARGO AND ANNE K. REAM

Bob Dylan and religion

By the late 1970s Bob Dylan had made his Christian turn, and many who had been accustomed to claiming him as free-thinking protest singer and prophet of modern peace felt betrayed. Among them was the music critic Michael Goldberg. Writing for the *New Musical Express*, Goldberg decried the sudden simplicity of Dylan's view of the world, comparing it to the beliefs of cultists who had gained so much attention throughout the 1970s. "Where are the de-programmers when we really need them?" he asked. Not lost on Dylan was the irony that many of his staunchest critics were former devotees, people who'd responded to the secular verve of his music in a religious spirit, tapping him as their very own social prophet (see Marcus, "Amazing"). At a 1979 concert during the tour for *Slow Train Coming*, his first album of gospel music, Dylan remembered how his critics had tried for years to tell him he was a prophet and overridden all his objections to the contrary, until one day he'd come around and declared Christ to be the answer – whereupon they turned on him, saying, "Bob Dylan's no prophet." A great many admirers found themselves excluded by the line Dylan was drawing between those with faith and those without, but in fact he'd always been drawing lines, many of them based on his loose and ever-changing concept of faith.

Dylan's turn to evangelical Christianity is one of the two most controversial episodes of the singer's sometimes infamous, often legendary biography; the other is his so-called rejection of the folk movement on the July day when Dylan went electric at the 1965 Newport Folk Festival and got booed for his troubles. What connects the two is conversion: in the first case a transition in musical style perceived as an ideological rift, in the second a revolution in personal consciousness perceived by many as having deleterious effects on his music. Nowadays most Dylanologists view his "Christian phase" as but one more example of Dylan's brilliant eccentricity. Nevertheless, just as Dylan's electric conversion and improvisational invention of "folk rock" brought to the surface influences that he insisted were always implicit in his person and music, so too his Christian or overtly religious phase, even apart from the views we may take on the specific credo espoused in the lyrics, realized an aspect of the music he'd been producing for two decades. In these songs he gave expression lyrically and melodically to a rock heritage that was dependent not only on black blues but on its heretic cousin, the gospel blues, each of which was also a folk genre, even as he mined the predominantly white folk movement for its traditional country ballads running back through Appalachia, and before that Scotland or Ireland, to religious hymns. In this chapter we presume a certain degree of religious consciousness in all of Dylan's music, even as we explore Dylan's varying attitudes toward the function of religion in culture. To assess the place of prophecy, proselytization, God, Jesus, and faith (both Jewish and Christian) in Dylan's songs is to encounter an artist who, in drawing on multiple religious traditions and attitudes, yokes them together by means of a marvelously syncretistic imagination.

Almost from the start, Dylan's criticism of American society worked in a prophetic vein. Envisioning a secular world characterized by wealth, privilege, and power, Dylan associated social status with corruption, speaking as a latter-day Jeremiah. His first album, on which there were only a couple of original compositions, was styled in the folk spirit, featuring morbid mock-spiritual laments about dying, ballads about wronged lovers, and songs of roaming couched in the idiom of Woody Guthrie. Especially in the songs about dying, Dylan traced a folk heritage that had ironically naturalized the religious contemplation of death. What the songs on this album lacked, however, besides the originality of Dylan's soon-to-be-invented improvisational, free-associative mode of writing lyrics, was the spirit of invective that would characterize his rise to fame.

For all of the debate about Dylan's folk credentials, the songs he wrote throughout 1962 and 1963 turned an attitude of discontentedness that might have come right out of the Hebrew prophets on almost everything he considered. Even in one of the simplest of his early compositions, "Blowin' in the Wind," there's a plainly prophetic, angry edge. Each of the song's conjectures about an era of Messianic peace is suspended in advance by an image of the incorrigible present stretching toward eternity, or by some intervening condition of physical impossibility. The third verse is the song's most resolutely biblical, with direct allusion to the mountains that tumble into the sea from Psalm 46, except Dylan has turned a conceit referring to the protection of God amidst adversity into one of anticipated apocalypse: "How many years can a mountain exist / Before it is washed into the sea?" In the song's very next line he vaguely evokes the Exodus narrative ("Yes, 'n'

how many years can some people exist / Before they're allowed to be free?"),
adopting one of the standard biblical tropes deployed by Martin Luther
King for the Civil Rights movement. Even as the song attempts to foresee
a peaceable kingdom, its chorus – as sung by Dylan in flat, low, tonally
uninspired notes – fails to predict much of anything.

At this point in his career, Dylan's use of biblical imagery was redemptive
only in the time-honored prophetic sense of uttering threats against the
powerful and the wayward people who follow them. This sensibility is
evident in "Masters of War" (1963), one of the best and angriest anti-war
songs ever written. Implicitly alluding to the Kennedy administration's
military activities in Vietnam, at a time when there was still officially no war
and effectively no protest movement against American policy, Dylan berates
a group of bureaucrats who orchestrate wars from behind their desks and
put guns in the hands of young people ordered to kill. "Like Judas of old" the
anonymous leaders of the American military–industrial complex perpetrate
a grand lie, in this case by propagating a Cold War that has gradually
assumed flesh and color. These early songs addressed to contemporary
sociopolitical problems were secular in their conception of motives and
consequences but possessed nevertheless of a prophetic rancor, sounded in
Dylan's compact phrases or the sharpening notes of his esoteric inflections.
In "The Lonesome Death of Hattie Carroll," written in response to the
killing of a Baltimore maid by a drunken socialite and released on 1964's
The Times They Are A-Changin', Dylan satirically observes the judge's
decision to give the socialite a "six-month sentence," remarking coolly on
his capacity to oversee "penalty and repentance." In one of the song's most
beautiful lines, associating Hattie Carroll with the ancient poor and forsaken
so often remembered by Isaiah or Jeremiah, Dylan speaks of her death as
betokening the destruction of "all the gentle," drawing the irony from the
last word with its Latinate origin as a term referring to the well-born. By this
clever inversion, a technique Dylan borrowed straight from the prophets, the
well-born have destroyed their claim to gentleness and passed judgment on
themselves, even if the corrupt judge won't do the same; and if any gentleness remains, in the way of virtue, it has been passed on to the servant class.

Like a true prophet, Dylan typically takes his stand against institutions,
often institutions that are stereotypical in their rigidity. For all of his strategic adoption of prophetic language, the early Dylan is tough on religion,
especially critical of the nexus whereby Church and State work their magic
together. The anti-war song "With God on Our Side" (1964) relentlessly
ridicules an American Christianity that has embraced the task of apologizing
for nationalistic myths such as "manifest destiny." Initially the song's true-
believing Midwesterner is disinclined to question the providential alliance

between God and the American nation, but an odd thing happens in the middle stanzas as he begins to doubt himself and his history. Following conventional twentieth-century history, according to which World War I sowed the seeds of modernist disenchantment with both wars and the nation-states in whose names they were waged, the speaker expresses bewilderment about God's sanctifying oversight of each world war, and soon finds himself indoctrinated in the ways of Cold War ideology ("I learned to hate the Russians") and anxious about chemical and nuclear weapons. By the time he flatly suppresses his own doubts, singing "And you never ask questions / When God's on your side," the doubts have become firmly lodged in us. The song ultimately questions the use of religion to rationalize the policies of the American State, but it also supposes that in its institutional function religion remains unaltered, encouraging the same old combative non-truths, serving as a force for conformity rather than thoughtful interrogation of the political status quo.

Much has been made of Dylan's adventures in pseudonymity – of the Robert Zimmerman who renamed himself "Bob Dillon" in 1960, and then "Bob Dylan" by the end of the year because the spelling looked cooler. In adopting the sensibility of a folk singer, Dylan not only changed his name but persistently reinvented himself, fabricating tall tales of a bohemian past that had been far more conventionally bourgeois than he let on. Although the new folk movement stood for truthfulness and authenticity, when it came to his own personal history Dylan took a cavalier attitude to such values. This has led some Dylanologists to perceive his folk-posturing as an opportunist's ruse. The name-change, as David Hajdu suggests, was most likely based on a supremely practical calculation, comparable to that of Ramblin' Jack Elliot in changing his name from Elliot Adnopoz. Each of these Jewish-born singers intuited that he was not "likely to be accepted as part of old-time America" with his given name (Hajdu 74). In the pseudo-biographical tales Dylan told of himself in liner notes, in songs, or in interviews such as the one given to Robert Shelton for the *New York Times*, he never spoke of his Jewishness. Then, at the beginning of 1964, *Newsweek* published an exposé on Dylan, which broke the news to the American public that the self-fashioned protest singer with the fabulous past was in fact a middle-class, Jewish kid from Hibbing, Minnesota. Richard Fariña, the budding folk star and novelist who would marry the other Baez sister, Mimi, was at the time Dylan's rival and close friend; and in an article on Joan Baez and Dylan written for *Mademoiselle*, he drew attention to the controversy only to dismiss it. On the apparent paradox between "name-changing and integrity," Fariña mused that Dylan had "stepped so cleanly away from his antecedents and into the exhilarating world of creative action as to make the precise nature of an early history look insignificant" (87).

Over the course of Dylan's career, critics, journalists, and fans would try to make an issue of the singer's past. Dylan himself was often dismissive of the personal past, on one occasion specifically linking its insignificance to the controversy over his name: "We allow our past to exist. Our credibility is based on our past. But deep in our soul we have no past. I don't think we have a past, any more than we have a name" (Cott, Jan. 1978, 193). He disavowed the influence of Jewishness on his world view: "I've never felt Jewish. I don't really consider myself Jewish or non-Jewish. I don't have much of a Jewish background. I'm not a patriot to any creed. I believe in all of them and none of them. A devout Christian or Moslem can be just as effective as a devout Jew" (Rosenbaum 234). As Dylan qualified his own identification with Jewishness to open himself to a promiscuous pluralism (saying this, paradoxically, less than a year before he would make his sudden turn to evangelism), he was by declining to be a "patriot" of any creed reiterating his longstanding suspicion of religion as a mode of nationalism.

When Dylan took stock of the social and political landscape of the 1960s, he perceived the religious temperament of everyday Americans in an ironical spirit not unlike that of Nathanael West in his 1933 novel *Miss Lonelyhearts* (Dylan knew West's work well enough to crib a song title from his novel, *The Day of the Locust*). In "On the Road Again," from *Bringing It All Back Home*, the singer rejects a girlfriend's pleadings for him to settle down in her hometown by recounting for her the strange doings of her family. As a guest at their house, he wakes up with frogs in his socks, notices the girl's mother in the icebox and her father wearing a mask of Napoleon Bonaparte; and things only get weirder from there. In the midst of it all, the singer has time enough to take notice of her living ancestry, a grandpa whose cane turns into a sword and a grandma who "prays to pictures / That are pasted on a board." The pictures on the wall are most likely prayer cards with pictures of saints, as Dylan characterizes Catholic Creoles as devoted to a cult of the weird. With his eye on the peculiarities of American culture, so often religious in their intensity, Dylan's satiric humor attained perfect pitch in the songs of this era.

Bringing It All Back Home, released in early 1965, was the first of three albums, along with *Highway 61 Revisited* (1965) and *Blonde on Blonde* (1966), that Dylan would later remember as having most closely approximated the music he heard in his head when the songs came to him. On these records Dylan blended a loose but sturdy musical form with lyrics generated spontaneously from within relaxed yet driving blues–rock rhythms. The musical style fit the improvisational irreverence of the lyrics, as Dylan not only caricatured the religious foundations of "manifest destiny" but perceived the collapse of redemptive biblical typologies. A sense of alienation, both from the customs of the country and from the God who ordains such customs, preoccupies these songs: "God said to Abraham, 'Kill me a son' / Abe says, 'Man, you must be puttin' me on.' The Abe of "Highway 61 Revisited" protests God's violent command in a way the biblical Abraham never does. Once cowed into submission, however, he prepares to murder a son, on that legendary artery of American blues music.

What makes Highway 61 an appropriate scene for biblical sacrifice? Doubtless Dylan meant to evoke the lore of open road and legendary deaths, including most famously that of Dylan's childhood hero James Dean. On such precedent, the American highway proves hospitable to biblical scenarios in which human beings are put to absurdist tasks, forced to rationalize hardship, misery, or their own confused violent actions as acts of providence. Once God has given his blessing to the mingling of violence and covenant, ordinary Americans of all sorts find their schemes similarly sanctioned on the highway. It's the perfect place for Georgia Sam to act out his grievances against the welfare state; or for Mack the Finger (taking his cues from a king) to unload red, white, and blue shoe strings and phones that won't ring; or for a polygamous father to worry about his fair fifth daughter's complexion even as his second wife may be committing incest with one of his sons; and it's also just the place for a rovin' gambler and promoter to put their heads together to arrive at a scheme for staging the next world war as a spectacle for American audiences. In short, Dylan's Highway 61 is like Herman Melville's and Mark Twain's Mississippi River, replete with confidence men and their cons, inclusive of schemes, sins, and the twisted workings of power. A brooding cynicism haunts Dylan's vision of America.

Dylan can populate so many of his songs with biblical characters precisely because he hears what Greil Marcus calls "the old, weird America," with its folk legacy of passed-on stories and legendary truths, as though it were continuous with the fantastic dimensions of biblical religion. "Traditional music," Dylan has said, "is based on hexagrams. It comes about from legends, Bibles, plagues, and it revolves around vegetables and death" (see Hentoff, "Crackin, Shakin'"). In such a world he can move between biblical and literary characters without missing a beat. On "Desolation Row" Cain and Abel share their forlorn fate with the hunchback of Notre Dame, a Good Samaritan dresses himself to attend a carnival, Ophelia anticipates her future as an old maid at 22, and Ezra Pound and T. S. Eliot square off in a captain's tower of the *Titanic*. In the world of "Tombstone Blues," Jezebel becomes a nun knitting a wig for Jack the Ripper even as John the Baptist tortures a man under military orders only to find that he, quite literally, doesn't have the stomach for what he's done. Dylan, steeped in the idioms of Jewish prophecy and exile, always perceives himself slightly apart from such scenes, cognizant of a rift between himself and a world in which he participates only with grave reservations, as though he might yet envision some place to stand other than in contemporary America. His biblical characters, like mythical stand-ins for the singer's own alienation, are also outliers; and the Abe who is mystified by a deity who could call so callously for blood on America's highways finds himself answerable, we deduce, not so much to the biblical God of Judaism as to a newly Americanized God, suited to the needs of the people of this strange land.

There is, however, another side to Dylan's approach to religion. Though his public turn to evangelical Christianity felt radical to those wedded to the notion that he was a "liberal humanist" (a term he once called "bullshit . . . it means less than nothing"), echoes of gospel music were present in his music long before he declared himself born again. Early Dylan is littered with references to saints, sinners, jokers, thieves, and faith healers, and sometimes he even casts himself, ironically, in the role of a Messiah. Just so he begs hospitality in "Bob Dylan's 115th Dream," reminding a rude American "you know they refused Jesus too." Even though the man confidently declares "you're not him," the song itself isn't so sure. Dylan's full of Christ-haunted characters, like the sword-swallower who crosses himself in "Ballad of a Thin Man"; and at times, as in "Sign of the Cross" from the famous basement sessions of 1967, the entire world lacks, or maybe requires, gospel-style salvation. There are a handful of Madonnas, some clothed in revelatory earnestness, as in "Visions of Johanna," others wrapped in metallic irony, like the motorcycle momma of "Gates of Eden," and still others steeped in the ways of comfort, like the mysterious woman in "Shelter from the Storm," who receives a Christlike stranger, relieving him of his "crown of thorns." Many of the metaphors have been secularized, as Dylan infuses erotic love with the passion of Christ, but the energy of such songs is borrowed from the motion and fluidity of gospel, which had poured for years from America's faith-haunted hills and its valleys of suffering.

To listen to Dylan's great spiritual influences – the Carter Family, the Soul Stirrers, and the Staples Singers – is to find oneself awash in otherworldly energy, witness to a scene in which mortals seek, reach out for, and reach the sacred even as the world they know shifts beneath them. Many of the songs collected as "social music" on Harry Smith's *Anthology of American Folk Music* (1952), long considered the "bible" of the folk movement, were Christian spirituals. Among Dylan's early concert standards were "Gospel Plow," which he sang regularly throughout 1961, and "Man of Constant

Sorrow," recorded for his first LP. At the Newport Folk Festival in July 1963, he closed with a haunting choirlike rendition of "Blowin' in the Wind," joined on stage by Joan Baez, Pete Seeger, the Freedom Singers, and more than a half-dozen others. For an encore, all on stage joined hands, swaying like a gospel choir, as they sang, "We Shall Overcome," that anthem of the Civil Rights movement adapted from Charles Tindley's 1903 spiritual "I'll Overcome Some Day." The next month Dylan was at the freedom march from the Washington Monument to the Lincoln Memorial in DC, sharing a stage with Martin Luther King, from which Dylan sang not only "Blowin' in the Wind" but also, joined by Len Chandler, the Negro spiritual "Hold On."

So completely did Dylan take possession of the songs he borrowed, sometimes as covers, at other times only as platforms for his own musical and lyrical compositions, that he became an influence on several of the artists who'd first captured his imagination. Early Dylan is rife with examples of his co-opting and reconsidering the music of his predecessors. He is often confident and creative in his appropriations, but at other times merely derivative. He could be slow to shine a light on direct influence, as was the case, famously, with the Reverend Gary Davis, the Baptist minister and gospel singer whose spirituals – including "Jesus Met the Woman at the Well," "Death Don't Have No Mercy," and "It's Hard To Be Blind" – Dylan covered and reinterpreted, for a long while without acknowledging his debt, although he made amends on this point in the late 1970s. Sometimes the flow of influence was convoluted and complexly reciprocal.

Consider the case of Sam Cooke, son of a Baptist minister and former lead vocalist of the Soul Stirrers, who abandoned a successful gospel career to become one of the most popular singers of the late 1950s and early 1960s. He began writing his Civil Rights spiritual "A Change is Gonna Come" in May of 1963, as a response to Dylan's "Blowin' in the Wind." Cooke's single was not released until late 1964, scoring a modest hit early in 1965 weeks after his murder; and years later Dylan would cover that very song. But Cooke's influence on Dylan can be apprehended from vocal stylings, piano-haunted gospel tunes, and even lyrics. Consider Cooke's 1956 gospel classic, "Touch the Hem of His Garment," a song based on a story from the Gospel according to Mark. Cooke begins the song with a growling "Whoah," as though little concerned with hitting the proper note. The cry is testimonial, attention-grabbing; it commands us to listen to a story about "a woman in the Bible days" who'd been "sick, sick so very long." Soon the mellow cadences of Cooke's voice settle in, above the softly rolling piano and gentle guitar, as he recounts the moment in which the woman tells herself, "if I could just touch the hem of his garment / I know I'll be made whole," but at several points in the song he strains his voice in soul-wrenching cries, sharpening his notes as if in physical or at least spiritual agony.

Dylan's own experiments in spoken rhythms and screamlike inflections may be indebted to various sources of inspiration, but surely one of them is the testimonial urgency we hear in Cooke's gospel voice. Only a month after Cooke's death Dylan released "It's All Over Now, Baby Blue," sung in a somber, haunting melodic roll over harpsichordlike piano notes. Dylan's Baby Blue, like the woman in Cooke's pop-gospel song, finds all her resources for self-preservation exhausted, having long searched for her own source of healing, but in bed sheets and in blankets now rolled up on the floor. Dylan counsels her, sounding not unlike that original itinerant preacher Jesus himself, who throughout the gospels encourages disciples, crowds, and random individuals to relinquish their possessions and past lives. This is gospel-singing as sermon, as the stirring up of promise and something new, which will be found only by letting go of almost everything one has until now held falsely to heart. The scriptural echo is fullest in the song's last verse, which begins, "Leave your stepping stones behind, something calls for you / Forget the dead you've left, they will not follow you." Dylan recalls a verse from the Gospel according to Luke, in which Jesus rebukes a man who asks permission to bury his father before undertaking discipleship by saying, "Let the dead bury their own dead" (9:60), and then in the next instant tells another man not to bother returning home to say his goodbyes. So urgent is the news of the kingdom of God that Luke would have us abandon even the most rudimentary of social courtesies, religious codes, and familial considerations. So too in "It's All Over Now, Baby Blue," Dylan calls for a severe rejection of the secular past, counseling Baby Blue with mellow mournfulness to let go of a past love and an entire way of viewing the world so as to move bravely into the song's promise.

Throughout the late 1960s Dylan continued to explore the idioms of faith, perhaps nowhere more prominently than on 1967's *John Wesley Harding*, which by one critic's estimate contains sixty-one biblical references. In songs such as "I Dreamed I Saw Saint Augustine" Dylan recounts biblical or religious legends as though their meanings continued to impinge on the present. In the early 1970s, songs such as "I Shall Be Released," first appearing on *Bob Dylan's Greatest Hits, Vol. 2* (1971), and "Knockin' on Heaven's Door," written for the soundtrack of *Pat Garret and Billy the Kid* (1973), discovered the latent religious content in criminality or Western-style justice. In "I Shall Be Released," the criminal's air of resignation yields a psalm-like profession of faith that he'll soon be delivered from imprisonment, but this release doesn't refer to the prospect of secular freedom. Rather it is founded on a light that comes shining from the West unto the East and on the man's having glimpsed his own reflection in the empty sky "so high above the wall." And in "Knockin' on Heaven's Door," a vaguely spiritual attitude is implied by the rolling yet lethargic melody, and then neatly complemented by the dying words of a wounded sheriff who, while knocking on heaven's door, can finally let go of the tools (badge and guns) of secular justice.

In 1978 Dylan released the LP *Street Legal*, which, though hardly a Christian record, was a harbinger of things to come. *Street Legal* featured some of the same complex biblical imagery that had previously peppered *Highway 61 Revisited* or *John Wesley Harding*. The use of three female back-up singers, sounding like a miniature gospel choir as they voiced harmonies reminiscent of influences Dylan had never completely forsaken, infused an unprecedented spiritual energy into his music. Perhaps most notably on "Changing of the Guards," this small mock-choir echoes Dylan and plumbs his disappointment, as the song repeatedly emphasizes the dominant chord only to resolve it in minor chords. The first-person narrator, having left "the good shepherd" grieving to follow instead a woman with a shaved head, witnesses scenes of destruction over which renegade priests and treacherous young witches strew flowers. As the woman he's been following strides finally amidst wailing chimes – our idea of her gilded by angels whose "voices whisper to the souls of previous times" – intimations of her pagan past suggest we may be entering a temple of the wrong sort.

All of this detail resolves in a stunning rewriting of the Samson story. Even if the initial allusion features the wrong head shorn of its hair, Dylan's revisionary allusion comes clear in the melancholy denouement:

> She's begging to know what measures he will now be taking
> He's pulling her down and she's clutching on to his long golden locks.

Dylan assumes the entirety of the biblical episode, conflating beginning and end of the story from Judges, alluding both to Delilah's method of discovering Samson's secret and to the time after he has been shorn, blinded, and enslaved by the Philistines. But Dylan's hero is already moving out of his role as moral weakling, his hair having grown back and the "broken chains" evidence of renewed strength. So he announces to the gentleman of an "organization," effectively recasting the nation of Philistines as a modern corporation, that he's done with his service of moving mountains and marking cards. "Eden is burning," he declares, "either brace yourself for elimination / Or else your hearts must have the courage for the changing of the guards." With an eloquence that the brute hero of Judges altogether lacks, Dylan's hero converts destruction into apocalypse, as imminent violence affords an opportunity for redemption.

The music of *Street Legal* marks a moment in Dylan's life, as well as the nation's. The post-Watergate hunger for redemption and institutional rebirth that led to the election of Jimmy Carter, the first avowedly "born again" president of the US, was implicit in Dylan's restlessness. He had gone beyond his customary metaphoric linkage of women and redemption to call for a new mode of relationship, and his next album *Slow Train Coming* (1979) was a brave experiment in a genre that could rightly claim to be the soul of American music. "When you listen to *Slow Train*," its producer Jerry Wexler would later recall, "it surely sounds different to anything else that he ever did" (Buskin 27). Indeed, as Robert Shelton has insisted, *Slow Train* has been undervalued largely because of the controversy following from Dylan's decision to become a "Jesus follower" ("Trust Yourself" 294). Much of the record moves effortlessly between the personal and the political, as Dylan comments on the state of the nation while weighing in on the erroneous ways of modern Americans:

> In the home of the brave, Jefferson turnin' over in his grave
> Fools glorifying themselves, trying to manipulate Satan
> And there's a slow, slow train comin' up around the bend.

The title track has the qualities of classic Dylan narrative, as he indicts corrupt authorities who've sold the country out to foreign oil, big-time negotiators, and a new breed of bureaucrats who, echoing the masters of war he'd denounced in 1963, are described as "[m]asters of the bluff and masters of the proposition." As Dylan turns to the solace of religion, embracing without reservation what Marx described as its opiate-like quality, he takes pleasure in listing all those who might wish to exempt themselves from servitude. Renewed by the threat of judgment, by the reductive scenario of choosing between the two bare alternatives ("it may be the devil or it may be the Lord / But you're gonna have to serve somebody"), the singer, although hardly exempt from judgment or servitude himself, is nevertheless eager for last things. As Dylan was surely aware, Christian converts, following the model of the Jewish Saul who was stricken by a brilliant light and temporarily blinded before becoming Paul, had for centuries changed their names to indicate spiritual transformation. Any change is permissible, Dylan declares after all these years, so long as it's in the service of some ultimate quest. Say what you will about the "either/or" approach to truth on *Slow Train Coming* or the subsequent Christian albums *Saved* (1980) and *Shot of Love* (1981): the music reflects the energy of a man who believes he has truth or God, or both, on his side.

As an artist, Dylan ought to be allowed his inconsistencies in vision, if only on the rationale of Emerson's famous excuse that "a foolish consistency is the hobgoblin of little minds." For much of his career he'd explored the possibilities of a largely secularized prophetic rancor, which was reinforced by his own exilic, or simply alienated, sensibility. In 1978's "We Better Talk This Over," he crooned about feeling "displaced" and then preemptively defended himself by taunting his interlocutor, "I'm exiled, you can't convert me." Of course the next year he would be converted, in defiance of the hobgoblins and a vast portion of his secular fan-base. But even without the rebirth of 1979, Jewish and Christian idioms persist in his work to such a degree that Dylan would have to be reckoned one of the most powerful interpreters of religious language and sensibility in all of American pop culture. In the midst of his "born again" period, 1979 through 1981, Dylan's songwriting was often at its best when he surrendered to inspirational Christianity as to a muse of spontaneity. Enthusiasm for the revealed truth even in its apocalyptic forms had served him well musically, although there were times when his lyrics became rather glibly proselytizing and the spiritual texture of the music became formulaic. His views would relax over time, as demonstrated in a 1997 interview for *Newsweek* in which he said, "I don't adhere to rabbis, preachers, evangelists, all of that." It's safe to say that this mood of complacency, or maybe only equanimity, had set in by the mid-1980s, leaving many critics wondering what to make of Dylan's religiosity.

After what many considered a string of forgettable 1980s albums, Bob Dylan soared once more with 1989's *Oh Mercy*, a ghostly collection of songs revealing a somber rather than enthusiastic version of Dylanesque piety. The album descends musically into moods of world-weariness, riffing on the slow, steady sway of the old Negro spirituals, and yet it always extracts enough in energy and hope to keep us coming back, less in the spirit of fundamentalist fervor than in that of a time-honored evangelical revival, with the preacher often mournful about the inevitability of sin in people's lives. Though he'd dropped the proselytizing tendency, Dylan could still testify to his faith in the necessity of change. Throughout the album Dylan intuits the persuasive malaise of modern nostalgia, interpreting himself as a sign of twentieth-century America's fondness for a mythic notion of itself. "We try and we try and we try to be who we were," Dylan said movingly in a 1997 interview, but the implication is that such edenic consciousness is futile, even delusional. Change is the rhythm of mortality, and so the singer keeps wandering, as if toward a morose end in which he proffers a quieter version of his relentlessly prophetic, often apocalyptic imagination:

> It's the last temptation
> The last account
> The last time you might hear the sermon on the mount
> The last radio is playing.

In this song our sense of last things is mournful, replete with loss as much as promise. The good people pray, in the spirit less of self-satisfaction than of somber reflection, as though tired of a world that keeps revealing its own demise. On *Oh Mercy* Dylan's religious vision is gentled, sung in a steady *sotto voce*, like the timeless echo of church bells or the reliable background noise of a radio that might still be playing gospel or blues or Bob Dylan on Judgment Day, though hardly, we hope, for the last time.

8

LEE MARSHALL

Bob Dylan and the Academy

On June 9, 1970, Bob Dylan took to the stage once more. This time, however, it was not to sing but rather to be awarded an honorary doctorate by Princeton University. Four months later, Dylan released a song documenting that day entitled "Day of the Locusts." "Darkness was everywhere, it smelled like a tomb" he sings, before concluding "Sure was glad to get out of there alive." Over thirty years later, in his autobiography, Dylan revisited his experience of that event. While the discomfort of the occasion is still vivid in Dylan's writing, he also suggests that he accepted the doctorate in order to undermine his countercultural credibility; "every look and touch and scent of [the degree] spelled respectability" (*Chronicles: Volume One* 134).

This ambivalent mixture of attraction and repulsion has characterized Dylan's attitude to those who study him since the 1960s. While he has repeatedly scorned those who seek to analyze him and categorize him, most scathingly in the withering putdown of Mister Jones in "Ballad of a Thin Man," it also seems likely that he is proud of his status as rock's most analyzed songwriter. Indeed, Dylan's management are rather generous in their granting of copyright permissions to aspirant authors, but there is always a requirement that a copy of any completed book be sent to Dylan's office to take its place among the vast library of work now completed on him. It seems that Dylan is rather interested in what people say about him.

This ambivalence works both ways. It would be wrong to suggest that Dylan has been wholeheartedly endorsed by the Academy; as my own experience of writing a book on Dylan attests, even today there is still skepticism generated by the medium in which he works. His place in the pantheon is less secure than James Joyce, say, or Arnold Schoenberg. Indeed, to write a chapter on "Dylan and the Academy" provides only a partial account of the critical work on Dylan because the majority of it has emerged from outside of the confines of academia and, even though its partisan nature and lack of critical rigor can sometimes be infuriating, the best of it – the work of Paul Williams, for example – is often more insightful than the work that has been completed by academics. In this chapter, I want to consider why this may be so.

The majority of academic work that has been published on Bob Dylan has emerged from English Literature departments. Browsing the Dylan book-shelf, the major academic works are by Ricks (2003), Scobie (2003), Day (1988), and an edited collection by Corcoran (2002), all of whom are pro-fessors of literature. And although he is not officially an academic, the lit-erary scholarship of Michael Gray (2000) can justifiably be added to this list. In books such as these, you can find frequent references to Bob Dylan being "a poet" (though the academic work on Dylan does not hold a monopoly on such claims). There is a problem, however, in treating Dylan as a poet, and that is the fact that he writes songs rather than poems. Although, at the start of their books, virtually all of the literary critics offer some kind of fleeting acknowledgment that Dylan's words are sung rather than read, this is sel-dom acted upon and the result is an over-emphasis on Dylan's lyrics. The outcome of such literary preconceptions is analyses such as this: "Dylan's lyrics construct an author–reader relation posited on the model of an irre-solvable enigma which is both the incitement to and the perpetual frustration of readerly desire" (Day, cited in Brown 193). Which is just about as distant from the experience of listening to Dylan as one could possibly imagine. It offers no insight into how we, as listeners, relate to the voice that sings the words to us. The idea being discussed is interesting, but it sounds like the author has never heard a Dylan song; it gives us no clue as to how songs work. Songs gain their emotional and artistic power not merely from the semantic meaning of the lyrics but from a constellation of *sound*. Dylan's words are *performed*: music, voice, and words come together to create a distinctive cultural artefact and not a verbalized poem. To analyze them effectively requires taking into account both the music and the vocal per-formance. Dylan himself raised this issue in his autobiography:

> For sure my lyrics had struck nerves that had never been struck before, but if my songs were just about the words, then what was Duane Eddy, the great rock-and-roll guitarist, doing recording an album full of instrumental melodies of my songs? Musicians have always known that my songs were about more than just words, but most people are not musicians . . . I was sick of the way that my lyrics had been extrapolated . . . (*Chronicles: Volume One* 119–120)

The quote from Brown above is not atypical. For example, one reviewer of Gray's recent *Encyclopedia* (2006) accused him of maintaining "a decisively literary, fundamentally unmusical bias – always privileging lyrics over sound . . . The 1965 [hit] 'Can You Please Crawl Out Your Window?' is a great record whose precise, lurid images emerge in quicksilver strikes from the fanatic swirl of a madly exciting performance: The sound makes it fly. But Gray merely asserts that 'the language of the song is at least as interesting as its music,' then devotes an entire entry to one while ignoring the other" (McKinney).

Given that he creates songs, the lack of attention given to Dylan's musicianship or his skills as a composer is remarkable. Only Wilfred Mellers's early work (1984) and Keith Negus's recent book (2008) have given explicit attention to the specifically musical aspects of Dylan's work. The inattention to Dylan's music is partly based on the popular cliché that Dylan uses "simple" chords and melodies as a backdrop to his "complicated" lyrics. According to Allan Moore, however, Dylan is not alone in having his musicality overlooked. Moore argues that the role of music in creating meaning has been underplayed in the vast majority of critical work completed on rock music, claiming that music is often relegated to being a pleasant background to the words. By contrast, Moore argues that it is essential to consider how music sets up a particular attitude within a song (186).

Ironically, what is probably one of Dylan's most quoted remarks refers to the musical qualities of one of his most highly rated albums. Here it is, placed in the context of the original interview from 1978:

DYLAN: I couldn't go on being the lone folkie out there, you know, strumming "Blowin' in the Wind" for three hours every night. I hear my songs as part of the music, the musical background.

PLAYBOY: When you hear your songs in your mind, it's not just you strumming alone, you mean?

DYLAN: Well, no, it is to begin with. But then I always hear other instruments, how they should sound. The closest I ever got to the sound I hear in my mind was on individual bands on the *Blonde on Blonde* album. It's that thin, that wild mercury sound. It's metallic and bright gold, with whatever that conjures up. That's my particular sound. I haven't been able to succeed in getting it all the time. Mostly, I've been driving at a combination of guitar, harmonica and organ, but now I find myself going into territory that has more percussion in it and [pause] rhythms of the soul.

(Cott 208)

Describing music as "metallic and bright gold" maybe a bit of a vague metaphor but it also offers a more intuitive sense of the musical qualities of Dylan's work than the majority of academic analyses of that work. It should also make us think about why *Blonde on Blonde* is such a good album. The lyrics, sure, but, more than anything, it's the sound that captures us. The lyrics to "Sad-Eyed Lady of the Lowlands" are vague and imprecise, with the potential to be dismissed as some of the worst excesses of Dylan's symbolist pretensions. The song's music wraps them up, however, contextualizes them and gives them their meaning, lending them both grace and warmth. The lyrics don't stand up as poetry on a page because they don't have to. By contrast, "Visions of Johanna" contains perhaps Dylan's most "poetic" writing, with the printed lyrics arguably standing up to academic scrutiny. But how much more exciting is the song than the poem! How much more sensual and more intimate because of the music! Note how the words themselves are carried along by the drumming, softly spoken yet with a military insistence, while the feeling of longing generated by the song is thrown into sharp relief by the spiky guitar lines that punctuate the verbal lines.

The intimacy and sense of longing generated by "Visions of Johanna" is not merely the result of the instruments, however; it is also created by Dylan's singing, and the fact that song lyrics are mediated by a performance is something regularly overlooked by those taking a literary approach to Dylan's work. When we read a poem, we read it in our own voice, at our own speed. With a song, we have no such control; the singer controls the pace at which we hear a song and the voice in which we hear it. In consort with the music, the singer gives us clues as to, for example, whether the authorial voice is male or female, or whether the words are sincere or ironic, that are not available in written poems. As Simon Frith argues,

> in songs, words are the sign of a voice. A song is always a performance and song words are always spoken out, heard in someone's accent. Songs are more like plays than poems; song words work as speech and speech acts, bearing meaning not just semantically, but also as structures of sound that are direct signs of emotion and marks of character.   (*Music for Pleasure* 120)

It is also worth noting that voices do not appear to us neutrally but rather are bound up in a wider set of meanings generated by popular music stardom (Marshall 14–48). This is particularly important for a singer like Dylan who has such a distinctive voice. When you hear that sound, you know who is singing, and what we know about Dylan affects how we respond to the song.

If we are to understand the emotional affect and artistic content of Dylan's songs, utilizing the assumptions underpinning the literary approach to Dylan may lead us in the wrong direction, over-emphasizing semantic meaning rather than sonic experience. Frith suggests that to understand how songs generate meaning, we should consider them as "speech acts" rather than as poems (*Performing Rites* 158–159). Rather than treating lyrics in the same way that we treat poems, we need to consider them as a form of rhetoric: "We have to treat them in terms of the persuasive relationship set up between the singer and the listener. From this perspective, a song doesn't exist to convey the meaning of the words; rather, the words exist to convey the meaning of the song" (166). This is something Dylan has argued in interviews: "When I do whatever it is I'm doing, if there's rhythm involved and phrasing involved then that's where it all balances out – in the rhythm of it and the phrasing of it. It's not in the lyrics" (Cott 323).

Given that treating Dylan's lyrics as poetry fails to address some of the most important aspects of Dylan's work, and given that Dylan himself has repeatedly argued that those analysing his work place too much emphasis on lyrics, it is worth asking why things turned out like they did. One reason, suggested by Kevin Dettmar, is a historical coincidence: the 1960s were the heyday of the study of poetry in English Literature departments. The dominance in the early 1960s of New Criticism – the approach to literature that eschews consideration of authorial intention and audience affect in favour of forensic analysis of the text itself – lent itself to the study of the complexity of poetry. If Dylan was to be studied at universities in the 1960s, then his work would have to be brought under the wing of this approach to literature. There was no place else for it to go.

When considering the academic study of Dylan's work, it is important to point out that we are not talking about some new messiah bashing down the gates of the ivory towers and shining a light into the souls of literary academics. Dylan was not immediately and universally accepted by the academic establishment as some great new poet. The introduction of Dylan into the classroom was surely opportunistic, with teachers wishing to appear hip to their students and to engage them "on their terms." Nonetheless, before too long Dylan was appearing in some literary anthologies and textbooks: Dettmar lists Lid's *Grooving the Symbol* (1970), Hogan's *The Poetry of Relevance* (1970), and Pichaske's *From Beowulf to the Beatles* (1972) as the earliest examples. Dylan did therefore make some inroads into the literary academy, and it is worth asking why. After all, Dylan didn't have to be studied in universities at all in the 1960s, and the fact that he was is itself something of a surprise. Universities are supposedly the guardians of high culture, rigorously defending the intellectual, the refined, the classical, and the unpopular from the talons of the trivial, vulgar, and commercial offerings available in daily life. How was it that a writer of popular songs became (partially) accepted into the literary canon?

It would be nice to argue that Dylan's appearance in scholarly circles was the result of the strength of the work – his songs were just of too high a quality to ignore. There are, however, more deep-seated explanations for the acceptance of a rock songwriter into literary life. Some of these refer to the wider social changes occurring in the 1960s, particularly the increasing challenge to intellectual authority and the changing role of universities in light of an expansion of higher education. These are beyond the scope of this chapter, however. What I want to consider is how changing ideas about the medium in which Dylan worked – popular music – affected his acceptance as a serious artist.

Dylan first became popular as a folk artist, of course, and such an emergence was vital in Dylan's acceptance as an artist. Folk music already had bourgeois respectability and was intimately tied to the ethnomusicological projects of folklorists such as Alan Lomax, who worked for the Library of Congress. The folk revival of the early 1960s contained within it a series of assumptions regarding the political and artistic flaws of commercially produced popular music. Indeed, the folk revival must be seen in the context of the more general critique of mass culture that was common during the 1950s – pop music was shallow, transient and commercially driven while folk music had depth, purity, and was produced authentically (this was at least partly delusional as the folk revival was itself part of mass culture). While Dylan's move into electrified "pop" music in 1965 was criticized by folkies as betraying folk's purity and honesty, in reality much of the intellectual authority granted by being a folk musician was carried forward by Dylan into a new genre of music.

Rock music is often portrayed as anti-intellectual, concerned with the sensual, bodily effects of music rather than with rational thought. This supposed character of rock fits nicely into the image of commercial music generated by the mass culture critique: rock music creates a generation of rhythmically obedient young people mindlessly reacting to physical stimuli. Rock, as commercial popular music, exists solely for quick thrills. Such a portrayal of rock, whether positive or negative, is misleading, however. Indeed, rather than rock being just another mainstream music, it emerged in the mid-1960s as a way of *stratifying* mainstream musical consumption, as a means of creating higher and lower levels of popular music. The basis of rock is the claim that, rather than all forms of popular music being mindless and disposable, certain elements of popular music are worthy of being taken seriously in their own right. Rather than merely assuming a difference in quality between serious/classical music and light/popular music, rock emerged to differentiate between serious, worthwhile popular music (rock) and trivial, lightweight popular music (pop). The gravitas Dylan attained from being a "serious" folk artist is important for the ideology of rock. Rather than merely "selling out" to rock & roll, Dylan's shift from acoustic to electric music precipitated those same ideas developing within the rock & roll mainstream. Dylan used "those aspects of the pop process that the folk world had defined itself against in the 1950s – not just the use of amplified instruments, but the trappings of stardom, packaging and promotion" to show the possibilities that popular music offered (Frith *et al. Cambridge Companion* 81). The ideology of rock thus emerged as a way of stratifying popular music into a layer of serious music that represented individual sensibility and communal experience (rock) against a lower stratum subject to all the commercial manipulation and trivial meaning that the folkies so despised (pop). Rather than polemicizing *against* popular music, rock polemicizes *within* popular music (Keightley 127). And, as Keir Keightley points out, it is actually this supposed seriousness, and not the alleged recklessness and anti-rationality of rock music, that endows it with its artistic qualities (129).

Because rock is purported to be a "higher" cultural form, one of the central beliefs of rock ideologists is the notion that those working within it are serious artists. This is a necessary justification for rock promoting both the quality of the work and the aesthetic motives of those producing it. For example, writing an article in *Sing Out!* in February 1966, Paul Nelson defended Dylan's new music as:

> A highly personal style-vision: Dylan's unyielding and poetic point of view represents a total commitment to the subjective over the objective, the microcosm over the macrocosm, man rather than Man, problems not Problems. To put it as simply as possible, the tradition that Dylan represents is that of all great artists: that of projecting, with the highest possible degree of honesty and craftsmanship, a unique personal vision. (Quoted in McGregor 74)

The growing emphasis on artistic self-consciousness can be seen in the increasing focus on originality as a prerequisite of rock authenticity, and it is within this context that an emphasis emerges upon rock lyricists as poets, with Dylan held up as the clearest example of the phenomenon. Dylan's skillful use of words resulted in him being described as a poet from early in his career. For example, when appearing on the Steve Allen TV show in 1964, the host introduced Dylan by saying that "He's primarily a poet. He's a very popular entertainer now, but I think one of the reasons for his popularity is that he has the mind of a poet," while Barry Kittleston in *Billboard* wrote that "Dylan's poetry is born of a painful awareness of the tragedy that underlies the contemporary human condition."

The introduction of Dylan into university study thus bought into some of the founding principles of rock itself. And, of course, by taking rock's claims to be a popular art seriously, the professors that adopted Dylan onto their courses reinforced rock's claims. The problem is that adopting Dylan as "literature" merely reinforced the problems caused by a binary high/low culture divide in the first place: namely, it resulted in an analysis of Dylan grounded in alien concepts. High culture and low culture have different qualities and achieve different things. Embedded within high and low cultural spheres are very different attitudes toward criticism, participation, and relevance that make them qualitatively different things. To study one in terms of the other will always do a disservice to the work in question. It does not just rob the work of its context, it fundamentally misinterprets the text itself.

The above points emerge from a changing attitude to the study of culture that is intrinsically related to the emergence of postmodernism (which, more than anything, is about the relationship between "culture" and "everyday life") and that have since coalesced into the discipline of "cultural studies." This approach recognizes that high and low cultural artefacts have different aims and achieve their effects differently. It also undermines the status of "high culture," deconstructing ideas of culture and making us aware of their inherently white, class-based, West-centric, and gendered elements. Cultural studies approaches have pluralized the notion of culture and weakened the idea that artistic value could only be found in one particular sphere. One outcome of this new intellectual attitude to culture is the great expansion of the study of popular culture in universities over the last thirty years or so. One may imagine, therefore, that the study of Dylan has developed in more appropriate ways since his early adoption onto curricula. However, cultural studies generally has paid very little attention to Dylan due, I think, to a couple of reasons. First, there is another historical coincidence: the emergence of cultural studies as an established discipline in the 1980s coincided with Dylan's lowest ebb in terms of recorded output and critical standing. He just seemed a less important cultural figure. More significant, however, is the matter of ideology. Dylan was damaged goods in the 1980s, tainted by the earlier attempts to elevate him into the pantheon of high culture. Rock had characterized itself according to the rules of high culture and, as those rules became challenged in the 1980s, rock itself found itself under fire. Rock was shown up not as a universal ideology, but a historically specific one that was pretty white, pretty male, and pretty middle class. If cultural studies is an intellectual attempt to wrest cultural status away from the dead, white, European males, then one of the ramifications of this is a tendency to study more marginalized forms of cultural production. Mainstream rock therefore tended to be overlooked in favor of more diverse, local, subcultural, and minority genres. Furthermore, questions of aesthetic quality became sidelined as questions of relevance and use became more prominent – issues of consumption trumped issues of production, and the canon was debunked as an historically specific social construction based on cultural privilege rather than inherent aesthetic worth. The claim that Dylan was worth studying because he was good was conspicuously absent. During the 1980s and

1990s, therefore, despite an increasing focus on the study of popular culture, Dylan's became a peripheral figure in the Academy.

The twenty-first century has seen some progress in this regard, but the study of Dylan has also been riven with some of the old problems. First, the positive developments: Dylan has become a more prominent figure in cultural studies in recent years. An increased interest in "traditional" musics (folk, blues, country), particularly in the USA, has coincided with a commercial and critical regeneration for Dylan that positions him squarely as an emissary of these older traditions. There have thus emerged a number of studies in which Dylan features as a key player in a wider story rather than as the central figure. This interest in tradition has also been one of the defining features of the writing on Dylan from outside of the Academy, in fanzines, music magazines, and on the web. Second, and although it is nowhere near fully developed, there have been some murmurings within cultural studies over the question of aesthetic quality. It has been argued by, for example, Simon Frith (1998) that we cannot ignore questions of aesthetic value by focusing merely on the populist, democratic, debunking elements of popular culture. There is good popular culture and there is bad popular culture: to ignore this fact does a disservice to the culture we study and abdicates our responsibility as cultural critics (Geraghty). The resurfacing of debates about aesthetic quality, small though they are, has facilitated the recent emergence of a number of single-artist studies within popular music (this very volume being one example).

So there are reasons to be cautiously optimistic about the future study of Bob Dylan within academic circles. There are, however, also causes for concern. Although there have been tentative steps toward considering issues of quality in cultural studies, aesthetic excellence is still the concept that dare not speak its name in cultural studies. Scholars are still far more likely to find something intellectually worthwhile because of its polysemous and "resistant" possibilities rather than because it is any good. Cultural studies and, in this case, popular-music studies, in particular, has yet to adequately address issues of quality. Where are the works from musicology, from performance studies, or from drama that could help us develop a critical vocabulary appropriate for the type of culture being studied? In part, the strengths of cultural studies are also its weakness: its subversive undermining of traditional hierarchies has resulted in a squeamishness about discussing cultural value in anything other than the most specific and particular circumstances; its ability to utilize insights from a range of different sources (its interdisciplinarity) has resulted in a magpie discipline that provides a series of insightful snapshots but fails to develop a coherent shared theoretical framework. The result is something of a vacuum in cultural studies which means that academic work produced on Dylan is still dominated by a literary studies approach that is inappropriate for his creative output (for example, the collection by Corcoran). As a matter of urgency, popular music studies needs to consider how best to deal with the matter of popular music texts – not just in their social context (though this is clearly important), but how they generate their affects aesthetically, through music, performance, and voice and not just words.

9

DAVID R. SHUMWAY

Bob Dylan as cultural icon

In the early 1960s, popular musicians were often called "recording artists," but they were not regarded by the press or the public at large as having a claim to making Art. From the middle of nineteenth century, the word "artist" was mostly reserved for painters, sculptors, writers, and composers, while the term "artiste" was sometimes used for actors and singers (Williams, *Keywords* 41). While in the US "artiste" evolved to mean something like "poser," we continue to distinguish between *art* meaning any skill or craft – for example, the art of wine-making – and *art* (or *Art*) meaning works or the best works of visual artists, writers, or composers, and others such as film-makers who increasingly are said to be artists.

Art was a contested domain in the early 1960s, and that contest had grown in the post-war era. The elite embrace of modern art did not immediately produce popular acceptance of it, but more Americans were becoming familiar with what had been tastes restricted to a very small percentage of the population. The rapid growth of higher education in the 1950s was one factor. Another was the growth of the media, which made more people aware of art and artists, both the accepted and the marginal. Everyone knew something about the Beats, for example, even though most people never read their work. The public remained suspicious that artists were, like "beatniks," lazy, slovenly radicals who refused "normal" work and family life. But they were also fascinated by the freedom these very characteristics seemed to entail, and, increasingly, by the strange new work such artists produced.

If in 1960 the wall between mass and elite culture was beginning to crack, popular music, especially rock & roll, was still widely regarded as the antithesis of Art. Folk music was somewhat less disparaged, having been granted a special dispensation as authentically primitive – a quality much valued in high modern art. In condescending to folk music in this way, the culture denied its practitioners the status of artist. Nevertheless, there were connections between the folk scene and the art world, especially in

New York. Bob Dylan experienced these connections, and they enabled him to acquire both some of the liberal education he ignored while briefly enrolled at the University of Minnesota, and an education that would have been hard to obtain anywhere else.

Dylan participated in activities of avant garde art, attending plays by LeRoi Jones and the Living Theater, and seeing films by Fellini and other European directors. Among visual artists, he singles out Red Grooms, part of the emerging pop art movement, as his favorite (*Chronicles: Volume One* 269). Pop art broke down the divide between high and low by making bits of mass culture and everyday consumer products into paintings that hung in elite galleries and, soon, museums. Dylan would attack the divide from the other side, making rock & roll that had the seriousness and complexity of high modernism.

In the 1960s, the appearance of popular musicians mattered a great deal. The Beatles' hairstyles – and to a lesser extent their clothes – attracted far more commentary in the US than their music. Adults were plainly threatened by this (relatively minor) violation of the gender code, which made the Four all the more Fab in the eyes of their young audience. After the Beatles breached the hair frontier, the Rolling Stones attacked accepted conventions of performance attire by looking as scruffy as possible. Dylan's earlier visual incarnations were carefully chosen, but they were not at odds with the expectations of the folk scene. On his first album, we see him in his cap and shearling jacket, looking the part of the folksinger. The clothes evoke work, but this is not a contemporary American worker, but one from some other time and place – from where folk music supposedly came. On his third record, *The Times They Are A-Changin'*, he appears in a black-and-white photo frowning, wearing an open-collared work shirt and relatively short hair. Here Dylan adopts a more obvious identification with contemporary American workers and the political left.

But Dylan's third album also pointed in a different direction. Instead of the traditional liner notes found on the first two, *The Times* featured Dylan's poetry. Called "11 Outlined Epitaphs," the poems in the main depict a world consistent with the lyrics and cover image, but they are apparently autobiographical and not explicitly political. They show the influence of modernist poetry even if they don't perhaps constitute particularly successful instances of it. While Woody Guthrie figures prominently, some other names mentioned are not those one would have at first associated with Dylan's persona as it had been known: François Villon, Bertolt Brecht, Brendan Behan, Edith Piaf, Modigliani, and William Blake among others. The poems are in free verse – with only occasional rhyme – and, while individual passages of them are clear enough, the reader is required to make connections that are not obvious if the whole is to be understood as an argument or narrative. These poems probably mystified most people who bought the record at the time, and in doing so, they began to make him seem more like an artist.

The new direction is much more apparent on his next release, *Another Side of Bob Dylan*. The cover photo shows Dylan dressed entirely in black, his hair longer and standing up in a wavy pile. He's frowning here, also, but the expression seems more thoughtful and less angry than in the photo on *Times*. Dylan, it seems, has morphed from a scruffy folksinger into a downtown artist. One who saw him a few months later at the Philharmonic Hall concert called him "the cynosure of hip, when hipness still wore pressed slacks and light brown suede boots" (Wilentz). This look conveys the image of sensitivity even as it also introduces Dylan as a man of taste, and in both respects it is consistent with Dylan's writing on *Another Side*. The liner notes are entitled "Some Other Kinds of Songs," and they consist of poetry similar in style to that found on the previous record, but they are not presented as autobiography and are considerably more opaque.

More important, the lyrics on *Another Side* are in a number of respects a departure from those on Dylan's earlier records. There are no topical songs on the album, and the majority are concerned with matters that seem more personal than political. There can be no doubt that Dylan saw *Another Side* as marking a shift in his career. As he told Nat Hentoff, who sat in on the recording session, "There aren't any finger pointing songs in here... Me, I don't want to write *for* people anymore. You know, be a spokesman. Like, I once wrote about Emmett Till in the first person, pretending I was him. From now on, I want to write from inside of me..." ("Crackin', Shakin'" 16). Dylan's songs offering explicit commentary on current events, and those that took explicit political positions – especially those that could be identified with a particular group or movement – were in conflict with the dominant conception of art. Artists spoke for themselves, *expressed themselves*. The folk community recognized the change, and an open letter to Dylan in *Sing Out* complained that his "new songs seem to be all inner-directed, inner-probing, self-conscious" after several of them were performed at the Newport Folk Festival the month before the album's release (quoted in Marqusee 104). One cut, "My Back Pages," was heard by many insiders as a "recantation," distressing Dylan's friends in the movement (Marqusee 113).

Dylan had actually always resisted pigeonholing, refusing to play the limited role of re-creating a single tradition. As Dylan put it, "Folk music was strict and rigid establishment. If you sang Southern Mountain Blues, you didn't sing Southern Mountain Ballads and you didn't sing City Blues. If you sang Texas cowboy songs, you didn't play English ballads ... Everybody had their particular thing that they did. I didn't pay much attention to that. If I liked a song, I would just learn it and sing it the only way I could play it" (quoted in Crowe). Dylan's quick move to writing his own songs also demonstrated his early distance from the preservationist impulse. While folk musicians like Pete Seeger had written some of their own songs, their personas depended on those songs seeming to be part of a tradition. The songs might be adapted for a new context from folk originals, but their efficacy strongly depended on their connection to a tradition. From the beginning, Dylan used such connections promiscuously for his own artistic projects.

Dylan's songwriting enabled a persona that differed from most other folksingers. Already on *Freewheelin'* he had established through the songs a distinctive personality of which they were the expression. While many songs were sung in the voice of another or written on behalf of oppressed others, there were also personal songs such as "Don't Think Twice, It's All Right," and "Bob Dylan's Dream." Moreover, the public conception of the artist's role included the idea of radicalism even as it also held that the artist was above politics. The tradition of the "lyrical left" goes back to the pre-World War I era when radical politics and artistic experiment went hand in hand. If it is true that in the 1930s the Communist Party tried its best to suppress that tradition, it survived elsewhere among Trotskyists, anarchists, and other heretics. And why was it that a mere singer and writer of songs could be so important to the old lefties whom Dylan would so quickly disappoint? Because this art was perhaps the only vibrant element of a movement that McCarthyism had recently decimated, but, in addition, that art was in itself understood as a politics, a rejection of the dominant capitalist culture.

Seen in this light, Dylan declaring himself an artist was a less sweeping break with his past. But it was, nevertheless, a break, because to be an artist in the sense of Eliot or Picasso is to be something quite different from a folksinger. Where the latter tried to keep old forms alive, the former was charged with, as Ezra Pound put it, making it new. If Dylan had previously sung the news, he now sought to make news. While *Another Side* had forecast this direction with "Chimes of Freedom" and "My Back Pages," Dylan's next album would fully embody it. *Bringing It All Back Home* was his first recording using electric instrumentation. One side featured these rock arrangements, while the other consisted of solo acoustic performances. But if the rock elements of the album are usually seen as its major innovation, it is worth considering the newness of the acoustic side as well. The first cut on that side, "Mr. Tambourine Man," is overtly about the power of art and the artist to take one away from the quotidian and self. Though it's sung as an appeal to the Tambourine Man, we might guess that Dylan imagines that he might play this role for his listeners, that he is Mr. Tambourine Man.

About the same time as *Back Home* was released, the Byrds' single of "Mr. Tambourine Man" became the first recording of a Dylan song to reach number 1 on the pop charts. The Byrds' version is defined by Roger McGuinn's chiming twelve-string guitar, and it's softer and sweeter-sounding than Dylan's recording. Moreover, the Byrds' cover omits several verses of the original, putting the emphasis on the chorus, and making whatever meaning Dylan had intended still more obscure. Perhaps for this reason – but certainly also because of the lyrics Dylan did write – the song became widely understood as being about drugs. While early 1965 was a bit before the words "take me on a trip" would automatically denote LSD, the song conveyed a more general sense of mind alteration that might be associated with marijuana or heroin. Drug use has long been associated with avant-garde artists, and Dylan's possible connection to it served to further redefine him.

The next song on the acoustic side of *Back Home*, "It's Alright, Ma (I'm Only Bleeding)," reveals another face of Dylan the artist. As Marqusee observes, it is "as much of a protest song as anything else Dylan had written: a sweeping vision of a corrupt and dehumanized society and the fate of the sensitive, autonomous individual within it" (127). But it is that last concern – or, more properly, the perspective of such an individual – that is new here. According to Nick Bromell, Dylan's earlier protest songs were "liberal" because they were sung on behalf of others, but with *Bringing It All Back Home* there is a radicalism rooted in "the perception of *oneself* as unfree, as oppressed" (131; quoting Greg Calvert). The singer now understands himself to be denied the freedom he once portrayed as denied only to society's Others, and the song's social critique combines surrealism, with more explicit charges:

> Advertising signs that con you
> Into thinking you're the one
> That you can do what's never been done
> That can win what's never been won.

This is not topical songwriting like we get in "Who Killed Davey Moore" or "The Lonesome Death of Hattie Carroll." It is a much more sweeping indictment, but one that implies that struggle is useless: "To understand you know too soon / There is no sense in trying." The film *Easy Rider* used "It's Alright Ma" to underscore just this point. Because activism is foreclosed, the artist is now free from its demands.

It makes sense, then, that the song also proclaims what might be called the artist's own creed, "That he not busy being born / Is busy dying." Dylan articulated this creed in the documentary *No Direction Home*, where he said "An artist has to be careful never really to arrive at a place where he thinks he's at somewhere. You always have to realize that you are constantly in a state of becoming." "It's Alright Ma" also proclaims the artist's freedom, "That it is not he or she or them or it / That you belong to." These last lines seem like a direct response to the claims that the old left and the folk purists had made on Dylan. As he recalled in *Chronicles: Volume One*,

> Ronnie Gilbert, one of The Weavers, had introduced me at one of the Newport Folk Festivals saying, "And here he is . . . take him, you know him, he's yours." I had failed to sense the ominous forebodings in the introduction. Elvis had never been introduced like that. "Take him, he's yours!" What a crazy thing to say! Screw that. As far as I knew, I didn't belong to anybody then or now. (115)

The adoption of rock & roll on the other side of the album was a stylistic assertion of this point, which demonstrated Dylan's interest in formal experimentation. By continuing to use folk sources, here, especially, the blues, but transformed into rock & roll, Dylan did not invent a new genre, "folk rock," a term which he always rejected, but rather a distinctive sound that was at that moment his alone. The lyrics of the songs redefine the singer's struggle. "Subterranean Homesick Blues," Dylan's first single to reach the pop charts, is a song mainly about obstacles to individual freedom and to aspirations of the young. "Maggie's Farm" turns a sharecroppers lament, "Down on Penny's Farm," into an angry proclamation of personal independence.

The rock tracks on *Bringing It All Back Home* don't sound like the records that were popular in 1965, what might be called the pre-bubblegum of second-tier British invasion bands and their American imitators. Needless to say, there was nothing sweet about Dylan's sound. While the rock songs on *Bringing It* borrow from rock artists such as Chuck Berry, they owe more to the precursors of rock & roll, including Jimmy Rogers, Robert Johnson, and, of course, Woody Guthrie. Perhaps to clue listeners in, the cover photo of what looks like a hip but bourgeois living room includes the album jacket of Johnson's *The King of the Delta Blues Singers*, but also the jacket of *The Folk Blues of Eric Von Schmidt*, by Dylan's contemporary in the Greenwich Village folk scene. Dylan was doing here what rock & roll innovators have always done, recombining the elements of various musical practices to make new forms.

"Subterranean Homesick Blues" only charted at 39, but Dylan's next single, "Like a Rolling Stone," was a genuine pop hit, making it to number 2. Greil Marcus, who has written an entire book about this record, finds virtually all of rock & roll summed up in its six-plus minutes, yet he also insists that it was immediately recognized as something utterly new. The record was startling, powerful, but it was also more recognizably rock & roll than anything Dylan had previously recorded. Mike Bloomfield's electric guitar and Al Kooper's Hammond B3 organ compete with Dylan's folk guitar and harmonica and, of course, finally dominate the mix. The record sounded like it belonged on the radio.

Its success, as Marcus observes, put Dylan in the rarefied company of the Beatles and the Rolling Stones as a star who reached the largest audiences and did so with work that defied the assumption of popular music's triviality. What did audiences find so attractive about this record? One answer is that it is "permeated by a kind of ecstasy of schadenfreude. The ensemble rises and falls on waves of bitterness. The guitar gloats. The voice taunts: 'How does it feel?'" (Marqusee 163). The song takes to new heights the attitude Dylan first expressed in "Don't Think Twice, It's All Right," of vindictiveness toward women – who seem as a group to have disappointed him. Where that song measures the attitude out, presenting it reflectively rather than emotionally, "Like a Rolling Stone" both reads and feels like an angry screed. This put Dylan in the very same terrain the Stones would mine over and over after "(I Can't Get No) Satisfaction," the number 1 record in the weeks preceding the release of Dylan's single. One could go farther, and argue that the song is the wish fulfillment of most high school students, male and female, since they suffer under the most rigid and oppressive social hierarchies.

But many have felt that the song's addressee is paradoxically also Dylan himself. He's the one who should know how it feels "To be on your own / With no direction home / . . . like a rolling stone." Muddy Waters and Hank Williams had both written about rolling stones, and Jack Kerouac and the Beats had styled themselves as such even if they hadn't used these words. The words seem to fit Dylan so well that two works about him have been titled "No Direction Home." I'm not sure how much this specific image of rootlessness attached itself to Dylan at the time, but all rock stars benefited from the presumption that they were not tied down to place or family or other mundane obligations.

Many of the songs from *Highway 61 Revisited* share a trait common to much modernist poetry: obscurity. "Desolation Row" in particular utterly resists paraphrase, as if it were written to illustrate the New Critical heresy. The song makes reference to two American fathers of modernist poetry: "And Ezra Pound and T. S. Eliot / Fighting in the captain's tower"; as these lines illustrate, the song, like their poetry, is full of allusions. The range includes Shakespeare (Romeo, Ophelia), Hollywood (Bette Davis), and the Bible (Cain and Abel, the Good Samaritan). Each verse describes a different scene, more or less coherent in itself, but related to the others only by the concluding words "Desolation Row." Such writing has given rise to an industry, unique to Dylan among rock stars: interpretation. At least four books are devoted solely to reading Dylan's lyrics, the most recent of which, *Dylan's Visions of Sin* – by Boston University professor, Eliot scholar, and right-wing culture warrior, Christopher Ricks – is 517 pages. This high-modernist take on Dylan is plausible because Dylan is perceived as an artist and not as a mere performer.

The ambition to high art can be found in many places in 1960s rock & roll, but Dylan is as much responsible for this ambition as anyone. Indeed, his lyrics may be the place where rock's sense of its own "seriousness," as Keir Keightley put it, was first apparent. The Beatles seem to have acquired their own sense of seriousness by listening to Dylan, which they began to do before Dylan had released any rock recordings (Coleman).

Dylan's high-culture borrowings and allusions are literary rather than musical. While his musical range shows the influence of virtually every sort of American popular music, he found this material more than sufficient for his purposes. There is no equivalent in Dylan's corpus to the violins backing the Beatles on "Yesterday" or the orchestral sound of "A Day in the Life." Dylan's modernism yokes together innovative, often difficult lyrics with music that remains, whatever its genre, primitive. Like modernist poets and novelists, Dylan relied on primitive artistic forms as a source of authenticity.

Unlike most other rock stars, Dylan had established his reputation first as a songwriter. Since his music was usually borrowed from folk sources, it was as a lyricist that he made his mark. This was a necessary but not sufficient condition for the perception that Dylan was a poet. The poems he used as liner notes were an indication that he aspired to poetry, but these texts were not those cited in the poetry debate. There was, of course, the widely repeated explanation that he named himself after Dylan Thomas. In 1965, the *New York Times Magazine* "ran a major piece on Dylan headlined, 'Public Writer No. 1?' The Subtitle ran, 'Who Needs Saul Bellow'" (Shelton, *No Direction Home* 227). In 1967, Ellen Willis could write, "It is a truism among Dylan admirers that he is a poet using rock-and-roll to spread his art... This misrepresentation has only served to make many intellectuals suspicious of Dylan and draw predictable sniping from conscientious B-student poets like Louis Simpson and John Ciardi" ("Sound" 77). Not all professional poets agreed. In March of 1966, Kenneth Rexroth claimed that "Probably the most important event in recent poetry is Bob Dylan" (quoted in Shelton 227). An informal survey of students at three Ivy League universities in 1965 found that Dylan was their favorite "writer" (Shelton, *No Direction Home* 227–228). While the lyrics of the Beatles and a few others were from time to time said to transcend the usual limitations of popular music, no other rock star was compared to Homer, Shakespeare, or Brecht, as Dylan was (228–234). By the end of the 1960s, the idea of rock poetry was widely accepted by ordinary listeners and many young poets, even if it was mainly pooh-poohed in the academy.

The fact that the professors – back then, anyway – did not accept Dylan and his ilk as poets or intellectuals did not necessarily damage their standing among youth – and perhaps did exactly the opposite. The generally negative reaction of the older generation to rock & roll was one of the grounds on which members of the younger one believed that they achieved a special kind of enlightenment. In short, they *got it*, while everyone else did not. Dylan gave this sense of communal knowledge and generational alienation powerful expression in many of his songs, including "Subterranean Homesick Blues" and "Positively 4th Street," but "Ballad of a Thin Man" is his most explicit statement of it. The song's chorus, "Because something is happening here / And you don't know what it is / Do you, Mister Jones," describes the condition attributed to most adults. The verses describe a series of surreal encounters that could easily have been filmed by Luis Buñuel, each suggesting more strongly than the last just how estranged Mister Jones is from reality.

One former *Time* correspondent claimed that Dylan had written "Ballad of a Thin Man" about him, and indeed the song does begin "You walk into the room / With your pencil in your hand." However, *Don't Look Back* suggests that Dylan may have had reporters in general in mind. While Dylan's contemptuous treatment of the press is often remarked, most of the journalists who interview Dylan don't seem to have a clue. Their questions reveal the abysmal state of popular music coverage in the 1960s, when most journals lacked specialists in the field. Journalists like Robert Shelton and Nat Hentoff, who wrote insightfully and sympathetically about Dylan, were mainly folk and jazz reporters. Dylan, along with the Beatles and a few others, would be one of major reasons that rock journalism would become a reality around 1970. In the meantime, Dylan had to put up with reporters asking questions that were at best ill-informed and at worst quite simply inane.

Dylan's artist persona was solidified by the release of *Blonde on Blonde* in the summer of 1966. The album also confirmed Dylan's status as a major rock star, including three songs that made it into the top 40 as singles. By this time, the expectation that Dylan should write topical or protest songs was no longer common in the US, though the tour of the UK that preceded the album's release – recorded in *Don't Look Back* – showed that it remained strong there. The record represents a return to the introspective and personal concerns of *Another Side*, but presented now in the form of rock & roll. Where *Highway 61* had continued to present social critique – however fragmented or surreal – *Blonde on Blonde* excludes that larger picture entirely. But the private world of which this album gives us glimpses is very strange indeed.

The music too was new. As Marqusee put it, "On *Blonde on Blonde*, Dylan made the familiar deliriously strange. He took inherited idioms and boosted them into a modernist stratosphere" (208). The various tracks on the album do not have a single music style, unlike *Highway 61* where almost every cut is blues-based. "Rainy Day Women #12 and #35" sounds like something you might hear a New Orleans funeral band play – at a party; "Visions of Johanna" is backed by the entire complement of studio musicians, but sounds restrained and soft, allowing Dylan's voice uncontested dominance. "Leopard-Skin Pill-Box Hat" sounds like rock & roll pure and simple save for Dylan's voice. "I Want You" borrows from traditional country music, while "Just Like a Woman" is a folk song with drums. At the time, the press lumped all of this variety together as "folk rock," but Dylan did not fit any genre, as his future stylistic shifts would confirm. It was the newness, the strangeness that resisted classification, that distinguished Dylan from all the would-be Dylans the industry tried to market.

Moreover, Dylan's appearance continued to evolve away from received categories of style. On the cover of *Highway 61* Dylan appears wearing a blue and pink print shirt open over a Triumph Motorcycle t-shirt. It's as if he is as intent on violating fashion codes here as he was in following them on his previous two album jackets. Beginning with this photo, his hair continued to get longer – or, as it appeared – bigger, so that in the *Blonde on Blonde* photos it curls up and out into a ragged orb. The look was captured in the pop-art poster distributed with *Bob Dylan's Greatest Hits* (1967) in which his hair is abstracted to what seems to be a large aura surrounding a smaller head. Dylan's appearance, like that of the Beatles, had finally become itself iconic.

Around the time *Blonde on Blonde* was released, Dylan was seriously injured in the motorcycle accident. He suffered a concussion and broken vertebrae, and was hospitalized for a week. The press portrayed "the accident as a near-death trauma," and at least one paper suggested that Dylan might never perform again (Heylin, *Behind the Shades* 269). Dylan canceled his planned tour of the United States, due to have begun in August and to last throughout the fall. Dylan would not tour the US again until 1974. It would be a year and a half until another album of new material, *John Wesley Harding*, was released. As a result of this withdrawal from the public eye, Dylan's enigma deepened. As *Time* put it, "Dylan *in absentia* loomed larger than Dylan in the flesh" ("Basic Dylan" 50). The press now seemed to be taking Dylan much more seriously. *Life*, *Newsweek*, *Vogue*, and the *Saturday Review* all gave *John Wesley Harding* respectful reviews or coverage.

Most of the headlines hailed Dylan's "return," but the *Saturday Review* described the album as a "Self-Portrait of the Artist as an Older Man." That allusion to James Joyce was followed by the assertion that "like most good writers, [Dylan] has successfully disguised his own involvement. Songs such as 'Just Like a Woman,' 'It Ain't Me, Babe,' and 'Positively 4th Street' are very much Portraits of the Artist as a Young Neurotic, but skillfully hidden ones" (Jahn 63). The new album, this reviewer thinks, is all about Dylan and the problems of identity that he speculates the motorcycle accident enabled him to address. The assumptions here are that Dylan's words are worth the trouble to interpret; he is being treated as one would treat an "artist" or a "good writer," but not previously a "pop hero."

In between *Blonde on Blonde* and *John Wesley Harding*, D. A. Pennebaker's cinema verité- style documentary of Dylan's 1965 tour of England, *Don't Look Back* appeared, first at a San Francisco premiere in May of 1967, and then on college campuses and in art houses. The critics' reaction to the film was mixed at best, though even the negative reviews often confirmed Dylan's artistic status. Ralph Gleason said the film was about "the problem of the artist communicating with his audience," while *Newsweek* commented that "it shows a singing genius who does not know where his songs come from" (Shelton, *No Direction Home* 299). Those sympathetic to Dylan who disliked the film complained that it not only was out of date – Dylan performed solo and acoustic – but also that it failed to capture the inner man (Goldstein). What the fans perceived is revealed by Pennebaker as he recalled Dylan's reaction to the film: "We showed him the first rough cut. What he saw must have made him look like he was bare bones. And I think that was a big shock to him. But then he saw, I think, the second night, he saw that it was total theater. He was like an actor, and he suddenly had reinvented himself as the actor within this movie and then it was OK" (*No Direction Home*). Dylan was undoubtedly performing for the camera, but in the very act of performing he was being the artist that his fans expected him to be. Dylan was revealed by his acting, by trying not to reveal himself.

Another element of Dylan mystique was added in June of 1968 when *Rolling Stone* published a long feature on unreleased Dylan recordings, "The Missing Bob Dylan Album." Soon after, bootleg recordings of what became known as the Basement Tapes began to appear. These recordings, made with the Hawks (later known as the Band) at various non-studio locations in and around Woodstock, New York, consisted of at least thirty new songs by Dylan (Heylin, *Recording Sessions* 57). The fact that copies of these recordings were unauthorized, illegal, and relatively difficult to obtain, made them all the more attractive. While interest in artists is often fueled by the rumor or knowledge of lost works, usually this must wait until after the artist's death. Dylan's "near death" and seclusion seem to have served the purpose, causing the Basement Tapes to become the holy grail of rock & roll. Their reputation endures to this day, with one critic calling the material Dylan's "greatest collection of songs," and another writing an entire book about them (*Recording Sessions* 57; Marcus, *Invisible Republic*).

Dylan in the 1960s evolved from a folk singer into the first rock musician identified as an artist. He presented himself as being in the same business as Ezra Pound, Pablo Picasso, and Igor Stravinsky. This persona enabled him to continue to comment on political and social issues without being classified as a protest singer. Because artists had since the mid-nineteenth century styled themselves as opponents of the bourgeoisie, Dylan's new persona continued to register as a form of radicalism. Yet it is also true that his songs became less political, and this fact was to some extent hidden by his identification as an artist. Dylan's claim to art made it possible for other popular performers to see themselves in this light (e.g., the Beatles) and to be taken seriously as artists by the media and the public. Rock stars from James Brown, to Joni Mitchell, to Bruce Springsteen, to Public Enemy, and Eminem, have benefited from Dylan's breakthrough.

PART II
Landmark albums

IO

ERIC BULSON

The Freewheelin' Bob Dylan (1963)

When Bob Dylan released his first album under an eponymous title with Columbia Records in March 1962, he was twenty years old. John Hammond, the producer at Columbia, first became interested in Dylan after seeing him play harmonica during a few sessions for Carolyn Hester's third album. At the time, Hammond was looking for someone who would allow Columbia to tap into the emerging folk-music craze; Dylan easily fit the profile. He walked, talked, dressed, and sang like a folkie. If it was all an act, something he learned by studying Woody Guthrie and Ramblin' Jack Elliott, his performance was authentic enough to convince everyone that he had some real talent. No one could have predicted just how long the act would last.

Bob Dylan is an album very much about the process by which Dylan found his voice. Of its thirteen tracks, only two are originals ("Song to Woody" and "Talkin' New York"). He was less interested in showcasing his originality than in paying tribute to a long list of influences that included Blind Lemon Jefferson, Woody Guthrie, Jesse Fuller, Hank Williams, and Reverend Gary Davis. The album cover is of the "meet the band" variety; a young, wistful boy dressed in a sheepskin jacket and cap has his hands clasped around the neck of an acoustic guitar. The expression seems earnest enough, but there is a devilish bend in the eyebrows that makes you think he's either full of himself or having fun with the idea. Dylan's first album didn't generate the sales that Columbia had hoped for, and there was some talk that they might drop him. Hammond, who agreed to record one LP with Dylan with the option to contract four more, decided to give his latest discovery another chance. It was a good thing he had the foresight to recognize that Dylan was just getting started. The second album, *The Freewheelin' Bob Dylan* (1963), did all the things that his debut could not: Columbia got its record sales (10,000 a month), and Dylan got his fame. When it was released, he was already teaming up with Joan Baez and arriving at all the major music festivals across the country as a full-blown celebrity.

In this second album, Dylan got repackaged for his audience (Gill; Riley; Benson). He had officially changed his name in between albums, and it's clear that he had a more coherent idea of who Bob Dylan was supposed to be. On the *Freewheelin'* cover, he walks down a slushy street with his hands in his pockets and a girl (then girlfriend Suze Rotolo) on his arm. Instead of posing for the camera, he looks as if he has been caught having a personal moment (it's worth noting that he's traded in his sheepskin jacket for a suede one along the way). Here already we have another side of Bob Dylan, the romantic, down-to-earth dreamer not afraid to get his feet wet. In the place of the generic folksinger, we are presented with the self-made freewheeler, someone steeped in the blues and folk traditions who belongs as well to the younger generation of Jack Kerouac and Allen Ginsberg. In interviews conducted at the time, he even began to sound more like a beat poet than a folkie. "My life is the street where I walk," he told Studs Terkel shortly after *Freewheelin'* was released; "That's my life, music, guitars, that's my tool, you know" (Cott 12).

Getting to know Dylan can be tricky. Even at his most down-to-earth moments, he can be ironic, detached, evasive, and cagey. "If I wasn't Bob Dylan," he once told an interviewer, "I'd probably think that Bob Dylan has a lot of answers" (Cott 233). In the early 1960s when his career was taking off, that was sometimes a problem. People were looking for answers to the social, political, and economic ills besetting America. Civil Rights activists, in particular, co-opted Dylan early on and expected him to play along. The more they pressed him, however, the more he retreated. Dylan didn't want to be a mouthpiece for any movement, and he resented the pressure that was being put on him to conform. He didn't have a problem lashing out at the hypocrites of the world: he just wanted to do it his own way. When asked to appear on the Ed Sullivan show on May 12, 1963, the same month *Freewheelin'* was released, he decided to play "Talkin' John Birch Society," a song that ridicules the right-wing anti-communist organization and includes a line comparing them to Hitler. Shortly before Dylan went on stage, the producers at CBS got cold feet and asked him to play another song: he refused and stormed off.

Freewheelin' occupies such a significant place in Dylan's sprawling cata-logue (forty-six albums and still counting) because it represents his first full-scale performance as a singer and songwriter. Only two of the thirteen songs are covers (a perfect inversion of the original/cover ratio from his first album), and he was writing, revising, adding, and omitting tracks up until the very last session. In fifty minutes, Dylan broke with his past and mapped out his musical future. When critics bemoaned his going electric in 1965, he directed them to "Mixed Up Confusion," a song he recorded for

Freewheelin' (released as a single, it was not included on the album). He was adapting and defamiliarizing all of the blues and folk forms he knew (12-bar and talkin' blues, epic ballads, and impromptu one-offs). The die-hard folkies weren't pleased with his experimental departure. The June 1963 *Little Sandy Review*, published in Minnesota, called *Freewheelin'* a "great disappointment." Dylan, they argued, was "too melodramatic as a songwriter," and he used "melodies more like popular than folk music." These reviewers were on to something about Dylan's metamorphosis, but they were a bit misguided about what had happened. The melodies, which sounded popular, were taken from British and American folk songs. They sounded strange because Dylan manipulated the timing and rhythm of the chords and overlaid them with dense image-laden lyrics. He was playing folk music on *Freewheelin'* – it just wasn't so easily recognizable.

The songs on *Freewheelin'* were recorded sporadically over the course of thirteen months (April 24, 1962 to May 27, 1963). They document a series of intensely personal meditations on the big questions: life, love, happiness, and death. As a whole, the album doesn't venture too far into hope or despair. The tracks have been arranged so that the tragic and comic balance one another out: the heavier, soul-searching four-song sequences are punctuated by moments of playfulness. That's one reason why "Bob Dylan's Blues" (track five) and "Talkin' World War III Blues" (track ten) appear where they do: they're moments of levity amidst his more somber musings. Dylan's songs were the products of intense, brief, bursts of inspiration. He tended to write lyrics quickly ("Blowin' in the Wind," he claims, took ten minutes), and then came up with a melody on his own or borrowed one from the vast repertoire of traditional folk and blues songs. "Bob Dylan's Dream," "Don't Think Twice," "Masters of War," and "Blowin' in the Wind" are examples of how successful he could be with borrowed melodies.

In *Chronicles: Volume One*, Dylan attributes a lot of his success as a songwriter to the Delta blues musician Robert Johnson (282). In an attempt to figure out Johnson's secret, Dylan copied down the lyrics and studied their structure and design. What he found there was "the construction of his old-style lines and the free association [. . .], the sparkling allegories, big-ass truths wrapped in the hard shell of nonsensical abstraction" (285). Dylan claims to be talking about Johnson here, but he's really getting at what he was learning to do in these early years. Two of the legendary songs on *Freewheelin'* ("Blowin' in the Wind" and "Hard Rain") are allegories built from the scraps of free association. Together they look for "big-ass truths" but do it in an unsystematic way. They challenge listeners to stretch their imaginations and refuse to provide any easy answers (try picturing ten thousand talkers with broken tongues). These startling and surreal images challenge listeners to see what he means, even if meaning is constantly abstracted and kept at a distance.

Freewheelin' was the first album where Dylan began to convert life experience into song. At times he can sound like a joker, a forlorn philosopher, or a blues man with a death rattle, but the spurned and spiteful lover is very much on display here as well. Not long after arriving in New York, Dylan became romantically involved with Suze. When she left for a trip to Italy in June 1962 (largely at her mother's bidding) and extended her stay until January 1963 (her mother's idea again), Dylan was heartbroken. Writing songs was one way for him to deal with it. He wrote four songs about Suze while she was away; two of them appeared on *Freewheelin'* ("Don't Think Twice," "Girl from the North Country"), and the other two ended up on his next album, *The Times They Are A-Changin'* ("Boots of Spanish Leather," "One Too Many Mornings"). All of them are finger-picked and built from the same chord progressions. This repetition is revealing: it's almost as if he had stumbled on a formula that worked, and used it to continue examining the various dimensions of his own sadness, anger, and pain. Each of these songs provides some mature reflection on the fragility of love and is resigned to the fact that a youthful love, once lost, can't be recovered.

Dylan never mentions Suze by name, though he does make one explicit reference to Italy in "Down the Highway." She's always the "gal," "honey babe," or "the one." "Don't Think Twice" is an extended monologue, the kind of one-sided conversation you might overhear right before or after a breakup. It anticipates the many bittersweet breakup narratives in Dylan's catalogue, including "Positively Fourth Street" and "Tangled up in Blue." The "gal" here takes a lot of the blame. The biggest insult, however, is saved for last: "you just kinda wasted my precious time, / But don't think twice it's all right." But if the lyrics are bitter, the upbeat melody leaves the impression that the narrator's not just trying to make himself feel better: he *is* traveling on and leaving her behind. "Girl from the North Country," which Dylan re-recorded with Johnny Cash in 1969, was also born out of this misery and confusion. It focuses on an estranged relationship that seems to have ended a while back, but the tone is considerably softer and more forgiving. The experience of intimacy and separation has already been converted into wisdom and there's an acknowledgment that loss in the past, like it or not, defines who we are in the ever-fleeting present.

The Suze cycle on *Freewheelin'* and *The Times They Are A-Changin'* shows that Dylan was learning how to use real and imagined situations, characters, and conversations to explore his emotions and ideas. A number of the other songs on *Freewheelin'* reveal that he had more on his mind than messy breakups. Dylan came of age during the Cold War, at a time when a nuclear attack on American soil was entirely possible (he even bought a Geiger counter when living in New York just in case). In "Talkin' World War III Blues," Dylan jokes around about commies, fallout shelters, and nuclear war, but he was seriously trying to come to terms with a very real fear about America's future. "Hard Rain," which has erroneously been characterized as Dylan's response to the Cuban Missile Crisis (it was written before), deals with this fear in a more indirect way. It's not so much a song about the fallout from a nuclear war as a song inspired by the threat of one. "I thought I wouldn't have enough time alive to write all those songs," he says in the liner notes "so I put all I could into this one."

"Masters of War" is organized around acerbic punch lines and accompanied throughout by a discordant refrain that never loses its edge. It is rage rationally expressed. Dylan was surprised by the unrelenting tone, but it was the only way to get across the hopelessness he was feeling at the time. "I don't sing songs which hope people will die," he explains in the liner notes, "but I couldn't help it in this one." "Oxford Town" is another song where Dylan vents his frustration about the injustice of this world. For this one, he latches onto a controversial news story for material: it is a songwriting strategy that has served him well over the years ("Ballad of Hollis Brown," "The Lonesome Death of Hattie Carroll," "Hurricane"). In September 1962, a young black student, James Meredith, won a federal court ruling that allowed him to enroll in the University of Mississippi. After a tense standoff between President John F. Kennedy and the governor of Mississippi, and the violent clash of an angry mob of white students and federal marshals that left 300 wounded, he was allowed to enroll for classes. Dylan doesn't single out the sinners and hypocrites as directly as he did in "Masters of War." Instead, he adopts the voice of a naïve observer, who has tried to make sense of it all but fails. The upbeat rhythm provides an ironic counterpoint to the lyrics and serves as a challenge to listeners; tapping your feet to the catchy rhythm would be the surest sign that you've missed the point. In Oxford Town, people are being beaten and killed "for the color of their skin."

On *Freewheelin'*, Dylan learned to be "Dylan": the poet, philosopher, protester, lover, and most of all musician discovering his powers as a singer and songwriter. He was arriving at Columbia's studios with masterpieces in his pockets, and the outtakes from the album reveal that this metamorphosis was taking place month by month. Four months after the album was supposed to be finished, Dylan recorded a last batch of songs ("Masters of War," "Girl from the North Country," "Talkin' World War III Blues," and "Bob Dylan's Dream") that significantly changed the texture of the entire album. With "Blowin' in the Wind" and "Hard Rain," few would disagree that Dylan had real talent, but these late tracks were a sure sign of his remarkable range and depth. In "Bob Dylan's Dream," which he recorded last, he looks back on his past and imagines that his old life is over (he was 23 years old). It is a song about the disenchantment that comes with adulthood, and the pact we all have to make when we exchange innocence for experience. For Dylan the freewheeler, looking back was just fine, but going back was out of the question. The street was there waiting for him to walk, and he was ready.

11

JEAN TAMARIN

Bringing It All Back Home (1965)

It seems almost silly to talk about an album produced more than forty years ago by an artist whose live performances re-imagine his earlier songs so dynamically that they feel like different songs altogether. Forty years is lifetimes ago: why dwell in the past when the present is exploding with mature work – both in performance and in the studio – of such satisfying depth and complexity?

Imagining a world before Dylan is like imagining a world before the Internet – the architecture of existence minus an entire dimension. *Bringing It All Back Home* (1965), more than any other rock album, was a watershed. It took rock and pop, not to mention folk and blues, to a plane of ideas, to the level of art, in which the lyrics were as important as the music – if not more so. Of course Dylan stood on the shoulders of some of our greatest musical treasures, from Hank Williams to Muddy Waters to Elvis. He threw multitudes into the mix, from Yeats to Baudelaire to Ginsberg, inventing a rock poetry that opened the doors for his equally hungry contemporaries – Paul Simon, Leonard Cohen, Neil Young, and Joni Mitchell among them.

Picture the times. JFK was dead. Motown was on the radio. The Beatles hadn't put out *Rubber Soul* yet. The Stones were just picking up steam. And Dylan was off in a corner, writing his masterpieces. Folk-music purists wanted to keep him for themselves. He was their messiah, their justification. "Blowin' in the Wind," "Chimes of Freedom," "Masters of War" – a modern troubadour had given birth to himself in New York City, had brought a rock-and-roll attitude to Southern traditional music born of the Church, and to Woody Guthrie's romance with America. Romantic Wild West stories, biblical lament, tragic love gone wrong and the righteous howling pain of what one man does to another (or to a woman) out of hate, ignorance, jealousy: this skinny white boy seemed to be singing from the soul of an ancient black man who had seen it all.

And then Dylan plugged in his guitar. In the documentary *The Other Side of the Mirror* (2007), which shows Dylan's performances at the Newport

Folk Festival in 1963, '64, and '65, we can see his progression from earnest, eager-to-please folkie, working hard to emulate his musical heroes, to postmodern celebrity – scornful, superior, probably stoned, and scared too, though hiding it for all he's worth. Before our eyes, he fashioned himself into our first rock icon – a kind of dark, mercurial god against whom all who followed him would measure themselves. Even he didn't know then the impact he would have on American music and culture.

The release of *Bringing It All Back Home* in March of 1965 – a few months before he faced his first live audience as a rock & roller in Newport – was a cultural as much as a musical event. To the emerging counterculture (before there was such a word), *Bringing It All Back Home* was what the Black Panthers were to the civil-rights movement – a call to arms. This was not evolution, it was revolution: it was the crack of the starting gun, the throwing open of the gates through which a new era would rush. Dylan going electric – a band playing behind his obscure, introspective lyrics – was like Dorothy in the *Wizard of Oz* going from black-and-white Kansas to Technicolor Oz. The skinny white boy who had written his own roots music was going back to the mother lode – the rock & roll that had come out of, or through, the black Church from which blues and gospel had also sprung.

He pulled a persona together from the old black blues musicians, from Elvis (who had done the same in his own way) and Buddy Holly. Elvis made black music accessible to white teenagers, but Dylan went further. He took the music and mixed it up with his own sensibility, his own reading of history, his own life as he was living it. From the beginning, he was an alchemist, creating music that was new, even as he stole, borrowed, and begged from old sources. He reworked older forms into a more complicated meld of sex, ideas, and surrealism; he delivered sex-plus-art, giving voice to a complex world of sexual relationships, emotional expression, and social protest.

Of course, those elements had always been part of rhythm and blues, albeit often in coded form, but pre-Beatles rock-and-roll had emasculated "race music" for white, middle-class teenagers. The likes of Frankie Avalon and Fabian were eroding the gutbucket influence of Elvis and Little Richard. With *Bringing It All Back Home*, Dylan added back the sex and the anger, but on an entirely different level, from a completely different direction. His sex was the tortured journey of a romantic, white, middle-class, Jewish intellectual trying to find his way through the minefield of relationships. For Dylan, loving a woman, or even just liking her, was never simple. He always seemed outside looking in, hurt or yearning or angry. He wasn't angry just 'cause his mama done him wrong: he elevated and deepened the anger of old blues songs into tirades and accusations, into conversations with friends, enemies, lovers. (It's still hard to tell the difference between lovers and enemies in Dylan's songs.) He was psychologically astute enough to manipulate with brio and passion. Mostly he was pissed off at anyone who dared to tell him how to think, what to think, how to be, who to be. His anger – as expressed in *Bringing It All Back Home* – was mythic, righteous, existential. Dylan's rock & roll – of which *Bringing It All Back Home* was the first formal expression – was a layered web of moral complexity, spiritual yearning, ambivalence, irony, uncertainty, historical context, and raw desire.

Dylan has always been intellectually restless, with zero tolerance for repeating himself. He's always pushing past the natural entropy that keeps most of us in our comfort zones. *Bringing It All Back Home* was a quantum leap in the creative risk-taking and self-reinvention that would come to signify his career: he was not going to meet people's expectations. He was not going to keep churning out liberal-lefty protest songs to please his white, middle-class, folkie fans. He needed a bigger canvas for a bigger vision. With *Bringing It All Back Home*, he made folk music sexy, and the blues smart. In 1963 Dylan had worn high-waisted, belted blue jeans, but in 1965 he was in tight black leather pants.

"Subterranean Homesick Blues": It's historic – a rock protest song. It's like running fast on a sheet of ice and then leaning back for a long, careening slide. It's a syncopated lyrical funhouse, the ultimate anti-authoritarian rap, a dizzying, fast-flying tirade that, as others have pointed out, is really hard to sing along with. (That fact is cleverly mocked in the famous opening sequence of D. A. Pennebaker's 1967 documentary of Dylan's last acoustic tour, *Don't Look Back*.) But you want to sing along anyway. This song still feels contemporary in its sarcasm, and all the more devastating for its brightness. The words pour out in sparkling, sharp-edged combinations, etching the myriad hypocrisies of the American dream. In 1965, you had to grab the words fast: no replay on a record player, and you couldn't Google the lyrics.

"She Belongs To Me": "She's got everything she needs / She's an artist, she don't look back." This stands among Dylan's most evocative love songs. As with most of Dylan's songs about women, the mixed emotions, the ambiguity and mystery are maddening. "She wears an Egyptian ring that sparkles before she speaks." You want to enter this mysterious, swirling dream. He imbued his women with power while simultaneously rendering them powerless. Like most of Dylan's women characters – archetypes all – the woman in this song wields great power, at least over him, but she is ultimately alone. The rhythm is fluid, almost jazzy. Dylan's voice is silky and tender, paying homage but with his edge of bitterness: if she will not be possessed, then neither will he. The music so warm and sweet, the words so bitter.

"Maggie's Farm": Snarly Dylan. Oracular and honky-tonk at the same time. The rhymes are so clever and his scorn so blistering that you can't help but identify with his global loathing of meaningless work and conformity. Of course he's also talking about his own audience at this point, and his record label and handlers:

> Well, I try my best
> To be just like I am,
> But everybody wants you
> To be just like them.
> They sing while you slave and I just get bored.

In his book *No Direction Home* Robert Shelton reminds us, "We may laugh at the plight of the narrator, until we realize that we're all working on somebody's farm" (272).

"Love Minus Zero/No Limit": A gorgeous classic, with Dylan singing in a rich, tender pitch. The song talks about love as complicated, paradoxical – the way it really is – though the song itself is simple. Images tumble forth: wind howls like a hammer, bridges tremble, love speaks like silence. Like so many of his love songs, it expresses a yearning that's always disappointed. It's hard to remember how revolutionary it was to write a rock song about love that wasn't "hey, hey baby." The images evoke deep feelings – especially longing, and a kind of humility before a complicated woman who "knows there's no success like failure / And that failure's no success at all." People of a certain age tend to insert Dylan lines like that one into conversation the way people used to quote the Bible and Shakespeare. Many moods and situations call to mind his intuitive grasp of paradox, chaos, and mystery – the essential mysteries of love and life itself. The line about success and failure is like so many Dylan lyrics: at first you think you understand it, but the more you parse it, the less sense it makes.

"Outlaw Blues": Propulsive, insistent, aggressive. Dylan wants to go away to some Australian mountain range where uncool people can't find him and kill his spirit, like Robert Ford killed Jesse James. Dylan challenges us to find our own truth and not mooch off his. "Don't ask me nothin' about nothin', / I just might tell you the truth."

"On the Road Again": More surreal, goofy images. I have no idea what it's about, but it's fun and makes you move your body. The character of Dylan-the-narrator is, as usual, in some chaotic situation. Anarchy's afoot: even the butler's got something to prove. It's a story, and we're coming in in the middle. Dylan gives a little laugh while addressing the "honey" of the song ("Honey, I can't believe that you're for real.") That goofy, stoned laugh in 1965 was revelatory: Dylan wasn't performing a song in the studio, he was living his life.

"Bob Dylan's 115th Dream": Dylan cracking up is the best part of the song. Another careening tall tale with clever, tight rhymes, talking cows, and lines like "I ordered some suzette, I said / 'Could you please make that crepe'" and "I said, 'You know they refused Jesus too' / He said, 'You're not Him.'" Dylan's sharp tongue is planted firmly in his sardonic cheek, and he's self-aware enough to poke fun at himself along with everyone else. A 1960s version of a hurdy-gurdy circus tune.

"Mr. Tambourine Man": Here the album turns acoustic. The song is passionately sung, not like the rushed, half-hearted version he performed at Newport the following summer. Much has been made of the fact that the song is about drugs. It's been called an homage to Rimbaud and "rock's paean to psychedelia" (critic Bill Wyman, salon.com). But it's more a search for transcendence. The singer is ready to go anywhere, to fall under the pied piper's spell, to go where all adventurers go who tire of "ancient empty streets too dead for dreaming." Drugs, in 1965, were a pied piper; but so was Dylan himself, so was music. The tambourine man is an archetype, perhaps the fool of the tarot deck willing to leap empty-handed into the void,

> Down the foggy ruins of time, far past the frozen leaves,
> The haunted, frightened trees, out to the windy beach,
> Far from the twisted reach of crazy sorrow.

Whatever drugs Dylan and everyone else was taking back then, there was an innocence to the whole album, this song in particular. Nothing had been irretrievably ruined yet. Bodies were young, hearts not yet broken. Minds blown, yes, but not blown out. The desire "to go anywhere," "to dance beneath the diamond sky with one hand waving free," to "forget about today until tomorrow" was a declaration of hope, not a cynical retreat.

"Gates of Eden": An epic, scary, slashing string of images, dark and relentless. Inside there are no kings, no sins, no justice, no trials. We enter the tight whirlwind nightmare where "the lamppost stands with folded arms," where no sound ever comes, where hound dogs bay at ships with tattooed sails, where you will not hear a laugh, where a gray flannel dwarf screams, where a foreign sun squints upon "a bed that is never mine." The images and phrasing burn into the mind. What is real, what is true, what is good, what is bad? This is a biblical, metaphysical protest song. Nothing is what it seems. We never have the satisfaction of feeling smart, of knowing what's going on. Dylan offers no comfort, no salvation – only death and oblivion:

> At times I think there are no words
> But these to tell what's true
> And there are no truths outside the Gates of Eden

"It's Alright, Ma (I'm Only Bleeding)": One of Dylan's most iconic songs, and one of his longest. Many famous Dylanisms are here, such as "money doesn't talk, it swears" and "he not busy being born / Is busy dying." I agree with Shelton that it's more sad than angry. A lament in which he insistently repeats, in verses that serve as a metronome, our diseases: fake morals, propaganda, dishonesty, hatred, game-playing, hypocrisy. The aching repetition of "It's alright, Ma" culminates in recognition that the lies, misdeeds, and despair are ultimately just part of the human play: "it's life, and life only."

"It's All Over Now, Baby Blue": Once again there's a breeziness to the melody that belies the pain in the lyrics: he has left his past behind, as we must leave ours. Dylan no longer needs us, his audience, in the same way he has up till now. From now on, he will write and perform for himself, and if we want to come along for the ride, well, that's okay; but he's not going to please us, he's going to please himself. No time for nostalgia: the seasick sailors are rowing home, our lover has just walked out the door. "The vagabond who's rapping at your door / Is standing in the clothes that you once wore." Everything that brought us, and him, to this point must be left behind. But something calls for us – we can strike a match to light our way and start anew. Dylan did.

12

ROBERT POLITO

Highway 61 Revisited (1965)

First the liner notes, and their magnificent candor. You can almost appreciate the notes for *Highway 61 Revisited* as a Dylan performance in anxious, mischievous anticipation of future press conference taunts, "What is your weird new record about? How do you write your strange new songs?" Yet his sly jacket stories focus his musical designs with generosity, even precision. Consider, for instance, that *about* question. On the sleeve Dylan's hint is forthright: "Lifelessness." So that if a listener didn't quite catch that line in "Desolation Row" where Ophelia's "sin" is "her lifelessness," or twig that her condition designates a spiritual despond circulating through the songs like a virus – the echoes everywhere: Miss Lonely's inclination to "let other people get your kicks for you" ("Like a Rolling Stone"), the "useless and pointless knowledge" decomposing inside "the old folks home and the college" ("Tombstone Blues"), Mister Jones's impotent mastery of "all of / F. Scott Fitzgerald's books" ("Ballad of a Thin Man"), the "very bored" gambler intent on staging "the next" world war ("Highway 61 Revisited"), the numb border-town dissipation of "I cannot move / My fingers are all in a knot" ("Just Like Tom Thumb's Blues"), "all this repetition" which Queen Jane might someday find herself "sick of" ("Queen Jane Approximately"), Dr. Filth's "sexless patients" ("Desolation Row"), the "broken" pipeline and the "lost" driver on the bridge of "From a Buick 6," and the singer's own admission in "It Takes a Lot to Laugh, It Takes a Train to Cry" that he "Can't buy a thrill" – if somehow a listener missed all that, then right there on the jacket of *Highway 61 Revisited* is a character named "Lifelessness," reenacting his recurrently bad faith:

> . . . when the Cream met savage Rose & Fixable, he was introduced to them by none other than Lifelessness – Lifelessness is the Great Enemy & always wears a hip guard – he is very hipguard . . . Lifelessness said when introducing everybody "go save the world" & "involvement! that's the issue" & things like that . . ."

Or consider that *how* question. Here too Dylan is direct, if impish. His new songwriting embodied a medley of voices and styles, blues, rock & roll, hardboiled, Western, Beat, and literary – "I need a dump truck baby to unload my head," as he sang in "From a Buick 6." The *Highway 61 Revisited* notes recast the singer as the conduit through whom language and history happen, self atomizing into otherness – "there is no eye – there is only a series of mouths" – after Arthur Rimbaud's infamous dictum, "I is another."

Could Dylan have made his case any clearer, or any wilier? Released on August 30, 1965, *Highway 61 Revisited* kicked off with "Like a Rolling Stone," the single that in 2004 *Rolling Stone* would enshrine as "the greatest song of all time." *Highway 61 Revisited* sits dead center of the 1960s fable ("Once upon a time . . .") that still is what most people mean by the words Bob Dylan. The nine songs track the moment where he finally pieced together his divergent pasts: the early love of R&B and rock & roll he chased in Hibbing High combos like the Golden Chords, and tentatively renewed for the electric side of his previous release, *Bringing It All Back Home*; his immersion in American traditional music, folk, blues, country, Woody Guthrie, Robert Johnson, Hank Williams, and Harry Smith's *Anthology of American Folk Music*; his reading of poetry and novels, John Steinbeck, Rimbaud, Bertolt Brecht, Allen Ginsberg, and Jack Kerouac. *Highway 61 Revisited* is also the first occasion Dylan might be styled a modernist, the crazy quilt of folk process blasting into Dada collage. Yet for music so fixed in a specific cultural instant, *Highway 61 Revisited* now registers curiously timeless, the lyrics as steeped in the 1930s, '40s, and '50s as the '60s. Greek mythology, Shakespeare, and Roman history bump up against Blind Willie McTell or P. T. Barnum, and Raymond Chandlerisms ("People'd call, say, 'Beware doll, you're bound to fall'") slide into jive patter ("get your kicks") or Eliotic lyricism ("stare into the vacuum of his eyes"). As "Desolation Row" obliquely but inescapably rewrites *The Waste Land*, so "Ballad of a Thin Man" rewrites Abbott and Costello's famous radio routine, "Who's On First?":

> You raise up your head
> And you ask, "Is this where it is?"
> And somebody points to you and says
> "It's his" . . .

Your classic explosion in a shingle factory, *Highway 61 Revisited* also manifests imperious control – the baroquely claustrophobic stanzas of "Desolation Row," the dead-end aaab//cccb verses of "Tombstone Blues," the virtuoso syntax that can snake a single sentence through six, eight, twelve rhymed lines. And Dylan probably for the first time on a record sounds his real age – as on June 15, three weeks after his twenty-fourth birthday, he entered Columbia's Studio A to start work on "Like a Rolling Stone."

Highway 61 Revisited inevitably traffics along the backstreets of 1960s gossip. Is Joan Baez also Miss Lonely, or just Queen Jane? If Miss Lonely is Edie Sedgwick, does that make Andy Warhol the diplomat on the chrome horse? Moving inside Studio A, Tom Wilson produced "Like a Rolling Stone," but why was he replaced by Bob Johnston for the rest of the sessions? Who played what on which song? Everyone knows the epic of how Al Kooper wound up playing organ for "Like a Rolling Stone," but it took half a century for Charlie McCoy to clinch his credit for the Spanish guitar on "Desolation Row." Even the final track list, and their sequencing, stayed in play. On August 2 Dylan left the studio carrying an acetate of the LP that still included the songs Columbia issued as singles in the wake of "Like a Rolling Stone" – "Positively 4th Street" and "Can You Please Crawl Out Your Window?"

So incessant are his reinventions that nearly any Dylan album might be tagged transitional, but *Highway 61 Revisited* is one of his three *necessary* recordings, in that full epochs of his career appear inconceivable without them. *The Freewheelin' Bob Dylan* (1963) reconfigured the blues and folk interpreter of *Bob Dylan* (1962) as a matchless songwriter, and that generational reputation hurled him through *The Times They Are A-Changin'* (1964), *Another Side of Bob Dylan* (1964), and into *Bringing It All Back Home* (1965). Similarly, *Time Out of Mind* (1997) revived Dylan as a popular artist of unique mastery, at once clarifying his past and mapping his future – "*Love and Theft*" (2001) *Modern Times* (2006), even *Masked & Anonymous* (2003), *Chronicles: Volume One* (2004), his hundred live shows a year, and into whatever comes next.

As a corny *It's a Wonderful Life* gesture, try to envision Dylan minus *Highway 61 Revisited* – no "Desolation Row," no "Ballad of a Thin Man," no "Like a Rolling Stone." Who would he have been? How would we view him? If Dylan somehow never realized this record, he'd likely be recalled as a symbol of protest, the author of some astonishing love songs, and also – alas – on the evidence of *Bringing It All Back Home*, another instigator of an ephemeral 1960s hybrid that rightly would limp along under the name "folk-rock," a phrase he despised. Side one of *Bringing It All Back Home* imposed electric instruments upon folk songs, the electricity hardly intrinsic or essential. Only retrospect reveals, say, "Outlaw Blues" as a blueprint for "Tombstone Blues," and even "Maggie's Farm" couldn't shock until Dylan blasted the tune open at Newport on July 25, just as Columbia shipped the first pressings of "Like a Rolling Stone" to stores.

Highway 61 Revisited pitched Bob Dylan into legend and myth. To speak personally – and Dylan always commands a personal response – I feel lucky to have coincided however briefly on this planet with Beckett, Nabokov, Borges, Balanchine, Callas, Welles, and Fellini. I got to meet Robert Lowell, Andy Warhol, Elizabeth Bishop, Sam Fuller, and was a friend in his last years of James Merrill. Giants walked the earth, and I wouldn't barter those experiences for everything south of Heaven. Yet Dylan's achievement over the past five decades looms so audacious, large, various, and singular that a hundred years from now it's his recordings and performances that will advance the signature narrative of what it was like to live and create during his lifetime.

If it's *Highway 61 Revisited* that starts to make this angle on Dylan imaginable, even plausible, the truth of course is that the album almost didn't happen at all. He exited his triumphant May solo acoustic tour of England restless, disconsolate, lost. "I was doing fine, you know, singing and playing my guitar," Dylan told Nora Ephron and Susan Edmiston. "It was a sure thing, don't you understand, it was a sure thing. I was getting very bored with that. I couldn't go out and play like that. I was thinking of quitting. Out front it was a sure thing. I knew what the audience was going to do, how they would react. It was very automatic" (Ephron and Edmiston 52).

Then, as Dylan expanded to Martin Bronstein, he stumbled on a way out – originating in "Like a Rolling Stone," but ultimately spurred by a bolder intuition of his aspirations for his songs: "I'd literally quit singing and playing, and I found myself writing this song, this story, this long piece of vomit about twenty pages long, and out of it I took 'Like a Rolling Stone' and made it as a single. I'd never written anything like that before, and it suddenly came to me that this is what I should do. Nobody had ever done that before . . . Because it was a whole new category. I mean, nobody's ever really written songs before, really . . ." (Bronstein).

By 2004 Dylan would recall "Like a Rolling Stone" as craft – "I'm not thinking about what I want to say, I'm just thinking, 'Is this OK for the meter?'" – and wonder : "It's like a ghost is writing a song like that" (Hilburn 432). Yet his own earlier reflections on his mood at his return from England in the spring of 1965 connect him to characters across *Highway 61 Revisited*. Dylan's comments to Ephron, Edmiston, and Bronstein, for instance, suggest he too was someone "tired of yourself and all of your creations"; that Lifelessness ("very automatic") then beckoned from his mirror as well.

Polyglot, mongrel, dramatic, his "whole new category" of songs performs multiple stories simultaneously, discovering parallels and contradictions, at once personal, collective, and political. The title track inscribes the album's strategy in miniature – five stanzas, five distinct yet analogous scenarios, veering from filicide through incest into World War III, Dylan's hellbent vernaculars variously hipster, noir, bluesy, everything set along Highway 61.

By calling the collection *Highway 61 Revisited*, Dylan dramatized a national past, as well as his own. As late as *Chronicles: Volume One* Dylan entangled the public and private whispers of Highway 61. "I was into the rural blues as well; it was a counterpart of myself. It was connected to early rock & roll and I liked it because it was older than Muddy and Wolf. Highway 61, the main thoroughfare of the country blues, begins about where I came from . . . Duluth to be exact. I always felt like I'd started on it, always had been on it and could go anywhere from it . . ." (240).

What *Highway 61* might mean for Dylan sounds inexhaustible, but isn't *Revisited* the tricky part? Revisited implies return, maybe rediscovery, or reawakening, and also something like their opposite – a second, harder look at early hopes for "fortune or fame"? Or even those sickening "repetitions" from "Queen Jane Approximately" that Dylan would revisit again on *Blonde on Blonde* (another repetition) as "Stuck Inside of Mobile with the Memphis Blues Again."

Through the overlapping story lines of *Highway 61 Revisited* the grace note is a slippery, complicated tone. A number of songs focus on a woman whose advantages, money, class, education, looks, and love can't stop her collapse, the singer perhaps trying to save her, perhaps luxuriating in her downfall. Over "Like a Rolling Stone" Dylan's contempt famously ascends into exuberance, even joy. "Confused – and justified, exultant, free from history with a world to win – is exactly where the song means to leave you," as Greil Marcus has written (*Like a Rolling Stone* 116). But what is the tone of, "Don't say I never warned you / When your train gets lost"? Is this revenge, a threat, I-told-you-so, sympathy? What's up in, "Well, if I go down dyin', you know she bound to put a blanket on my bed"? Is Dylan sardonic, tender, mean, funny?

"Ballad of a Thin Man" juggles many of the same knives as "Like a Rolling Stone" – including a recurrent, "How does it feel?" – but here Dylan sustains the vengeance. The cunning intro tilts a roving reporter into a Freudian totem of male humiliation: "You walk into the room / With your pencil in your hand . . ." Other songs, such as "Tombstone Blues," swap bedrooms for boardrooms, classrooms, backrooms, and war rooms, sexual maneuvering for City Hall, the University, and Vietnam. The corrupt spectacles of "Desolation Row" open on the Duluth lynching of June 15, 1920 ("They're selling postcards of the hanging . . ."), but spread past politics across a culture, the idle vanity of Miss Lonely's "finest school" inseparable from the idle vanity of the century's finest poets: "Ezra Pound and T. S. Eliot / Fighting in the captain's tower . . ."

Bob Dylan is nowhere, but everywhere inside the *Highway 61 Revisited* stories. He might sound like Queen Jane, as we've already heard, and he's Miss Lonely too, now, with no direction home, whether the home that no longer can protect or sustain him is Hibbing, Minnesota, or the folk-music establishment, he's invisible, he's got no secrets to conceal, he's Pound, Eliot, a calypso singer, the king of the Philistines, Cecil B. DeMille, and when he judges Queen Jane, or Miss Lonely, whoever they are, any of them, he's also Mister Jones.

Which is why, I think, Dylan concludes "Desolation Row" and *Highway 61 Revisited* on empathy – empathy and candor: "Don't send me no more letters no / Not unless you mail them / From Desolation Row."

13

MICHAEL COYLE AND DEBRA RAE COHEN

Blonde on Blonde (1966)

In all the micro-documented history of rock & roll it's hard to imagine a more incisive description of the paradox of rock-star fame – the kind of fame that later hastened the deaths of Ian Curtis and Kurt Cobain – than these lines from "Visions of Johanna": "Now, little boy lost, he takes himself so seriously / He brags of his misery, he likes to live dangerously." To see these lines as self-descriptive is and isn't, as we'll see, to take them out of context. *Blonde on Blonde* – let's acknowledge it as *BOB* – represents the first of Dylan's many attempts at a self-portrait, but it undertakes self-portraiture in a defiantly anti-exegetical way. Tired of being saddled with the heavy interpretations of fans, critics, journalists, and scholars, Dylan amplified and exposed the songwriting strategies that informed his earlier albums. The self-consciously surrealist textures of *BOB* at once invite and ridicule attempts to divine their meaning. Like the French poets from whose books he lifted more than a few pages, Dylan immerses his listeners in the twinned processes of weaving and unweaving myth – which is why the songs of *BOB* seem so often self-interfering and contradictory. The least didactic of the albums of Dylan's second period, the album where, as Ellen Willis has written, Dylan proves "no longer rebel but seismograph," *BOB* compels listeners to take responsibility for their own interpretations (Willis 235). It offers the specious promise "anybody can be just like me, obviously": the promise is specious because the obvious *isn't* obvious – the obvious is offered up as bait and quickly yanked away.

The story of how the author of "Blowin' in the Wind" or "Masters of War" got to this point has been often told, and his movement away from the folk scene where he first established his career is now itself the stuff of legend. Less often considered is where the astonishing success of what had at first seemed a career-killing move had left him. After *Highway 61 Revisited*, Dylan was again feeling cornered. Once again, legions of fans were claiming him and seeing his vision as their own. Dylan's response, both to those who hailed him as prophet and to those who called him "Judas," was to suggest that "time will tell just who fell / And who's been left behind, / When you go your way and I go mine." *BOB* diverges from *Highway 61* not just because it was recorded in Nashville rather than in New York, employing both a new producer and a new band: it parts from *Highway 61* in what it claims for tradition, in how it relates to tradition, and in how it relates to its audience.

The shift to Nashville was salient. So too was Dylan's involvement with a new and varied cast of musicians with an equally varied set of musical referents. Although Al Kooper and Charlie McCoy contributed to both *Highway 61* and to *BOB*, they were now surrounded by Nashville session men, hired by producer Bob Johnston, who had little or no experience of rock music. In fact, according to McCoy, at the time he was the only one among them who even knew who Dylan was (Spitz 334–342). The recontextualization of the *Highway 61* musicians allowed Dylan an ironic distance from his own celebrity, as well as from all that rock was taken to represent. The Nashville milieu facilitated his recombinations of American musical vernaculars, his attempts to renew tradition by playing with it, often literally.

On *BOB*, the songs that draw most aggressively on the vernacular – especially on blues – prove to be the most overtly ironic. The most telling example is found in the first song from *BOB* to be released as a single – "Rainy Day Women #12 & 35." As drummer Kenny Buttrey remembers, when Dylan said he wanted the track to sound like a Salvation Army band, the musicians responded by swapping instruments, and even by disassembling them, taking the slide off the trombone or laying the bass drum down across a couple of chairs (Spitz 339). The literal deconstruction of "tradition" here, the tongue-in-cheek recombination of musical elements to produce a drunken stagger of a march, a parodic invocation, serves as a metaphor for Dylan's broader compositional practice on *BOB*. He deliberately foregrounds his choice of value-laden musical and lyrical signifiers in order to frustrate any attempt to reduce them *to* that value. On this opening track, for instance, the deliberately slapdash brass-band tootling seems at first to underscore the obvious import of the song's refrain: "Everybody must get stoned." Annoying and abrasive, even arrogantly so (especially as the album's first statement), the song seems to exemplify old-model, anti-Establishment Dylan, a couldn't-care-less kiss-off to the possibilities of radio play (and paradoxically successful because of it). Yet a closer look at the lyrics makes clear that the "stoner" refrain is purposeful coat-trailing; red flag to the morals police, tip of the hat to critics who espy drug references everywhere, it bears only oblique relation to the text of the verses: "Well, they'll stone you and say that it's the end. / Then they'll stone you and then they'll come back again. / They'll stone you when you're riding in your car.

/ They'll stone you when you're playing your guitar." "Getting stoned" here is public stoning, tied explicitly to musical performance. The "stoned," carnivalesque brass-band swagger is retroactively recast as New Orleans funeral. Both music and lyrics, recontextualizing each other through alternative lenses, serve as an anti-exegetical warning, even as the lyrics themselves depict one outcome of that exegesis: getting "stoned."

The game of exegesis that informs the title of "Rainy Day Women #12 & 35" – why #12 and #35 and not, say, #13 or #36? – plays out in other titles, too: "4th Time Around" or "Obviously Five Believers." The absurd numerological specificity of these titles raises the equally absurd question: just how many different *Bob*s are possible? That question echoes throughout the songs themselves: we get "the six white horses" of "Absolutely Sweet Marie," the "fifteen jugglers" of "Obviously Five Believers," or "the twenty pounds of headlines" in "Stuck Inside of Mobile." Even as he is offering up a self-portrait, Dylan is suggesting that none of these portraits could ever be final or definitive. The numbers in and of themselves are arbitrary; their function as signposts is not.

This fooling with numbers is only the most blatant way in which Dylan refers to the impossibility of presumptive knowledge – of reaching trustworthy and *final* conclusions based on apparent evidence. He rings titular changes on epistemological processes – pointing to taxonomic categories ("Just Like a Woman") even while undercutting them, holding out the lure of conclusive knowledge (*"Absolutely* Sweet Marie," *"Obviously* Five Believers") and then reneging. "One of Us Must Know," for example, undercuts the seeming inevitability suggested by the title in a number of ways. As the core of the song unfolds in the future subjunctive, a peculiarly non-specific form of the inevitable ("sooner or later one of us must know") develops. Despite the word "must" in the chorus, the song doesn't perform the assuring function it seems to advertise: the song doesn't tell us who the two parties are, which of them is going to know, or when they're going to know it; and the thing that will then be known isn't even that Dylan loved the woman but only that he "really did try to get close to [her]." Dylan's overt oscillation between knowledges that reveal themselves (or declare themselves, as in "Temporary Like Achilles" or "Most Likely You Go Your Way (And I'll Go Mine)") to be merely provisional serves as a mechanism for the exposure, even parody, of his own songwriting processes and the manner in which they've been characterized. The musical vernaculars assembled on *BOB* serve as the necessary frame for his self-exposure, expanding listeners' notions of what a "Dylan song" might be even as his lyrics cater to and then mockingly explode such expectations.

Part of what had marked a "Dylan song" at least since "Mr. Tambourine Man" (1964) was his penchant for surreal imagery: "Then take me disappearin' through the smoke rings of my mind / Down the foggy ruins of time, far past the frozen leaves / The haunted, frightened trees." Indeed, it's largely on such imagery as this that his grandiose reputation as poet and prophet rests – or at least rested in 1966. But, on *BOB*, surrealism represents neither occasional moments nor mere indices of either tone or atmosphere. On *BOB* surrealism begins to assume new functions – sometimes several in a single song, some of which aim to conceal rather than reveal. Consider "Stuck Inside of Mobile," for example:

> Well, Shakespeare, he's in the alley
> With his pointed shoes and his bells,
> Speaking to some French girl,
> Who says she knows me well.

The pointed shoes and bells, for all that they evoke the jester or fool, suggest that Dylan means for us to see Shakespeare himself, rather than a modern who simply carries that nickname, but otherwise it functions as Dylan's claim of fraternity with the Bard, even to the extent of sharing women. This isn't the Shakespeare of American classrooms, but a poet of the streets, who knows that it's on those streets and not in parlors that real life and passion are to be found. In other words, this passage isn't just decorative: it presents an elaborate trope that requires listeners to tease out its implications. This is surrealism as a structural element of the song. But in the very next verse Dylan tells "Mona" of a railroad man who "just smoked my eyelids / An' punched my cigarette." In this case, surrealism is the butter-cream frosting that doesn't add much more than topping to the cake: it's Dylan trying to confuse or dazzle "Mona" simply by reversing the direct objects of a complex sentence. The sentence is perfectly comprehensible without changes in perception; this reversal represents a self-conscious manipulation of the surreal rather than an actual use of it, less a way of thinking than a kind of performative display. "Stuck Inside of Mobile" is from our vantage a great song partly because it displays its own self-parodic function.

Surrealism functions in other new ways in "Most Likely You Go Your Way." In the bridge, Dylan warns:

> The judge, he holds a grudge,
> He's gonna call on you.
> But he's badly built
> And he walks on stilts,
> Watch out he don't fall on you.

The rhyming of "judge" and "grudge" is familiar enough to listeners of blues, but the image of a judge on stilts functions in several ways simultaneously: the spectacle of serious justice awkwardly working a child's toy is funny, but the stilts also suggest the artificial eminence the law gives to such public servants. The quality of being "badly built" would seem more pertinent to stilts than to the judge himself unless, as a comment on his physique, it reminds us that he is underneath the robes just a man. Dylan's verse here affords rich play; his language comments on justice without ever being, as this chapter must be, didactic.

But it's also characteristic of *BOB* that its musical textures – as we mentioned above in connection with "Rainy Day Women" – further complicate this linguistic play, this frustrating of exegetical expectations, by alternately pulling with and against the tendencies of the lyrics. Pacing the lyrical allusion and resistance to didacticism in "Most Likely You Go Your Way," Buttrey's military drum-rolls on the snare emphasize the song's underlying structure as a march. At the same time, the circus jangle and swagger of the keyboard and lead guitar push against the tendency to lockstep, a push that plays out both on the level of musical form and also of ideological formation. That is, this musical tension ultimately contributes to what we have been calling *BOB's* anti-exegetical impulses: although the words would seem to be directing us to particular conclusions, the song as a whole undermines its own authority.

This destabilizing impulse appears throughout *BOB*, but most crucially in those songs ostensibly about or addressed to women. In many cases, especially in the ballads, the musical texture of the songs provokes expectations of confessional immediacy that wind up being belied by closer attention to the lyrics. The clearest example of this is "Just Like a Woman," where the almost saccharine sweetness of the acoustic finger-picked counterpoint is burned away by the corrosive irony of the lyric – which in certain ways genericizes the woman, robbing her of the particularity necessary for desire. Kooper's organ maintains a steadying presence. Even though here, as elsewhere, it invariably evokes the sincerity of gospel, there's a lushness that holds out the promise of emotional depth. The organ seems to align itself with authentic feeling and truth-telling, the empathy that one expects from the speaker in a ballad, especially one addressed to a lover. It almost cradles the lyric so that for moments at a time it's easy not to listen to what the lyric is actually saying. The song begins with a statement of *his* pain, then goes forward to complain about the woman. By the second stanza, after resolving once again to see Queen Mary, "Dylan" wearily tells us with the unsurprise of experience that

> Nobody has to guess
> That Baby can't be blessed
> Till she sees finally that she's like all the rest
> With her fog, her amphetamine and her pearls.

As these lines are delivered, Kooper continues the distinctive organ line, while Hargus Robbins produces piano arpeggios that essentially echo the guitar work. All of this is very sweet. All of it feels tender, perhaps even loving. All of it differs painfully from the words we've just quoted. In this context, what would it even mean to be "blessed?" In this context, "Baby" doesn't even have a name. There's a struggle here, but it's not really between "Dylan" and "Baby"; the struggle is in Dylan himself:

> And your long-time curse hurts
> But what's worse
> Is this pain in here
> I can't stay in here

Given this pain, to say "you fake just like a woman" opposes the woman's naïveté to Dylan's own consciousness of self-construction. "Baby can't be blessed" until she recognizes and/or understands this process. This process is finally the very one represented in *BOB* itself. This process *is* BOB. The difference between Dylan and the album's women is that Dylan knows the extent to which he's a fake. Indeed, women are oddly absent from the songs that purport to be for or about them. Whether they exist as phantoms that allow the heroicizing of Dylan's own desiring persona ("I Want You" or "Visions of Johanna") or as accessories in both senses of the word ("Pledging My Time" or even "Leopard-Skin Pill-Box Hat"), they serve as foils for the process by which Dylan examines "Dylan."

But the issue here is not whether Dylan is or isn't sexist or even misogynist: the point is that *BOB* is a self-portrait. To be sure, Dylan's self-personifying impulse can be said to have been there from the beginning – if we regard the early part of his career as having been about establishing the Dylan mythology that he would later come to regret, and that *BOB* deconstructs. Even the title of his fourth LP, *Another Side of Bob Dylan* (1964), calls attention to the business of self-portraiture. And, not surprisingly, the process has continued to the present day. Dylan's least successful album, both popularly and critically, was the much-maligned *Self Portrait* (1970); but thirty-five years later it clearly represents an attempt to celebrate musical origins over the demands of marketplace and fans. *Biograph* (1985) extends those values, transforming the career overview from a packaging of "greatest hits" to the documenting of personal changes. Even Dylan's recent DJ work for Sirius radio, "Theme Time Radio Hour," exemplifies this documentary impulse. But *BOB* differs from these and others of his self-personifying gestures in that it is a deliberately unresolving self-portrait. The songs pull against each other even as they pull against themselves.

"Sad-Eyed Lady of the Lowlands" is the song that pulls hardest against everything else on *BOB*, the one song that straightforwardly asks to be read as sincere – without the scare quotes that would make it "sincere." Its original positioning as the fourth side of rock's first double-LP set physically separates it from the other songs – a particularity that has lost its force in the digital age. But, in truth, there never was a practical necessity for the separation: "Sad-Eyed Lady" clocks in at only 11:21 (even "In-A-Gadda-Da-Vida" plods along for 17:05). *BOB* is actually a 3-sided album – a "sesquialbum." The reasons for isolating "Sad-Eyed Lady" on a separate side have more to do with how Dylan wanted the song to be experienced.

Other songs on the record set themselves up to be taken as "sincere" or "literary" – the trap for the exegete or the biographer – but then reveal themselves as subverting the process. They lure the listener into responding to "Dylanesque" surrealism, what was once touted as "anti-establishmentarianism," only to reveal these as aspects of surface, not as essence of the song. "Sad-Eyed Lady" seems to reembrace all of those sentimentalities that the rest of the album not only mocks but derides *as* tropes. If the rest of the album is about Dylan even when it purports to be about others, here the celebration of his new wife, the Petrarchan catalogue of her qualities, implies the humbling limitation of the persona the rest of the album enacts. He offers up his "warehouse eyes" – the prophetic vision that empowers him to be the transformative observer – and the "Arabian drums" that add spiritual potency to his chronicling of surfaces, and proposes to leave them at her gate. It's a gesture as emphatic (and yet as unactualized within the work) as Prospero drowning his book. That the gesture *is* incomplete represents the final irony in this profoundly ironical work; even in this concluding paean to sincerity, Dylan is impossibly entangled in the very mythologies he is attempting to demystify. *BOB* is the moment, however, where Dylan began to allow his audience to watch him in the process of mythmaking – and this anti-exegetical, because unresolving, process was, paradoxically, never again so . . . revelatory.

14

ALEX ABRAMOVICH

The Basement Tapes (1967; 1975)

Midway through the dark woods of the 1960s, Bob Dylan took his Triumph motorcycle for a country ride and lost his balance, or hit an oil slick, or (according to the mythopoetic account Dylan himself would give) stared too long into the sun and found himself momentarily blinded.

The specific circumstances are cloudy. But we do know that Dylan was burned out after nine months of a grueling, seemingly endless, still-ongoing tour; that the proofs of his first novel, *Tarantula*, had arrived and that Dylan, who seems to have written the book in a methamphetamine haze, recognized them to be unreadable and embarrassing; that there were hundreds of hours of films to edit for a forthcoming documentary, and constant demands for new recordings. Dyan's responsibilities had multiplied exponentially, and vast sums of money were at stake.

We can only imagine the toll these expectations, and others, took on his central nervous system: "Different anachronisms were thrust upon me . . . " Dylan wrote in his 2004 memoir, *Chronicles: Volume One*. "Legend, Icon, Enigma (Buddha in European Clothes was my favorite) – stuff like that, but that was all right. These titles were placid and harmless, threadbare, easy to get around with them. Prophet, Messiah, Savior – those are tough ones" (124). Bob Dylan was 25 years old.

Dylan crashed his Triumph in July of 1966. His close friend, the folksinger and novelist Richard Fariña, had died in another motorcycle crash a few months earlier. The carousel was out of control.

Dylan would never again play the "thin wild mercury music" you hear on pre-motorcycle-crash albums like *Highway 61 Revisited* and *Blonde on Blonde*; the two albums which followed – *John Wesley Harding* and *Nashville Skyline* – were countrified, conservative, and muted in comparison. Dylan wouldn't appear in public again until January of 1968; by all outward appearances, he sat 1967 out entirely. And yet, in the spring, summer, and fall of that year Dylan and four or five members of his band (who were arguing over whether to call themselves "The Honkies" or "The Crackers") retreated to the 12 foot × 12 foot basement of a nondescript, three-bedroom ranch house – "Big Pink" – located some ways down a dirt road in Saugerties, New York, and recorded well over a hundred tracks. The output dwarfed that of the seven studio albums Dylan had cut for Columbia Records (those albums contained a total of eighty-one tracks). And because the "basement tapes" were never released in anything approaching their entirety, pirated versions of the recordings acquired the status of cult objects among collectors (it's quite likely that the first records we'd describe as "bootlegs" were bootlegged copies of *The Basement Tapes*).

Greil Marcus, who sometimes functions as a critical arm of the Bob Dylan Industrial Complex, would see the results as a deep dive into the "old, weird America" of Harry Smith's *Anthology of American Folk Music*. But *The Basement Tapes* weren't quite a return to the amniotic, old-timey aesthetic that Smith's *Anthology* epitomized. If traditional works like "Wildwood Flower" and "See That My Grave Is Kept Clean" took pride of place, so did songs by Johnny Cash, Hank Williams, John Lee Hooker, and the Impressions. A number of the original compositions – "Nothing Was Delivered," "Tears of Rage," "Odds and Ends," "Yea, Heavy and a Bottle of Bread," "This Wheel's on Fire," "You Ain't Going Nowhere," "Million Dollar Bash," and quite a few others – were carefully reworked, and recorded multiple times. The results aren't rough-hewn because they represent a stab at recapturing the *ersatz* authenticity of Dylan's early, acoustic albums. They're rough-hewn because they're works-in-progress. So while there's a great deal to recommend Greil Marcus's take on *The Basement Tapes*, it's just as easy to see Dylan's removal from the public eye as a tactical retreat – an attempt to conquer the pop charts via other means, through the auspices of other musicians.

A storekeeper's son with a fine head for business, Bob Dylan knew that, as far as the market was concerned, Dylan albums weren't as successful – or remunerative – as albums of Dylan songs recorded by other artists: Peter, Paul, and Mary, or the Byrds, whose debut album was named after Dylan's "Mr. Tambourine Man," contained four Dylan songs and reached number 6 on the *Billboard* chart (the title track topped the charts in America and England both). When it came to singles, Dylan fared no better. The image had become ubiquitous – and the attention might have been oppressive – but the music itself sold best when smoother voices sang it. *The Basement Tapes* were "done out in somebody's basement," Dylan explained. "They weren't demos for myself . . . I was being pushed again into coming up with some songs" (Heylin, *Recording Sessions* 68).

Pressed to acetate, and passed out to members of the musical elite, the recordings weren't quite pop songs. (The oddly affecting "Quinn the Eskimo," which became a hit single for Manfred Mann the following year, was a notable exception.) But they were remarkably influential: the Byrds included two songs – "Nothing Was Delivered" and "You Ain't Going Nowhere" – on their 1968 country–rock cornerstone, *Sweetheart of the Rodeo*. That same year, the Crackers/Honkies rechristened themselves as the Band and released *Music From Big Pink*, which included three songs – "This Wheel's On Fire," "Tears of Rage," and "I Shall Be Released" – written by or with Bob Dylan, and on her 1969 album *To Love Somebody*, Nina Simone turned "I Shall Be Released" into something like a spiritual. The transformation made sense: At their best, these demos suggested the majestic, devotional qualities of songs Dylan had yet to write. ("Knockin' on Heaven's Door," which appeared on Dylan's 1973 soundtrack for *Pat Garrett and Billy The Kid*, wouldn't have been out of place on *The Basement Tapes*.)

Some of the lyrics you'll find on *The Basement Tapes* were as straightforward, and beautiful, as anything Dylan would write: "I see my light come shining, / From the west unto the east / Any day now, any day now, / I shall be released." Others were whimsical, half-baked, or almost entirely absurd: "Well. The Comic Book and me, just us, we caught the bus / Poor little chauffeur, though, she was back in bed / On the very next day, with a nose full of pus / Yea! Heavy and a bottle of bread" ("Yea! Heavy and a Bottle of Bread" [Take no. 2]). Or: "Well a big, dumb blonde with her wheel all gorged / And Turtle, that friend of hers with his checks all forged / His cheek's in a chunk, with his cheese in the cash / They're all gonna be there at that million-dollar bash" ("Million Dollar Bash" [Take no. 1]). Or: "See you later, croco-gator (See you later, croco-gator) / After a while, smock-a-while (See you later, Allen Ginsberg)" ("See You Later, Allen Ginsberg").

At first, at least, it might seem that Dylan was keeping one foot planted in the stream (or gush, or, occasionally, tidal wave) of consciousness which had gotten him through *Bringing It All Back Home*, *Highway 61 Revisited*, and *Blonde on Blonde*. But it's worth keeping in mind that, while some basement tapes are fully formed demo recordings, most are simply rehearsal tapes – accidental records of works-in-progress which never were fleshed out. This isn't to say that they don't have their moments, or that the moments aren't exquisite. But the pleasures they afford are, in part, the pleasures of getting an informal, insider's view of Dylan's method. The demo recordings collected on Columbia's official *Bootleg* series sounded different from anything you'd hear on the radio (e.g., "Like a Rolling Stone," played in waltz time) but the lyrics were more or less the lyrics we knew. On the unofficially bootlegged *Basement Tapes* we hear Dylan sing sounds which (do or don't) turn into symbols: each one is an object lesson in just how intimate the relationship between words and music can be.

Which is also to say that the charm of *The Basement Tapes* might have less to do with the quality of the songs themselves than with the informal, experiential qualities of the recording: the false starts, botched verses, buried vocals, and muttered obscenities which mark any given set of home recordings, as well as the no-fidelity which gives home recordings an aura of low-rent, *audio*-verité authenticity. To hear *The Basement Tapes* was also to strike a bargain with Dylan and his band: listeners plowed through five-plus hours of intermittently brilliant material, not simply to pluck out the gems, but to get a sense of what it might have been like to sneak into Big Pink's basement and eavesdrop a while. And so, the precise moment of Dylan's withdrawal from the public eye was also the best chance yet to catch him at his most private and unguarded.

Many of those qualities went missing from *The Basement Tapes* that Columbia Records released – as a remixed, truncated, overdubbed two-album set, a third of which consisted of Band demos that Dylan had had little or nothing to do with – in 1975. But, by then, the laid-back Americana Dylan and his band pioneered at Big Pink had become its own idiom, and a core element of the overall rock & roll aesthetic – a soundtrack, of sorts, to the nation's own withdrawal from the promises and disappointments of the previous decade. ("That was some other era, burned out and long gone from the brutish realities of this foul year of Our Lord, 1971," Hunter S. Thompson had written, four years earlier (23).) Greil Marcus provided liner notes for the release; the "Dean of American Rock Critics," Robert Christgau, who graded records as if they were homework assignments, awarded it an A+; consumers turned out in great numbers, pushing *The Basement Tapes* into the Billboard top ten, and surprising Dylan himself. "I thought everybody already had them," he said.

As for Big Pink, it's still standing, ricky-ticky, at an address formerly known as 2188 Stoll Road in Saugerties (Stoll Road now has a new name, which the house's current owners asked me not to disclose). The house spent years on the market (and went unsold), enjoyed visits from the occasional (Japanese) tourist, and served as the home base for a local DJ and importer of classical albums. For the past ten years, it's been owned by a musician and audio engineer, who produces bands in the basement, on a project basis. It still looks very much like the house Dylan and the Band inhabited.

15

CARRIE BROWNSTEIN

Blood on the Tracks (1975)

Blood on the Tracks was recorded in the month and year in which I was born, September 1974. I mention this for the sake of full disclosure – namely, I don't know what life was like without it. I wasn't in high school or college that year, experiencing my own heartbreak; I didn't rush out to buy the vinyl when it was released in 1975, nor have any expectations at all about Bob Dylan. If anything, I was learning to crawl or maybe getting pieces of bark pulled out of my mouth by my mother. Like the album, I was brand new and open to interpretation. My parents were probably listening to Emerson, Lake, and Palmer, Dan Fogelberg, or if I was lucky, Joni Mitchell. For myself, part of the challenge of listening to *Blood on the Tracks* is to determine what it means to live concomitant to it. Since I have always lived in a world where the album existed, I have had to figure out ways of appreciating it apart from the noise that has surrounded it since its release.

Blood on the Tracks created an emotional dialogue as well as an emotional landscape around music. Whether Dylan intended it or not – and he likely didn't – it became a love album, a salve, for his fans to sing not only to themselves but also back at him; it emboldened fans with a vocabulary. The album expounds on the complexities of love, but it also embodies the contradictory feelings the fans had about Dylan, music, the times they live(d) in, and themselves. *Blood on the Tracks* is Dylan's civil war; from his secession from the union, to bloody battles, and an eventual but tepid reconciliation, *Blood on the Tracks* leaves both the artist and the listener scarred. It can be listened to as a series of individual battles, discovered one piece at a time, or one can step back and let the mess of it be revealed as a whole. Either way, it circles back onto itself, spinning, beautifully but also slightly out of control. *Blood on the Tracks* is a self-elegy; it sings to itself, and it breaks its own heart.

In the early 1970s, Dylan was growing hazy in the public imagination. Mystery is alluring to music fans, but vagueness that crosses into distortion can be frustrating to an audience. Dylan had been churning out stubbornly confounding albums, such as *Self Portrait* and *Planet Waves*, frustrating both the critics and his listeners. He had been in relative hiding since 1966 – living the domestic life with his wife Sara Lowndes Dylan and the four children they had together. Then, in April of 1974, Dylan emerged from Woodstock, NY and escaped to New York City. There, he took painting classes with Norman Raeben, whom Dylan considered more of a magician than an instructor. Raeben instilled in Dylan the idea that looking and seeing were vastly different. Painting also allowed him to play with temporality and meaning, to create shades and layers that could be understood both individually and as part of a whole. Sometimes you need to be challenged outside the perimeters of your expertise in order to reimagine your own art or as a means of finding your way back to your own medium. By examining music from a visual perspective, with colors and lines instead of notes and chords, Dylan laid out the canvas that would be *Blood on the Tracks*.

Blood on the Tracks was recorded once, reconsidered, and then recorded again. Common as this practice is, here it is noteworthy because of the album's thematic content. The songs that comprise *Blood on the Tracks*, tunes full of heartache and venom, were dragged halfway across the country to a new frontier; maybe that was the only way for Dylan to make sense of them, to hear what the songs had to say.

Dylan first recorded at A&R Studio on 54th Street with producer Phil Ramone, who had worked with everyone from Frank Sinatra to Quincy Jones and had been Dylan's live engineer during his 1974 tour with the Band. Dylan, with the help of Ramone, chose the musicians the day of the recording. Eric Weissberg and his band Deliverance, fresh from their success with "Dueling Banjos," became the New York session players.

When the recording was completed, Dylan had a few months to sit with the tapes. He was dissatisfied with what he heard. "Some songs just weren't being presented to their best advantage," Andy Gill and Kevin Odegard write in *A Simple Twist of Fate*. "It was largely his own fault, for not coaching his musicians more, and for insisting on inspired immediacy over a more considered approach" (91). In December, he went to the industrial side of South Minneapolis to record the album again with an entirely new set of musicians. Dylan enlisted his brother, David Zimmerman, to locate the musicians, the studio, and the instruments he wanted. This time the session players had a jazz background, and some of them were homegrown Minnesota boys.

The result, and what appears on *Blood on the Tracks*, is a hybrid of the two sessions. Sensitive ears, or finicky ones, can pick them apart, but it's not necessary. In the end, it is one glorious mess of songs, one tangled story, told and then retold because that's how you commit something you love to memory – or how you exorcise despair from your mind.

Like the landscape of a relationship itself, perhaps these songs could simply not be captured in a single place. It's an homage to its subject that *Blood on the Tracks* crossed the country, that the end turned out so different from the beginning. To traverse miles, to pick up and start again, to set up in a new space, to stretch out in different rooms, under the glare of different lights: that's what it feels like to be in love. It's a combination of what we know – our own cities, our own country, our own language – and what we don't know. It's constantly striking a balance of the foreign and the familiar, the contradictory urges to feel new again with someone, yet to want to be ourselves and still, somehow, better than ourselves. You can't do that in one studio or one space. You have to pick up and move, set yourself down in a new location, and see yourself in a new way. And that's what Dylan did.

Blood on the Tracks begins with a single unimpeachable color on the canvas. "Tangled Up in Blue" is a journey of both the artist's and of the lover's, and it conflates past and present. It is an American story of humble beginnings, with far-reaching hopes and colossal disappointments. At the start, the lovers and the narrator himself occupy a cohesive space. But the context begins to shift and unravel, not unlike the political era during which the song was written. Thus, making sense of a particular truth, or of an individual self, becomes increasingly fraught. The song sets up the album as a series of fractures, a dismantling of ideas and relationships that one used to count on for solidity and permanence.

"Tangled Up in Blue" is followed by "A Simple Twist of Fate"; here the story moves beyond tangible boundaries toward a metaphysical and psychological sphere. "I still believe she was my twin," Dylan sings. We see for the first time that the lovers are part of a larger universe over which they have little control. Yet the tragedy unearthed in the song is also personal in scale, and tells of accountability that cannot be blamed on destiny; it is the inability to rid our minds of doubt and to let go. In the end, the narrator "walks along with a parrot that talks" – the parrot being himself, going through the motions, speaking words without any meaning but with no way of regaining what has been lost. The twist of fate is an opening in the psyche, a window of vulnerability, near impossible to maintain.

"Idiot Wind" is a stunning beast. "Idiot" is a clumsy word to sing and Dylan has to stretch and fuss to get around it. In the song, his voice is a tornado, picking up dust and debris, growing stronger and more dangerous with each line. It is Dylan at his most acerbic, and the melody gets lodged in your head and burrows under your skin. "Idiot Wind, blowing through the flowers of your tomb," Dylan sings. It is a relentless rage, a tormentor so pernicious that even death will not free you. The song also depicts fragility teetering on disdain: "I can't feel you anymore, I can't even touch the books you've read." Everything has been tainted, and the song leaves an indelible mark on the album. It is the moment when everything breaks apart.

"Shelter from the Storm" acts as the balm to the vituperative gusts of "Idiot." "Shelter" is a song of reassurance and the protective walls with which new love surrounds us. Lullabylike and welcoming, the song becomes a reprieve for both the weary lover and the weary listener. It promises a return to wholeness or speaks of what could have been. Other songs are more forgiving, even resigned. In "You're a Big Girl Now" and "If You See Her Say Hello," feelings of regret are mixed with acceptance. "Buckets of Rain" might be the precursor to every sensitive-boy rock or folk song ever written, from Bright Eyes to Neutral Milk Hotel, Pete Yorn to Wilco. "Buckets" captures a naïve longing and breaks heartache down to its most rudimentary: "Life is sad / Life is a bust." It encompasses the philosophy of both the newly jilted and the embittered.

For most fans, *Blood on the Tracks* was a return to form. It confirmed Dylan as the preeminent songsmith of his generation and reassured his audience that he was worthy of the genius title they had bestowed upon him. Though at the time, *Rolling Stone* critic Jon Landau declared, "*Blood on the Tracks* will only sound like a great album for a while," the vaticination proved false. That very publication, along with countless others and the general public, has ultimately concluded that *Blood on the Tracks* is one of the best albums ever made. The album's gnarled truth, the ugliness exalted and transmuted, has helped it outlive its era.

Though the album endures mostly because of how people relate to its poetic candor, for Dylan the suggestion that *Blood on the Tracks* is a personal dissection has been more problematic. "It's hard for me to relate to that," he said in a radio interview with Mary Travers of Peter, Paul, and Mary. "I mean, people enjoying that type of pain" (Gill and Odegard 15). Dylan also stubbornly refutes that there is anything autobiographical on the album, claiming he was inspired by Chekhov stories.

It matters how and when you hear a piece of music, and whether it is a collective experience or an individual one. Being around to see Janis Joplin, Jimi Hendrix, the Clash, or Nirvana, is vastly different from hearing about them later, downloading a song onto your computer, or reading about them after their moment has expired. Through a collective memory, we can appreciate the impact of the Isle of Wight Festival or Woodstock, the Beatles on *The Ed Sullivan Show*, the vertiginous ride that is *Rock 'n' Roll Circus*; and the collective memory can make it feel like it's a part of our own history, because in some ways it is. But not all of us can say that we awoke one morning to those events, that we felt whole lives shift, that we saw the tide roll in and watched it take away beliefs and things we thought we knew.

That it left us with a changed shoreline and an inability to remember what it resembled before.

For anyone carving out their own song, straining to find the beauty in the uglier fragments of their life, it matters when you first heard Bob Dylan's *Blood on the Tracks* because of what it has left in its wake. To be born in the time of the album is to speak using the lexicon it has created, and in some ways, it is to take for granted the breadth of its language.

The challenge of *Blood on the Tracks* is to listen to it as more than the headwaters to a massive, undammable river of imitators and apprentices. If you can listen to it as a document of wars, the battles within us and around us, and as a struggle against dividable forces, then *Blood on the Tracks* is not just an old story that has been passed down through the years – it is a new tale, and it is one worth telling.

16

JONATHAN LETHEM

Infidels (1983)

To consider *Infidels* is to wade into the perplexity of Bob Dylan's 1980s, generally viewed as his lost decade, or at the very least an era for Dylan of intermittent lost faith in his relationships both to his audience and to his working methodology (such as it was). The *Infidels* recordings appear a focused attempt at statement-making by an artist who had lately been in a losing argument with his audience, if not himself, over the value of devotional biblical study to his art; the record has the mixed fate of seeming one of his most deliberate, and most wrecked. (If it is too much to claim it as Dylan's equivalent to Orson Welles's *The Magnificent Ambersons*, perhaps it may qualify as his *Lady from Shanghai*.) Musically, Dylan's purpose was expressed by the assembling of an unusual and fluent studio band, some of them strangers to one another before the work began (Dire Straits's keyboardist Alan Clark and guitarist–auteur, Mark Knopfler, who also participated in the record's production; Rolling Stone Mick Taylor, and the Jamaican rhythm-section-for-hire, Sly Dunbar and Robbie Shakespeare), rather than the use of a received group or of Dylan's current touring unit. Yet by the evidence of "bootlegs" both officially sanctioned and not, the set of songs released as *Infidels* in 1983 was only an iceberg's-tip exposure of the power, charm, and persuasiveness of the material recorded with this band. A devotee is forced to conclude, despite any reservations against psychobiography, or even simple second-guessing of a genius's purposes, that in 1983 Bob Dylan's art was vulnerable to a rather savage ambivalence on the part of its maker.

At least, a version of *Infidels* briefly prepared for release would have freed "Foot of Pride" and "Blind Willie McTell" from their fate as underground recordings until 1991's *The Bootleg Series, Vols. 1–3*. By the time they were revealed there, accompanied by more of the sessions' results – "Tell Me," "Lord, Protect My Child," and "Someone's Got a Hold of My Heart" – even a listener who obeyed Dylan's injunction against purchasing unauthorized recordings would begin to project for himself an ideal *Infidels* quite different from the original release. Deeper exploration adds the furious, unreleased, biographical rant "Julius and Ethel," plus a tender cover version of Willie Nelson's "Angel Flying too Close to the Ground" (which snuck into official release as the B-side to a European 45) and the fact that *Empire Burlesque*'s "Clean Cut Kid" ("how did he come up with the toughest Vietnam-vet song yet?" – Robert Christgau, *Record Guide* 131) also originated as part of the *Infidels* work.

Putting aside *The Basement Tapes*, there's no body of delayed or suppressed releases in Dylan's work to compare to this wealth. And *The Basement Tapes* were rehearsals and experiments, private play among friends. *Infidels* was intended, by every indication, to make an impression. What's odd is that it did anyway, garnering a rave review from *Rolling Stone* that stood for a general consensus (however soon abandoned) that this might be Dylan's "best album since the searing *Blood on the Tracks* nine years ago, a stunning recovery of the lyric and melodic powers that seemed to have all but deserted him" (Connelly). The record sold better than its two predecessors, and has continued to loosely demarcate some sort of "comeback," a status reinscribed by its inclusion as the only 1980s album beside *Oh Mercy* in the *Dylan Remasters* box set.

Well, what better measure of a titanic creator's sway with his audience that intention might be taken for result, or that shreds of greatness are sometimes nourishment enough? *Infidels*, as released, provided more than shreds in at least one instance: "Jokerman," side 1, track 1, a sublimely intricate and elusive song which, though it may seem to advertise itself as Dylan self-parody, refuses to do anything but gain force and beauty in the repeat-listener's contemplation. But before analyzing specific tracks, it may be worth emphasizing further the context of *Infidels*'s reception. That is to say, the narrative of yearning, on the part of an audience ostensibly still feeling betrayed by Dylan's public avowal of born-again Christianity in 1979, for proof of his reversion to a figure who could support the romantic projections of a counterculture (one meandering, with its idols, toward middle age, making romantic projections all the more urgent). *Infidels* was taken for that proof, and a great sigh of relief was issued in reply. Never mind that Jesus was still lyrically in the mix if you listened. Never mind that the preceding record, 1981's *Shot of Love*, had already offered secular imagery and love songs, and in some ways presented a warmer and more spontaneous whole than *Infidels* – *Shot of Love* contained a song with the threatening title "Property of Jesus," and had lousy jacket art. On the *Infidels* jacket Dylan looked cool in Wayfarer shades. And since both *Saved* and *Shot of Love* had sounded rather murky, Dylan's embrace of "contemporary" production methods – like that unpleasant etched reverb on the drums, which has dated so pitiably – also seemed to stand for Dylan's willingness to please us again.

Let us begin, then, as *Infidels* does, with the best – but not restrict ourselves to the released *Infidels*. "Jokerman" and "Blind Willie McTell" are the masterworks here. Let me offer myself as one listener, though, who didn't trust "Jokerman" the first few dozen times I heard it. The kaleidoscopic visionary verses seemed both vague and willed and, despite the overt biblical references, too evidently an attempt to write in an earlier mode. Topped with the ecstatic, but gnomic chorus: "Jokerman dance to the nightingale's tune, / Birds fly high by the light of the moon, / Ooh, ah, Jokerman!", the song embarrassed me. Later, after I'd learned to live inside, rather than resist, the verses' brilliant uncertainties, and to embrace the instinctive epiphany the chorus represents, I recalled the similar embarrassment I'd felt learning to surrender myself to "Mr. Tambourine Man" and "Chimes of Freedom" – the nearest precedents for "Jokerman" in Dylan's catalogue. ("Changing of the Guards" may be another, but though stirring, that song remains stuck in the middle distance, a parade one can admire but never join.) Like them, it explores grandiose feelings of self- and world-possession simultaneously, and doesn't trouble with modesty, offering warmth instead. Unlike them, however, "Jokerman" is inflected with worldly exhaustion beneath the exhilaration, and is deepened by its explicit continuity with Dylan's oeuvre-in-progress. That's not to say "Jokerman" is a song for initiates only, but that it's unimaginable without the context of previous work.

"Blind Willie McTell," though it was ironically available only to initiates for eight years, is the opposite: a vision of the original sins of human history through the lens of a memorial blues, a casual epic totally unified in terms of tone, imagery, and narrative implications. Though its depths can hardly be sounded at a dozen listenings, it tends to persuade anyone on first listening, Dylan fan or not (or, perhaps most typically, Dylan fan who restricts himself to 1975-and-before) that they've encountered a masterwork. McTell was a real figure, of course, and the glimpses Dylan offers here, from the "chain-gang on the highway" to the view from "the window of the St. James hotel" suggest a dire documentary montage narrated by the gravest voice of exhausted conscience Dylan or his callow early advocates could have ever hoped or feared he'd grow into.

Lagging one lap behind these two (and no shame in that) is the released *Infidels*'s second-best track, "I and I." Striking for Dylan's adoption of Jamaican idiom, this song has atmosphere in spades, placing introspective bitterness in a Reggae frame and letting it elegantly seethe there. The sinister precision and restraint of the studio track, with Mark Knopfler at his most

Dire and a Sly-and-Robbie slither that verges on shivery Muzak, point the singer toward those future Daniel Lanois-produced musical settings which risk the bogus in their ominous theatricality – "Man in the Long Black Coat" and "Love Sick" – but "I and I," while not skirting the bombastic, earns doom with a tough lyrical undercurrent. Like *Desire*'s "Isis" (on whose title "I and I" may be seen to pun), "I and I" allegorizes a journey from home and hearth, but here Dylan never returns, the last verse dissolving on the singer "barefoot" on "the narrow lanes." In a sense, this song presents *Infidels*'s paradigmatic face, declaring an important statement and withholding it at the same time. The revelation "I and I" never quite delivers is worth going back to try for. And the shade of depressed stoicism points ahead to *Time Out of Mind*.

Nothing in the remaining six tracks of the original *Infidels* strikes me as being as vital, lasting or (certainly) strange as "Foot of Pride," from *The Bootleg Series, Vols. 1–3*. A summit of Dylan's "manic preacher" mode, this poetically disjointed (and truthfully, cryptic) track takes another tour of "Desolation Row" yet replaces that song's dispassionate sorrow with the admonitory fury of the singer of "Idiot Wind." While visiting the *Bootleg Series*, let's also collect for our ideal *Infidels* "Lord Protect My Child," an achingly candid blues-plea which, as a rare glimpse of Bob Dylan-the-parent interests a great deal more than the anthemically vague "Forever Young"; "Tell Me," an odd, sneaky, lilting song of courtship in an imperfect and rather middle-aged world; and most intriguing of all, "Someone's Got a Hold of My Heart," a gregarious and truly catchy pop song (albeit built on the bones of the Velvet Underground's "Sweet Jane"), one nearly as insouciant as "I Want You." For all the polish and charm of "Someone's Got a Hold of My Heart" – which is not to slight the intricately allusive verses between the hooks – this song would turn out to function as merely a rough sketch for *Empire Burlesque*'s "Tight Connection to My Heart (Has Anybody Seen My Love?)," a rewrite that substituted a number of transposed Humphrey Bogart-movie dialogue lines for Dylan's own, and replaced the original's vulnerable tone with a Bogartishly hardboiled one. This overt collage technique is of course another forecast of future work, and the rewrite is impossible to completely dismiss, but many listeners may prefer the *Infidels* sketch to the *Empire Burlesque* final result. Among the replaced lines is the superb, tossed-off, "What looks large from a distance, / Close up ain't never that big"; among those the rewrite retains is the marvelously conflated confession, "Never could learn to drink that blood / And call it wine / Never could learn to hold you, love / And call you mine." Whether or not this is seen as a deft redressing of the certainties expressed in songs of religious and sexual redemption, like the (gorgeous) "Precious Angel" from *Slow Train Coming*, "Someone's Got a Hold of My Heart" would have graced any album.

But, back to the real-world *Infidels*. "Sweetheart Like You," the album's small radio hit (and one of Dylan's last) is a song one would hardly wish to claim either as "underrated" or as a complete and organic success, yet it easily passes the test of flawed Dylan balladry, both by staking out territory for future work, and by sustaining interest over years of listening. Sometimes the radio knows a thing or two. It secures this interest largely by the exquisite delicacy of the vocal, which could be said to address its subject tenderly even when wielding a scalpel. In Dylan annals, the song seems mainly remembered as an affront to feminists, for the title phrase, a seemingly obnoxious and banal seducer's line: "What's a sweetheart like you doin' in a dump like this?", and for the verse couplet "A woman like you should be at home, / That's where you belong / Taking care of somebody nice who don't know how to do you wrong." If the song must take its place in Dylan's feminists' hall of shame, it has fine company there in "Just Like A Woman"; for most listeners the lines will be redeemed by both context and presentation, and the song's narrative fragments place singer and addressee in a film-noir dive.

The method at hand, of entrenching "received" cultural stuff (film dialogue, blues archetypes) not in the margins of his songs, but at their center, would become increasingly familiar to Dylan's listeners in the *Time Out Of Mind/"Love And Theft"/Modern Times* era; it's worth pointing out that use of a phrase like the song's chorus, once bitterly disenchanting to those cherishing Dylan's status as an imaginative phrasemaker, are precisely the gestures now widely celebrated by proponents of "postmodern" Dylan. As Dylan love songs go, "Sweetheart Like You" occupies a midpoint between an older strategy of "real" confessional intimacy (in successes like "Spanish Harlem Incident" and "If You See Her Say Hello" and failures like "Ballad in Plain D") which invite the listener's interest in the singer's authentic persona, however protectively diffused into surrealist metaphor, and the utterly abstracted intimacy of Dylan's elder-statesman stance (consider, say, "Sugar Baby," or "Nettie Moore"). Recognizing a channeler of archetypal stories, whether rooted in blues mythology or other sources, few I think would bother to begrudge Dylan a recent line like "I want some good woman to do just what I say" or his mentions of "booty calls"; that is to say: who would take such usages personally? This gap describes differences in the state of feminism (or should I say "gender studies"?) and Dylanology both, for better or worse. Finally, "Sweetheart Like You" makes room for a consummately generic Dylan restatement of power's operation: "Steal a little and they throw you in jail, / Steal a lot and they make you king." The odd implication being that the "dump like this" in which the sweetheart finds herself is a Default Dylan Song – a dump for stray lines.

Another love song, "Don't Fall Apart on Me Tonight" raises similar problems and offers similar fugitive pleasures – yet fewer of those pleasures (beguiling harmonica, a genuinely catchy chorus) survive the irritations of long exposure to this particular lyric, into which Dylan seems to have dumped a chilly shrug or two. Michael Gray, in his *Bob Dylan Encyclopedia*, hears "prime examples of nasty California therapy-speak" in the chorus (186). Certainly the song disappoints in the comparison begged by its placement as the album's final track: "I'll Be Your Baby Tonight," "Tonight, I'll Be Staying Here With You," and "Where Are You Tonight? (Journey Through Dark Heat)" were all album-closing "tonights." One of these is not, alas, like the others.

The last of *Infidels*'s acceptably-diminished-returns is the choogling "Man of Peace," a jubilant catalogue of Satan's prime indicators ("He can be fascinating, he can be dull / He can ride down Niagara Falls in the barrel of your skull!" and "He knows just where to touch you, honey, and how you want to be kissed!"). It seems to me as infatuated a portrait, really, as that of Joey Gallo in "Joey," or of Catfish Hunter in "Catfish." Class this song not with the evangelical stuff, but with Dylan's joke blues, like "Leopard-Skin Pill-Box Hat." The test "Man of Peace" passes is that of a silly and raucous Dylan vocal showcase: just the way he grins his way through the phrase "full of grease-hah!" could get an eight-year-old child jigging around the room at its foolish fury.

Brian Hinton, in his *Bob Dylan Complete Discography*, asks, "Why on earth wasn't *Infidels* a double album? It would have rivaled *Blonde on Blonde*" (275). Well, no. Anyway, rather than merely adding outtakes, my own ideal *Infidels*, unlike Hinton's, would also shed three tracks (and therefore fit on a single disc). That is to say, as hurriedly as I'd welcome "Blind Willie McTell" and his compatriots in from the cold, I'd kick "Union Sundown," "Neighborhood Bully," and "License To Kill" to the curb. "Union Sundown," and "Neighborhood Bully" simply fail the test of minor, riffing album-filling Dylan rockers; with their half-assed topical lyrics, they rankle. As Paul Williams remarked to me, being a fan of 1980s' Bob Dylan can sometimes be like being in love with the ugliest girl in the world. If a listener wishes to hear Mark Knopfler and Mick Taylor duel on guitar, I recommend two iPods playing *Making Movies* and *Goat's Head Soup* simultaneously. Or seek out "Julius and Ethel," which is at once richer and stranger than these two.

"License To Kill," a pallid "Masters of War" rewrite, disappoints more elaborately, though it may originate in an impulse like that which gave rise to "Union" and "Bully": Dylan, if one may again speculate on motives, seems to have been feeling the burden of producing social commentary to demonstrate his "return" (a point of comparison for this sense of duty is perhaps 1971's "George Jackson"). The saving grace of this leaden song is the manner in which Dylan sings "But there's a woman on my block, / She just sits there facing the hill, / She says who's gonna take away his license to kill?" Yet the lyric's complacency hovers over that same image. That woman on his block: does she truly never frame *any* question beside "Who's gonna take away his license to kill?" Possibly you distrust Dylan when he castigates women as objects of intimate perfidy; I distrust him when he blurs them into wan moral paragons. Certainly the song sits uneasily on an album on which the singer eagerly prints up a killing license for his favored "Neighborhood Bully."

Enough. Perhaps I've persuaded you (I hope I have) that *Infidels* doesn't exist, at least not completely. Instead, it's a kit: construct your own. Surely there's a version you'll award four stars. However, if contrasted with the fulfillments of 1960s, '70s, and post-'80s Dylan, the foggy Dylan of the 1980s – he who wanders from evangelical certainties through self-effacing stints with the Heartbreakers, the Dead, and the Wilburys, and whose albums so often seem half-regretted sheddings – still troubles you, be assured: songs as consummate as "Jokerman" and "Blind Willie McTell" *do* exist. Passing every test of full-blown Dylan masterpieces, these will be objects of wonder and devotion as long as anyone cares for Dylan, or songs. So, for that matter, will "Foot of Pride," and "I and I," and "Every Grain of Sand," as well as "Brownsville Girl," "Angelina," and "When the Night Comes Falling from the Sky," other gems cast aside in dismay in the years neighboring *Infidels*. In these instances, Dylan's art found its way home.

17

ERIC LOTT

"Love and Theft" (2001)

Leslie Fiedler, in a book whose title I riffed on for my *Love and Theft: Blackface Minstrelsy and the American Working Class* (a little bit of larceny in its own right), famously suggested that US narrative is continually possessed by the idea of two men, one white and one dark, alone together in the American void, Huck and Jim, Kirk and Spock, Dre and Eminem. The minstrel show's miscegenation in one body – the white man inhabiting black – literalized this imaginary proximity, the fascination with and heisting of black cultural materials. When Bob Dylan turned to "Jack Frost" to produce his great 2001 album *"Love and Theft,"* he generated another mask to handle the cultural mash he advanced, where, as he put it in an interview, the original influences are represented but not any more in their original form, like barley into whiskey. If Dylan's mash is a little sour, it's because it's so fully aged. Dylan could only have made this record at 60, not just because it showcases a ripped and ragged voice but also because of its incredible range, literary, musical, and philosophical. I'll argue here that in addition to its reflections on the musical relations of race and artistic borrowing generally – its theory of culture – Dylan's *"Love and Theft"* advances as well an intricately related musical theory of affective life in late middle age. If once he used "ideas as . . . maps," he's older than that now, feeling his way, pledging his time, lyin' in winter, mapping his country ("My Back Pages," *Another Side of Bob Dylan*, 1964).

In the words of Dylan's publicist, "Mr. Dylan neither confirms nor denies a connection between the title of his album and the title of that book."[1] (And that was it: no word with me or anyone else before or after on why he chose his title, the only one of his forty-four album titles to date to be placed in quotation marks. Just another professor who liked his looks, I guess.) Greil Marcus put it to me this way: "I don't know that [Dylan's] read your book but wouldn't be surprised; he's a true scholar of old American music and all that goes with it."[2] I suspect Dylan liked my title for its general resonance, in which stolen hearts and emotional misdemeanors stalk the sweetness of love, as they usually do in Dylan's songs. More particularly, though, he knows full well the cross-cultural indebtedness of music in the Americas, his included, and alludes to it in the songs as well as the title, itself stolen, of *"Love and Theft."*

"High Water (For Charley Patton)," with its banjo, tambourine, and other clattering percussion, is the *"Love and Theft"* song that sounds the most like nineteenth-century minstrel-show music, which is interesting not only since it's influenced by and dedicated to Delta bluesman Patton (cf. Patton's "High Water Everywhere" and "High Water Everywhere, Part Two"; see Woods, especially 110–112, 118–119; Lomax; and Gussow) but also because it's a song of high seriousness, as though ultimate truths are rooted in cultural plunder. "Some of these bootleggers / They make pretty good stuff / Plenty of places to hide things here / If you want to hide them bad enough," Dylan affirms on the record's "Sugar Baby." Moonshiners, sure, but pirated recordings, too, perhaps Dylan's most enduring legacy, and pirated sources as well, which floated many of those recordings. On *"Love and Theft"* alone the range and number of these is astonishing: they include, at the very least, Lewis Carroll, Tennessee Williams, the myth of Icarus, Robert Johnson, Johnny Cash, Elmore James, a Parchman farm prison song, the work song "Rosie," Elvis, *The Great Gatsby*, Blind Willie McTell, W. C. Fields, *West Side Story*, Stephen Foster, *Romeo and Juliet*, Charley Patton, Joe Turner, *Jane Eyre*, Clarence Ashley, Dock Boggs, *Night of the Hunter*, "Ode to a Nightingale," John Donne, P. T. Barnum's Chang and Eng, *Othello*, "The Three Little Pigs," knock-knock jokes, Howlin' Wolf, *Don Pasquale*, the Bible, and "Darktown Strutters' Ball," as if Dylan's daring us to accuse him of theft – which people subsequently did (again) when it was discovered that he'd lifted quite a bit of the song "Floater" from a Japanese gangster memoir, Junichi Saga's *Confessions of a Yakuza* (1991), or that the very melody of "Sugar Baby" was boosted from a 1928 Gene Austin pop number called "Lonesome Road" (Pareles, "Plagiarism"; bobdylan.com). Who's gonna throw that minstrel boy a coin?

This is not to say that Dylan's simply a blackface artist, as Michelle Shocked – a little too abjectly – proclaimed herself to be on her 1992 album *Arkansas Traveler*, the cover of which was originally to feature her in blackface make-up. No: cultural "miscegenation" – a stupid word, not only because of its racist origins but also because you probably can't show me an instance of culture that isn't somehow mixed in kind – is on the contrary a spur to newness and uniqueness for Dylan. "If there's an original thought out there I could use it right now," Dylan jokes in "Brownsville Girl" (1986), that opus spun out of Wild West movies, border ballads, gospel music, Dust Bowl sagas, Sam Shepard plays, Alamo fables, and parables and paradoxes and a hundred other sources. Yet however much he's borrowed and stolen, and as we all know that's *a lot*, Dylan's music has always been full of original thoughts. What's fascinating with great artists is that it's usually tricky to specify where minstrelsy or obvious cultural appropriation stops and something different and fresh begins. Sometimes they coexist outright, in (say) Biz Markie or the Beastie Boys. It's far easier to spot lame bizzers like crooners Michael Bolton or Robert Palmer than it is to say how an obvious borrower like Dylan or Elvis nonetheless somehow makes the music his own. While the ingrown persistence and cold corruptions of blackface still structure our feelings, at least we know better now how much American pop music jes grew out of the gold-standard rush of minstrel-show writers like Stephen Foster and Dan Emmett – both of whom, by the way, Dylan has covered.

What interests me about *"Love and Theft"* is that it seems bent on demonstrating all this. I don't mean to turn a fabulous record into a dull dissertation, but it does cap in knowing ways the artistic process Dylan (re-) discovered in the 1990s on *Good as I Been to You* (1992), *World Gone Wrong* (1993), and *Time Out of Mind* (1997), albums full of blues, ballads, and other timeless tunes that constitute, as Dylan put it in the liner notes to *World Gone Wrong*, a "physical plunge into Limitationville." Its borrowings are voluminous and pointed, but, unlike the covers on *Good as I Been to You* and *World Gone Wrong*, they are sublated into Dylan's own compositions, and unlike the "party's-over" vibe of *Time Out of Mind* (perhaps three of whose eleven songs aren't end-obsessed blues),[3] *"Love and Theft"* makes loss and unwholesome gain an occasion for cultural and autobiographical self-consciousness. The album's governing terms, "love" and "theft," become multi-dimensional metaphors for heartbreak, crime, and time unredeemed as well as Dylan's career and musical choices – these latter ranging from rockabilly ("Tweedle Dee and Tweedle Dum"), jump blues ("Summer Days"), and soft-shoe shuffles ("Bye and Bye") to country swing ("Floater"), Tin Pan Alley pop ("Moonlight"), and roadhouse blues ("Honest With Me"). That is, if love-and-theft can be taken as the defining relationship not only of minstrel-show but probably all American music, Dylan knows that the terms of his title point in at least two directions. "Love" is that cross-cultural attraction among US musical formations responsible for the heady mix Dylan has always tapped. "Theft," on the other hand, points to the exploitative conditions – from chattel slavery to the chitlin' circuit and beyond – that have often afforded the sharing of Anglo- and African-American musical influences, inflections, forms, phrasings, verses, and titles. We might indeed play on the sense of "title" as ownership and note that Dylan doubly undermines his claim to the mixed-up musical territory on *"Love and Theft,"* no matter how striking or original it is in

Dylan's hands: he wryly implies his thievery in the album's name, and with scare quotes calls attention to his thievery *of* the name.

But it's not as though the cultural relations of love and those of theft can be so sweetly separated. It would be pretty to think that the terms of cross-cultural attraction are free and clear, but the society in which current rockers live is still (if in transmogrified ways) the society structured in dominance that gave rise to the musical loves of white minstrel men, to say nothing of the black music they loved. Just as there's probably no racially unmixed instance of American culture, so there's no mixed instance not marked in some way or other by inequalities of power. Love is shot through with theft, and theft with love. Think about "High Water." Where in the long musical history by which plantation slaves invigorated Anglo-Irish folk tunes with a post-African percussive sensibility only to be commercially represented on the US theatrical stage by white men who gave rise to generations of "white" rural string music, eventually to be taken up in homage to black blues musician Charley Patton by somebody (self-)named Bob Dylan ("Hm, Bob Dylan, I wonder what it was before," Marshall Berman reports his mother musing when she first heard the name forty years ago) on an album called *"Love and Theft"* – where in all this can you even think of escaping the rigors and mortises of racialized cultural life in these United States (73)?

By the same token, I'd guess that Dylan regards minstrelsy, say, whatever its ugliness, as responsible for some of the US's best music as well as much of its worst – without the wishful fantasies of musical racelessness that mar Greil Marcus's invocations of the "old, weird America" (*Invisible Republic* 124). I've argued elsewhere that the emancipatory depictions of Jim in *Adventures of Huckleberry Finn* (such as when Jim and Huck are reunited on the raft after their separation in a fog) are no less indebted to minstrelsy than the more stereotypical ones, which is to say there's no "transcending" or circumventing through sheer will the internally contradictory structures of blackface feeling (Lott 129–152). Stephen Foster's "Oh! Susanna" (1848), written in "black" dialect with some less than palatable suggestions about African American mental capacity, is nonetheless a great song that exhibits a good deal of sympathetic identification with the black family separated by slavery depicted in it.

The blues formats that Dylan chooses to say something about cultural borrowing on *"Love and Theft"* give rise in turn to its insistence on age and loss – lost love, lost relatives, lost time. *"Love and Theft"* is preoccupied with loss and futility in direct proportion to its refusal to give up – "never say die," as Dylan sings on "Po' Boy." Song by song, the singer's pathway stones are announced and recuperated by the general buoyancy of his wit and his music. The oscillation between death drive and pleasure principle isn't unique to

"Love and Theft," of course, but is a structuring principle of all blues; the music's repetitions don't aim to drown in sorrow but to exorcise it, allow the repressed to briefly return on its way out of the psyche. The *sound* of loss and trauma returning in order to be remade comes in the "dirty" tones, the falling pitches, the flatted Es and Bs of the blues scale – and on *"Love and Theft"* in the voice of gravel that intones whole realms of aging and struggle (see Murray; Griffin 56–57; Scandura, ch. 3). Dylan does seem singularly intent here, though, on capturing a state Freud termed "melancholia": not the failed mourning of his 1917 essay "Mourning and Melancholia," even less a synonym for depression, but a middling state in which, as Freud summed it up in *The Ego and the Id*, the lost love object is retained as a (historical) component of the self. In these terms, the content of one's emotional life is nothing less than the transferential sum of abandoned or lost loves, a nexus of ghostly emotional attachments, "the sedimentation," as Judith Butler has put it, "of objects loved and lost, the archaeological remainder, as it were, of unresolved grief" (Freud 18–20; Butler 133; and especially Flatley). Loss inevitably undergirds the self, on this view, and if that tends in a variety of ways to haunt us it also connects us concretely and materially to the past, to history. It thus has an immensely productive aspect for thinkers and creative artists, which is why I'd argue that the key line on the whole of *"Love and Theft"* is "I wish my mother was still alive" ("Lonesome Day Blues").

Beatty Zimmerman died in late January of 2000. To make too much of this fact would be as foolish as thinking it had nothing to do with the feel and spiritual vibe of the album Dylan wrote and recorded a little more than a year later. The line above seems to come out of nowhere, at the end of a disjointed verse in the middle of the internally dissociated "Lonesome Day Blues," as though live and direct from the unconscious. Closer inspection reveals the connections, which have the odd effect of making the song seem even more self-exposing. Singing against a heavy blues downbeat, the song's speaker sits thinking, his "mind a million miles away." It is on the whole a roving set of reflections on drastic loss. He left his long-time darlin' standing in the door; his pa died and left him, his brother got killed in the war; Samantha Brown lived in his house for four or five months but he didn't sleep with her eeeeven once. Then comes this:

> I'm forty miles from the mill – I'm droppin' it into overdrive
> I'm forty miles from the mill – I'm droppin' it into overdrive
> Settin' my dial on the radio
> I wish my mother was still alive

In some deep current of feeling, mother and radio are bound up with each other: it's a genius couplet. Both are major modes of cultural and more specifically musical transmission (which incidentally realizes the punning intention of "droppin' it into overdrive"). The mother is the pre-linguistic source of all music, her heartbeat the first rhythm we hear, her hum among the first melodies; losing her in the process of individuation is our first loss, the first lost object to be introjected as part of the ego's melancholia and one template for our later relationships. The radio mimics the mother's subsequent status as ghosted, disembodied musical source (I'll refrain from speculating on the radio dial's anatomical analogue), and its status as a technological anachronism in an age of downloading, music-sharing, and iPods casts upon it a similarly vestigial and recursive shadow (that is to say, when you hear the radio you remember the first times you ever heard the radio; the same goes, unconsciously, for the pull – or push – of your mother's voice). So it's no real surprise that the two references might come one after the other, or, as the syntax of the line suggests, that the radio itself might remind the singer of his mama. The phrase "love and theft" finds an especially poignant resonance in the context of Dylan's mother being stolen away; such is the power of her originary position, moreover, that she might even *be* the long-time darlin' the singer last left standing in the door. In any case, Dylan singing about his mother opens rather effortlessly onto singing about music and by implication his career, and given that doing so has helped create a powerful song on a powerful album, we might say that loss is recuperated here by, and in the service of, a melancholic art.

It's the memories that haunt you, things acquired, loved, and lost. "Some of these memories you can learn to live with and some of them you can't" ("Sugar Baby"). So many things cluster here: the people you once clung to, the wrongs you couldn't help ("So many things that we never will undo / I know you're sorry, I'm sorry too," Dylan sings in "Mississippi"), the very sources of your energy and your art. "These memories I got, they can strangle a man" ("Honest with Me"), not a good thing for a singer, but understandable if what you've got in your throat are traces of a thousand different songs from apartheid America. Race, memory, and music meet in musical melancholia, where you get by with materials you barely remember taking in the first place: you were too young, or they were too available, or both, and they work so well, speak so solidly to your condition. You reach back to your roots, you work through your masks, and you find yourself again in the land where the blues began.

NOTES

1 Reported to me in 2001 by David Yaffe, who upon the album's release wrote an article for *Lingua Franca* about the relation between Dylan's record and my book

(the magazine folded before the article appeared). I thank David for his extensive support and brilliant contributions to my thinking about Dylan's work.

2 Greil Marcus, email communication, 17 July 2001.

3 The line comes from the song "Highlands," but it applies generally to the album on which it appears, *Time Out of Mind* (Columbia, 1997).

WORKS CITED

Allen, Lynne. "Interview with an Icon: Bob Dylan grants an audience." In *Younger than that now: The Collected Interviews with Bob Dylan*, New York: Thunder's Mouth Press, 2004.

Attali, Jacques. *Noise: The Political Economy of Music*. Trans. Brian Massumi. Minneapolis: University of Minnesota Press, 1985.

"Basic Dylan." Rev. of *John Wesley Harding*, by Bob Dylan. *Time* (Jan. 12, 1968): 50.

Bauldie, John. "Jacques Levy and the *Desire* Collaboration." In *All Across the Telegraph: A Bob Dylan Handbook*, ed. Michael Gray and John Bauldie. London: Sidgwick & Jackson, 1987.

Wanted Man: In Search of Bob Dylan. New York: Kensington, 1998.

Benson, Carl, ed. *The Bob Dylan Companion: Four Decades of Commentary*. New York: Schirmer, 1998.

Berman, Marshall. "Love and Theft: From Jack Robin to Bob Dylan." *Dissent* (Summer 2002): 73.

"Bob Dylan and the NECLC": www.corliss-lamont.org/dylan.htm

Bromell, Nick. *Tomorrow Never Knows: Rock and Psychedelics in the 1960s*. University of Chicago Press, 2002.

Bronstein, Martin. "February 20, 1966 interview." *Jewels & Binoculars: 1966*. Vigotone, 2000.

Brown, Richard. "Highway 61 and Other American States of Mind." In *Do You, Mr Jones? Bob Dylan with the Poets and the Professors*, ed. N. Corcoran. London: Chatto and Windus, 2002. 193–220.

Buskin, Richard. *Inside Tracks: A First-Hand History of Popular Music from the World's Greatest Record Producers and Engineers* (New York: Avon, 1999).

Butler, Judith. *The Psychic Life of Power: Theories in Subjection*. Stanford University Press, 1997.

Christgau, Robert. *Christgau's Record Guide: The Eighties*. New York: Pantheon Books, 1990.

"Look at that Stupid Girl." *Village Voice* (June 1970); www.robertchristgau.com/xg/bk-aow/stupid.php

"Rock Lyrics Are Poetry (Maybe)." In Benjamin Hedin, ed., *Studio A: The Bob Dylan Reader*. New York: Norton, 2004. 62–63.

Cohen, Scott. "Bob Dylan: Not Like a Rolling Stone Interview." *Spin*, 1:8 (Dec. 1985) 37–42, 80–81.

Cohn, Nik. *Awopbopaloobop Alopbamboom: The Golden Age of Rock.* 1968; New York: Grove, 2001.

Coleman, Ray. "Beatles Say – Dylan Shows the Way." *Melody Maker* Jan. 9, 1965: 3. Rpt. in *The Bob Dylan Scrapbook 1956–1966.* Ed. Robert Santelli. New York: Simon & Schuster, 2005. 39.

Connelly, Chris. "*Infidels.*" *Rolling Stone* Nov. 24, 1983: 65–67.

Conquergood, Dwight. "Between Experience and Meaning: Performance as Paradigm for Meaningful Action." In *Renewal and Revision: The Future of Interpretation.* Denton, TX: Omega (1986). 26–59.

Cott, Jonathan (ed.). *Bob Dylan: The Essential Interviews.* New York: Wenner Books, 2006.

Crowe, Cameron. Liner Notes. *Biograph.* Columbia Records, 1985.

Day, Aidan. *Jokerman: Reading the Lyrics Of Bob Dylan.* Oxford: Blackwell, 1988.

DeCurtis, Anthony. "Interview with Jakob Dylan." *New York Times* May 10, 2005.

Dettmar, Kevin J. H. "Among School Children: Dylan's Forty Years in the Classroom." In *Highway 61 Revisited: Bob Dylan's Road from Minnesota to the World,* ed. Colleen Sheehy and Thom Swiss. Minneapolis: The University of Minnesota Press, 2009.

Don't Look Back. Dir. D. A. Pennebaker. Leacock–Pennebaker, 1967.

Durbin, Karen. "Can The Stones Still Cut It?" *Village Voice* (June 23, 1975): 6–9.

Dylan, Bob. "Bob Dylan in His Own Words." *Los Angeles Free Press,* Sept. 17–24, 1965.

    Chronicles: Volume One. New York: Simon & Schuster, 2004.

    Liner notes, *World Gone Wrong.* Columbia Records, 1993.

Dylan Speaks. Eagle Rock Entertainment, 2006.

Eliot, T. S. *Selected Prose of T. S. Eliot.* Ed. Frank Kermode. New York: FSG, 1988.

Ephron, Nora and Susan Edmiston. Interview with Dylan, "Positively Tie Dream," Aug. 1965, in *Cavalier,* Feb. 1966. Rpt. in *Bob Dylan: The Essential Interviews,* ed. Cott. 52.

Fariña, Richard. "Baez and Dylan: A Generations Singing Out," *Mademoiselle* (Aug. 1964). Rpt. in *The Dylan Companion: A Collection of the Essential Writing About Bob Dylan,* ed. Elizabeth Thomson and David Gutman. New York: Delta, 1990.

Fiedler, Leslie. *Love and Death in the American Novel.* New York: Stein and Day, 1966.

Flatley, Jonathan. *Affective Mapping: Melancholia and the Politics of Modernism.* Cambridge, MA: Harvard University Press, 2008.

Freud, Sigmund. *The Ego and the Id.* Trans. Joan Riviere. Ed. James Strachey. New York: Norton, 1960.

Frith, Simon. *Music for Pleasure: Essays in the Sociology of Pop.* Cambridge: Polity Press, 1988.

    Performing Rites. Oxford University Press, 1998.

Frith, Simon, ed. *The Cambridge Companion to Pop and Rock.* Cambridge University Press, 2001.

Gates, David. "Dylan Revisited." *Newsweek,* Oct. 6, 1997: 62–68.

Geraghty, Christine. "Aesthetics and Quality in Popular Television Drama." *International Journal of Cultural Studies* 6:1 (2003): 25–45.

Gill, Andy. *Classic Bob Dylan 1962–65: My Back Pages*. Zurich: Edition Olm Zurich, 1998.

Gill, Andy and Kevin Odegard. *A Simple Twist of Fate: Bob Dylan and the Making of Blood on the Tracks*. Cambridge, MA: Da Capo Press, 2004.

Gilmore, Mikal. "Bob Dylan." *Rolling Stone*, 882 (Nov. 22, 2001): 56–69.

Goldberg, Michael. *New Musical Express* (Nov. 1979).

Goldstein, Richard. "Dylan: 'We Trust What He Tells Us.'" Rev. of *Don't Look Back*, dir. D. A. Pennebaker. *New York Times* Oct. 22, 1967: D25.

"Satellite Dylan." *Nation* May 15, 2006: 11–15.

Graham, Bill and Robert Greenfield. *Bill Graham Presents: My Life Inside Rock and Out*. Cambridge, MA: Da Capo Press, 2004.

Gray, Michael. *Song and Dance Man III: The Art of Bob Dylan*. London: Cassell, 2000.

Bob Dylan Encyclopedia. London: Continuum, 2006.

Griffin, Farah Jasmine. "Who Set You Flowin'?" In *The African-American Migration Narrative*. Oxford University Press, 1995. 56–57.

Gussow, Adam. *Seems Like Murder Here: Southern Violence and the Blues Tradition*. University of Chicago Press, 2002.

Hajdu, David. *Positively 4th Street: The Lives and Times of Joan Baez, Bob Dylan, Mimi Baez Fariña, and Richard Fariña*. New York: Farrar, Straus, and Giroux, 2001.

Hasted, Nick. "Bob Dylan Presents the Never Ending Tour." *Uncut Legends #1*, n.d., 106–111.

Helm, Levon and Stephen Davis. *This Wheel's on Fire: Levon Helm and the Story of the Band*. Chicago Review Press, 2000.

Hentoff, Nat. "The Crackin', Shakin', Breakin' Sounds." *New Yorker* October 24, 1964. Rpt. in *Younger than that Now: The Collected Interviews with Bob Dylan*, ed. James Ellison. New York: Thunder's Mouth, 2004, 13–30.

"Playboy Interview: Bob Dylan." *Playboy*, 13:3, March 1966: 41–44, 138– 142. Rpt. in *Bob Dylan: The Essential Interviews*, ed. Cott.

"Shoes for Everyone." *Bluerailroad Magazine* (May 2007): bluerailroad.com/shoes/0507.html.

Heylin, Clinton. *Bob Dylan: Behind the Shades Revisited*. New York: Harper Collins, 2003.

Bob Dylan: The Recording Sessions, 1960–1994. New York: St. Martin's Press, 1997.

Hickey, Neil. "The *TV Guide* Interview." In *Younger Than That Now: The Collected Interviews with Bob Dylan*, ed. James Ellison. New York: Thunder's Mouth Press, 2004.

Hilburn, Robert. Interview in *Los Angeles Times*, April 4, 2004. Rpt. in *Bob Dylan: The Essential Interviews*, ed. Cott. 432.

Hinton, Brian. *Bob Dylan Complete Discography*. New York: Universe, 2006.

Hishmeh, Richard. "Marketing Genius: The Friendship of Allen Ginsberg and Bob Dylan." *Journal of American Culture*, 29:4 (Dec. 2006): 395–405.

I'm Not There. Dir. Todd Haynes, 2008. DVD: The Weinstein Company, 2008.

Jahn, Mike. "Self-Portrait of the Artist as an Older Man." Rev. of *John Wesley Harding*, by Bob Dylan. *Saturday Review* May 11, 1968: 63–64.

Karwowski, Michael. "Bob Dylan's Dilemma: Which Blond?" *Contemporary Review*, 279 (Sept. 2001): 1628.

Keightley, Keir. "Reconsidering Rock," *The Cambridge Companion to Rock and Pop*, ed. Frith, 109–142.

Kokay, Les. *Songs of the Underground:Rolling Thunder Revue*. Private publication, 2000.

Kotkin, Joel. "Renaldo and Wasso." *New York Times*, Feb. 6, 1978: 44–45.

Lethem, Jonathan. "The Genius of Bob Dylan." *Rolling Stone*, 1008 (Sept. 7, 2006): 74–80; 128.

Light, Alan. "Travelling Wilburys." music.msn.com/music/remasters/travelingwilburys; June 1, 2007.

Loder, Kurt. "Interview with Bob Dylan." *Rolling Stone* (June 21, 1984).

"Interview with Bob Dylan." *Rolling Stone* (Nov. 5–Dec. 10, 1987): 301–303.

Lomax, Alan. *The Land Where Blues Began*. New York: Pantheon Books, 1993.

Lott, Eric. *Love and Theft: Blackface Minstrelsy and the American Working Class*. New York: Oxford University Press, 1993.

"Mr. Clemens and Jim Crow: Twain, Race, and Blackface." In *The Cambridge Companion to Mark Twain*, ed. Forrest G. Robinson. Cambridge University Press, 1995.

Madison, D. Soyina, and Judith Hamera. "Performance Studies at the Intersections. " In *The Sage Handbook of Performance Studies*, ed. D. Soyina Madison and Judith Hamera. Sage Publications, 2006. xi–xxv.

Marcus, Greil. "Amazing Chutzpah." *New West* (Sep. 24, 1979). Rpt. in *The Bob Dylan Companion*, ed. Benson.

Invisible Republic: Bob Dylan's Basement Tapes. New York: Holt, 1997. Reissued in paperback as *The Old Weird America*.

Like A Rolling Stone: Bob Dylan at the Crossroads. New York: Public Affairs, 2005.

The Old, Weird America: The World of Bob Dylan's Basement Tapes. New York: Picador, 2001.

Marqusee, Mike. *Wicked Messenger: Bob Dylan and the 1960s*. New York: Seven Stories, 2005.

Marshall, Lee. *Bob Dylan: The Never-Ending Star*. Cambridge: Polity, 2007.

McGregor, Craig. *Bob Dylan: A Retrospective*. London: Picador, 1972.

McKinney, Devin. "Eat the Document." *Village Voice* 19 June 2006: 95.

Mellers, Wilfred. *A Darker Shade of Pale: A Backdrop to Bob Dylan*. London: Faber and Faber, 1984.

Mischel, Lawrence and Jared Bernstein. *The State of Working America, 1992–93*. Ithaca, NY: Cornell University Press, 1993.

Moore, Allan F. *Rock: The Primary Text*. Aldershot: Ashgate, 2001.

Murray, Albert. *Stomping the Blues*. New York: McGraw-Hill, 1976.

Negus, Keith. *Bob Dylan*. London: Equinox, 2008.

No Direction Home. Dir. Martin Scorcese. DVD. Paramount Home Video, 2005.

Notes to *Dave Van Ronk: The Folkway Recordings*. Smithsonian Folkways, 1991.

Noyes, Russell, ed. *English Romantic Poetry and Prose*. Oxford University Press, 1956.

The Other Side of the Mirror: Bob Dylan Live at Newport Folk Festival 1963–1965. Sony, 2007.

Pareles, Jon. "Plagiarism in Dylan, or a Cultural Collage." *New York Times*, July 12, 2003: B7, B14.

"A Wiser Voice Blowin' in the Autumn Wind." *New York Times*, Sept. 28, 1997. Rpt. in *Bob Dylan: The Essential Interviews*, ed. Cott.

Polito, Robert. "Bob Dylan: Henry Timrod Revisited." n.d., n.p.; www.poetry-foundation.org/archive/print.html?id=178703

Pollack, Della. "Performing Writing." In *The Ends of Performance*, ed. Peggy Phelan and Jill Lane. New York University Press, 1998.

Posner, Richard. *The Little Book of Plagiarism*. New York: Pantheon Books, 2007.

Reynolds, Simon and Joy Press. *The Sex Revolts: Gender, Rebellion and Rock 'n' Roll*. Cambridge, MA: Harvard University Press, 1996.

Ricks, Christopher. *Dylan's Visions of Sin*. London: Penguin, 2003.

Riley, Tim. *Hard Rain: A Dylan Commentary*. New York: Da Capo Press, 1999. 52–67.

Rosenbaum, Ron. "Interview." *Playboy* (Mar. 1978); reprinted in *Bob Dylan: The Essential Interviews*, ed. Cott. 199–236.

Rowley, Chris. *Blood on the Tracks: The Story of Bob Dylan*. New York: Proteus Books, 1984.

Scandura, Jani. *Down in the Dumps: Place, Modernity, American Depression*. Durham, NC: Duke University Press, 2007.

Schou, Solvej. www.usatoday.com/life/music/2007-08-22-1778358558_x.htm

Scobie, Stephen. *Alias Bob Dylan Revisited*. Calgary: Red Deer Press, 2003.

Shank, Barry. " 'That Wild Mercury Sound': Bob Dylan and the Illusion of American Culture." *Boundary* 2 29:1 (2002): 97–123.

Shelton, Robert. *No Direction Home: The Life and Music of Bob Dylan*. Cambridge, MA: Da Capo Press, 2003.

"Trust Yourself." In *The Dylan Companion: A Collection of Essential Writings About Bob Dylan*, ed. Elizabeth Thomson and David Gutman. New York: Delta Books, 1990. 291–295.

Shepard, Sam. *Rolling Thunder Logbook*. Cambridge, MA: Da Capo Press, 2004.

Simmons, Allan H. "Read Books, Repeat Quotations: A Note on Possible Conradian Influences on Bob Dylan's 'Black Diamond Bay.' " *The Conradian* 20:1–2 (Spring–Autumn 1995): 103–108.

60 Minutes, Dec. 7, 2004, CBS.

Sloman, Larry "Ratso." *On the Road with Bob Dylan*. London: Helter Skelter, 2005.

Smith, Larry David. *Writing Dylan: The Songs of a Lonesome Traveler*. Westport, CT: Praeger, 2005.

Sounes, Howard. *Down the Highway: The Life of Bob Dylan*. New York: Grove Press, 2001.

Spitz, Bob. *Bob Dylan: A Biography*. New York: McGraw-Hill, 1989.

Thompson, Hunter S. *Fear and Loathing in Las Vegas*. New York: Modern Library, 1998.

Van Ronk, Dave. *The Mayor of Mcdougal Street: A Memoir*. Cambridge, MA: Da Capo Press 2005.

Vega, Suzanne. "The Ballad of Henry Timrod." *New York Times*, Sept. 17, 2006: WK 15.

Wenner, Jann. "Slow Train Coming." *Rolling Stone* (Sept. 20, 1979).

Wexler, Jerry (with David Ritz). *Rhythm and Blues: A Life in American Music.* New York: Knopf, 1993.

Wilentz, Sean. Liner notes. *Bob Dylan Live 1964.* Sony BMG Music, 2004.

Williams, Paul. *Bob Dylan Performing Artist. 1960–1973: The Early Years.* London: Omnibus, 1990.

    Bob Dylan Performing Artist: The Middle Years 1974–1986. London: Omnibus, 1992.

    Bob Dylan Performing Artist. Volume 3: Mind Out Of Time 1986 and Beyond. London: Omnibus, 2004.

    "Dylan – What Happened?" in *Bob Dylan Watching the River Flow: Observations on His Art-in-Progress 1966–1995.* London: Omnibus, 1996 (1997).

Williams, Raymond. *Keywords: A Vocabulary of Culture and Society.* Oxford University Press, 1983.

Willis, Ellen. "Dylan," *Cheetah,* 1967. Rpt. in *Bob Dylan: A Retrospective,* ed. McGregor, 218–239.

    "The Sound of Bob Dylan." *Commentary* Nov. 1967: 71–78.

Woods, Clyde. *Development Arrested: The Blues and Plantation Power in the Mississippi Delta.* London: Verso, 1998.

Zinoman, Jason. "Theater: When Bobby Met Brecht, Times Changed." *New York Times,* Oct. 8, 2006: AR7.

INDEX

CPSIA information can be obtained
at www.ICGtesting.com
Printed in the USA
LVHW08s1506170918
590420LV00016B/347/P